CONTENTS

Acknowledgments

The editors would like to thank the Telus Distinguished Visitors Program at the University of Calgary for providing the financial support that made *How Canadians Communicate* possible. The program has given life to many crucial projects that have left an important legacy to the university and the community. Colin Snowsell, a young and gifted student, assisted in organizing the conference from which this book originated. His hard work and insights were instrumental in making the conference the success that it was.

Kathleen Scherf, Dean of the Faculty of Communication and Culture, and David Mitchell, then Director of Graduate Studies in the faculty, provided both financial and moral support for which we are very grateful.

A great deal of thanks must go to Walter Hildebrandt, Director of the University of Calgary Press, who gave his unwavering support to this project. His dynamism and professionalism have done much to make the press an increasingly important institution in Canadian publishing. John King and Peter Enman did an excellent job in copy-editing. Their skill and perseverance made an enormous difference.

Joan Barton went beyond the call of duty in ensuring that the manuscript went through the publishing process with speed and efficiency. Sona Khosla, Ann Cowie, and Becky Naiden all contributed in different ways. They set up meetings, kept us on schedule, and offered needed encouragement.

We would also like to thank two anonymous reviewers for their helpful and constructive comments. Our greatest debt of thanks is owed to our contributors. Their knowledge, insights, and willingness to speak and write forthrightly about the common concerns that we share makes this book what it is. Our hope is that our readers will be moved in some way by the ideas and passions that flow through this book. It is to them that the book is dedicated.

THE NEW WORLD OF COMMUNI- CATIONS IN CANADA

David Taras

How a country communicates with itself and sees its own reflection is central to the health of its public and economic life and its prospects for survival as a vital community. Newspapers, music, libraries, workplaces, and TV programs are where a culture takes place – where it lives and breathes and grows. These are forces and institutions of immense power and persuasion. They convey meaning. They locate us in time and place. They allow us to learn who we are, where we have been, and where we are going. Todd Gitlin, the influential media scholar, once observed that the mass media has the power "to name the world's parts" and "to certify reality as reality" (Gitlin 1980, 2). The Canadian experience is largely defined by the communications habits and experience of its people.

In 2000, Canadians over the age of eighteen spent over three hours a day watching television. Indeed, 85 per cent reported having watched television the day before they were surveyed. This means that a typical Canadian spends over one full day out of each week, or over ten years out of their lifetime, watching TV – an extraordinary commentary on the way that we live our lives. Many, if not most, Canadians have TVs in their bedrooms and watch TV while they are eating. Mealtime, once the bedrock of family life, the great time of sharing and togetherness, has all but disappeared from many Canadian homes. We also spend over two hours listening to the radio and half an hour reading the newspaper each day. Listening to drive-time radio and reading newspapers over a morning cup of coffee or after supper are a part of the daily ritual for most Canadians (Communications Management 2002). Christopher Dornan reports that newspapers still attract a substantial readership; 57 per cent of Canadians over the age of eighteen read a newspaper during a regular weekday, while 64 per cent read a newspaper over the weekend. All of these forms of communication are part of our waking up and part of putting the day in context before we go to sleep.

While newspaper readership has declined sharply during the last decade, the amount of TV watching and radio listening has remained roughly the same for at least a generation. Other patterns also seem to have hardened into place. Almost half of all Canadians over the age of eighteen read or flip through a magazine at least once a day, over 70 per cent have read a book in the last year, and over 60 per cent will go to a movie theatre at least once during the year. Interestingly enough, over 60 per cent of those surveyed will read a book by a Canadian author, and 30 per cent will see at least one Canadian film during the year (MacAfee 2002, A3).

But the old media are only part of the story. The Internet has changed the landscape in ways that were unimaginable eight or ten years ago. Over a third of Canadians over the age of eighteen, and a lot more who are under the age of eighteen, visit cyberspace every day.

The Internet, of course, has become a central experience for most Canadian young people. Whether it's doing homework on computers, communicating with friends through e-mail, downloading music, or playing video games, young people have a familiarity and a dexterity with computers that is the envy of most of their parents. One researcher has noted that the time that young people spend on the Internet has not come at the expense of going to movies, watching TV, or listening to music; it's come at the expense of sleeping, doing homework, talking to family members, or exercising. The Internet has also thrust young people in particular into an interactive world in which fantasy and reality can often be confused. The interactive entertainment business, which garnered close to US$11 billion in revenue in 2001, allows enthusiasts to "wrestle Hulk Hogan, hit a home run in Yankee Stadium or inhabit the body of skateboarder Tony Hawk" (Kushner 2002). People can assume different identities, walk the streets of imaginary worlds, have conversations with characters that they meet inside a game, and even attend concerts that take place only in cyberspace.

Few Canadians would disagree with Gitlin's contention that we live our lives amid a "sensory uproar." Our life experience "has become an experience in the presence of media" (Gitlin 2002, 46, 20). But what is crucial to understand is that communications is not only the focal point for vast changes in the way that we live our lives but is also a battleground in a wider struggle between global economic forces and the state. Where the state was once there to insure the survival of cultural institutions and did so through a phalanx of public corporations, subsidies, tax breaks, and technological fixes, global economic and institutional forces are now so strong and technological change so deep and all-pervasive that the state has had to relinquish much of the role that it once played. As David Cameron and Janice Stein have noted:

> At the beginning of the twenty-first century ... the reach of the state has retreated from a portion of the economic and cultural spaces that are important to citizens.... The disjunction is clear: political boundaries continue to remain largely fixed, while cultural and economic spaces are reconfiguring. (Cameron and Stein 2002, 141)

While some observers would be pleased to see the erosion of state power and the emergence of new global forces and identities, it is important to note that the state is still the institution most closely tied to democratic institutions and able to address the needs of its citizens. In fact, one can argue that we are beginning to witness a turning of the wheel. After the events of 9/11, corporate scandals at Enron and Worldcom, and the tragedy at Walkerton, people are no longer willing to tolerate the withdrawal of the state from some of the key roles that it once played. Unbridled corporate power and unfettered globalism are no longer seen as the saviours that they once were.

The goal of this volume is to describe how Canadians communicate with each other and with the world in the widest possible sense. The book describes the major trends and developments that have taken place in government policy, in corporate strategies, in creative communities, and in various media – newspapers, films, the Internet, libraries, TV, music, and book publishing. We also examine how new communications technologies are transforming the workplace and medical practice.

The book originated out of a conference sponsored by the University of Calgary's Telus Visiting Scholars Program, which was held in November, 2001. Six prominent scholars were invited to Calgary and then to Banff to interact with students and the community, to share ideas, and to focus on developments that had taken place in the institutions and cultural and communication industries that they study. The distinguished visitors were joined by scholars from a number of faculties at the University of Calgary. We wished to ensure that this book would cover a wide range of issues and topics and include a rich broth of viewpoints and perspectives.

The book mirrors the tensions that exist between the power and influence of global media and the needs of citizens and local communities. It also reflects another crucial tension – the clash between the power of market forces and the needs of the state. Many of the articles celebrate the dynamism of Canadian culture and communication – the vibrant populism of Canadian music, the achievements of Canadian authors (some of whom now command a world stage), the presence of high quality commentary and critical journalism in newspapers and on TV, and the considerable potential that exists in areas such as telehealth. Much of this has to do with taking back, or in some cases preserving, what the authors see as genuine and authentic voices and expressions. The emergence of a distinct Aboriginal media system, the expanding of venues where Canadian films can be seen, and the market for Canadian music that has been carved out both by government support and regulations and by popular demand are hard won achievements. But they are also examples of how fragile and vulnerable many of our cultural industries have become.

Most of our authors believe that powerful economic and technological forces are overwhelming and curtailing our capacity to hear our own voices. Canadian messages are being lost amid the cacophony – the endless din of American and global communications. Increasingly we are prisoners to economic arrangements over which we have little control. It is in some ways a frightening time. Identity and citizenship are at stake.

How Canadians Communicate chronicles some of the extraordinary changes that are shaking the foundations of Canada's cultural and communications industries at the beginning of the twenty-first century. Some would argue that these changes have been so deep and so pervasive that in some ways we are facing a new world, a world where many of the old assumptions, the old dependable relationships, have been eroded. Others contend that arguments about the reach of globalization and the diminished capacity of the state may be exaggerated. Globalization is not a predictable process. It can recede in some areas even as it expands in others. "Globalization is a 'layered' process. Some of the threads of globalization may thicken more quickly than others, and, indeed, some may thin out," as Cameron and Stein point out (2002, 142). While the state may be "shape-shifting" – changing its contours and its responsibilities, its power may be increasing in some ways while shrinking in others (Pal 1999, 2).

Marc Raboy, one of Canada's leading experts on communication and globalization, has identified at least four areas in which dramatic changes have taken place. The first is that the sovereignty of nation states is being challenged and indeed curtailed by the emergence of transnational and multilateral institutions such as the European Union, NAFTA, and the WTO. Second, the world economy is becoming integrated due to the rise of global communications and entertainment conglomerates. The economic repercussions are enormous, but so are the ideological ones. Raboy's argument is that:

> Global economic integration comes packed with a particular seductive ideology that emerges powerfully in the sphere of culture and communication. The global cultural industries market not only a set of products but also a vision of a certain way of life. Thrust on to the global stage, all industrialized cultural production is reduced to entertainment, and its only value is commercial (Raboy 2002, 115).

Raboy's third point is that advances in technology have reduced time and space and provided extraordinary economic and cultural opportunities. But while these new technologies have reduced barriers in some ways, they have also created new gaps between rich and poor. They have also created new meeting places, but they have destroyed others.

Another of Raboy's arguments is that these shifts in the geological plates of global communication have fostered a counter-reaction. There is strong resistance and a struggle to reclaim and reformulate local and national identities. There is also a strengthening and a renewed search for other ways of connecting and cross-connecting – particularly a deepening of gender, ethnic, linguistic, and religious experiences and associations.

While our authors do not deal with all of these points explicitly, they do touch on each of them implicitly. All of these developments wash across the volume in one way or another. At the heart of what Raboy has described are two phenomena that are intimately linked; digitization and convergence. I would like to describe each of these forces in some detail.

Fragmentation, Convergence, and the Digital Revolution

The advent of digital communication has not only made it possible for an almost infinite expansion in the availability of TV and radio signals but has made it possible for signals to be read and transmitted across media. One key aspect of this development is that virtually all media are converging on the Internet. The Internet allows us to hear radio broadcasts, read newspapers, listen to music, play video games, search databases, e-mail friends, and watch videos.

Cell phones and other hand-held devices are also leading examples of technological convergence. The flip-up screens on the new generation of cell phones will allow users to send e-mail messages, play games, read news headlines, and watch movies.

One aspect of the digital revolution is the splintering and fragmentation of audiences. Again, the new digital technology allows many more signals to be carried in the same amount of space. We have seen the number of channels explode from twenty to two hundred in fifteen years. And that number is likely to multiply as digitization begins to take hold. While Canadian television has not yet reached that range of choice, the CRTC's licensing of dozens of new digital channels could change the landscape of Canadian television. The potential fallout for Canada's major TV networks could be dramatic. In a three-hundred-channel universe driven by boutique channels devoted to sports, news, documentaries, lifestyles, and movies, they may have great difficulty assembling sizable audiences. Where a new dramatic series, a national newscast, or a rock concert by a Canadian group was once almost guaranteed to attract a large TV audience, there are now few guarantees. Canadian nationalists fear that these once powerful vehicles of national expression will simply not find an audience amid the endless kaleidoscope of choices that are now or will soon be available. Indeed, in their contribution, Bart Beaty and Rebecca Sullivan document the degree to which audience and advertising shares for Canadian TV networks have already plummeted.

Compounding the problem are the grey and black markets for American satellite systems that allow viewers to bypass the Canadian market entirely. An estimated 700,000 Canadians have chosen to exit the country in terms of TV reception. Despite the availability of Canadian satellite systems that offer a myriad of choices, and the prospect of fines and even jail sentences, many Canadians refuse to accept any limits on their right to watch more and more American TV programs. The financial investments made in Canadian programming – in terms of Canadian content regulations, the Canadian Television Fund, tax laws and credits, and support for public broadcasters – amounts to very little if large numbers of Canadians can simply opt out of the system, electing to receive TV signals from another country.

Another critical development is the advent of personal video recorders. PVR's allow viewers to download up to ninety hours of programming on a hard disk. According to Amy Harmon of *The New York Times*, the tendency will be for viewers "to watch what is on the machine rather than what is on TV" (Harmon 2002). They can ignore network schedules and cut through advertising to their heart's content. This also means that the daily calorie count of Canadian TV programming is likely to be reduced even further. And all of this could have a major effect on Canadian music, sports, and film, among other areas.

But technological convergence is only one aspect of a wider drama. Technological convergence has helped to propel the rush toward corporate convergence. Media giants such as AOL Time Warner, Disney, Bertelsmann, and Viacom now control media empires that span a vast horizon. The same conglomerates that own film and TV studios now also own music labels, cable operations, Internet services, TV networks, publishing houses, sports franchises, and theme parks. Almost every aspect of communications is integrated with every other aspect, and media "products" are endlessly linked and cross-promoted. While this has many repercussions for global marketing and indeed ideology, one particular consequence is that, as media conglomerates tend to rely on their own internal food chains, it may be much more difficult for Canadian media companies to sell their products in the American market.

As Vincent Carlin and Christopher Dornan demonstrate in their articles, Canadian media corporations have also been captivated by – have fallen prey to – the promise of convergence. The telecommunications giant,

BCE, recently acquired two of the great jewels in the Canadian media pantheon, CTV and *The Globe and Mail*. The Asper family's CanWest Global, arguably Canada's most financially successful TV network, moved suddenly in 2000 to buy the Southam newspaper chain, including the *National Post*, from Conrad Black. Quebecor, which controls much of the print business in North America, has acquired the French-language TV network, TVA, and Videotron, which dominates the cable industry in Quebec. Its treasure chest of media properties also includes the Sun newspaper chain and recently purchased radio stations from Astral. Rogers Communications, which has outposts in cable, cell phones, video stores, and the magazine industry (*Maclean's*), recently added the Toronto Blue Jays to its stable of properties.

Convergence has created a new set of problems for Canadian media corporations. First, in order to make these acquisitions, corporations have saddled themselves with debt. The irony is that, as they have grown larger, they have also become weaker and more vulnerable. Arguably, their ability to take chances, to invest heavily, and to promote Canadian magazines, music, TV shows, or newspapers has been weakened. But convergence has also raised questions about the nature of journalism and its role in ensuring that the country benefits from a lively and open debate about issues that are critical to the future. Critics contend that, when ownership falls into too few hands, abuses of power are more likely to occur. In his article, Christopher Dornan of Carleton University chronicles the controversy sparked by the Asper family's supposed unwavering support for Prime Minister Jean Chrétien. Editors and journalists working for the Southam chain were told that they must adhere to the positions taken in national editorials written at corporate headquarters in Winnipeg. To many this meant that the freedom needed to reflect attitudes in their communities or to question the actions of government leaders – both basic ingredients in a vibrant and progressive democracy – had been drastically reduced.

In June, 2002, CanWest again imposed what some described as a "gag order" on journalists who had been critical of Prime Minister Chrétien. This time, some forty former publishers, editors, and directors of Southam published an open letter warning that the free expression necessary for democratic debate was being imperilled. In their view:

> CanWest has awakened us to the daunting potential of concentration of newsroom ownership – particularly when a single firm owns other media. We can picture a time when one or two multi-channel media giants, each with a single national voice, will be

telling us what to think. One danger, of course, is a loss of diversity of voices – a diversity that is the essence of free speech, democracy and pluralism. The challenge is how to adjust the balance between "the right of owners" and the "public interest." (*Globe and Mail*, 6 June 2002, 7)

Communications and Canadian Identity

In analyzing the changes to the communications environment that Raboy has described, one must keep in mind that Canada has little of the hardwiring that has kept vital cultural traditions in place in other countries. Our country did not emerge, was not consecrated, in a bloody revolution or a fierce struggle for independence; it is not united by a distinct language or religious tradition; we do not enjoy a common education system; and our political institutions are viewed with suspicion and cynicism by a vast majority of Canadians. We also lack the ethnic hardness of countries such as Ireland, Japan, Sweden, the Netherlands, or Italy.

Much of what has made Canada such an exceptional experiment in human relations – our openness to new ideas, our acceptance and celebration of different and multiple identities, our postmodern sensibilities, and our strong belief in individual rights – also makes us exceptionally vulnerable to outside forces. It is difficult to guard frontiers in a country that remains so open to the flow of people and ideas.

Optimists argue that our very openness and flexibility and our impressive capacity for resistance and self-expression will allow the country to survive the torrential sea that now threatens to engulf us. Scholars such as John Meisel (1996) contend that we now have an educated middle class that demands and will pay for Canadian literature, music, and art and will watch Canadian TV programs if they are made available. While Canadians are exposed to large doses of American culture, Canadian culture is flourishing, and Canadian nationalism is at high tide. One of the contributors to the volume, the extraordinary Canadian writer Aritha van Herk, has expressed her optimism in the following way:

My tentative conclusion is that culture is seeking to reinvent itself now as it inevitably must. It is looking to the local and the regional. It is not looking to that national discourse. It is not looking to the centre; it is not looking to succeed in Toronto. It is looking to what it is doing here and now at this particular moment, without sanction to a government sanctioned discourse at all. The energy that I am seeing in the local and the regional is phenomenal. It is an energy that somehow manages to keep itself going, sustain itself and that has wonderful fights and arguments and is simply explosive. And if Canadian culture is going to survive it is going to be there. (Banff symposium, November, 2001)

Others are not so sure. They see government policies with respect to book and magazine publishing, film and television production, and competition policy as weak and ineffectual. Historically, Canada was able through an act of extraordinary national will to create spaces in which Canadians could perform, act, write and publish, and make TV programs. As Richard Schultz observes in his contribution to the volume, the government's capacity to effect change, and indeed to maintain even the limited space that was once reserved for cultural expression, has been greatly diminished. In area after area, from TV programming to film, from music to publishing, our authors document the degree to which the state's capacity for investment and intervention has withered. Their fear is that in many cultural fields we will be left with little but the wreckage of what once was.

The articles in this volume focus for the most part on the inner life and workings of various communications industries. In almost every case, our authors chronicle how a vibrant and creative inner world is being shaped and buffeted by harsh external forces and by extraordinary changes in technology.

★ ★ ★

The book begins with an article by Richard Schultz, a political scientist at McGill University who is one of Canada's leading experts on government regulation. Schultz's contention is that the federal government's ability to control consumer choice through its flotilla of regulations and incentives has largely failed. As Schultz points out, the foreign share (i.e., the American share) of Canadian cultural markets – from books, to films, to TV programs, to sound recordings – is, if anything, growing. Popular tastes, the openness of borders, and new technologies that allow consumers to "exit" the Canadian media system, combined with a failure of will and imagination by policy-makers, have made the government merely a bystander on a host of communications issues.

The second article, written by Vince Carlin, formerly a senior CBC executive and now a professor at Ryerson University and one of the country's most thoughtful commentators on Canadian journalism, can be seen as a companion piece to that written by Schultz. Carlin examines the flip side of government policies – the strategies being pursued by the private sector. His main concern is with how the theory of convergence has dominated the actions and operations of Canada's leading media giants. His argument, however, is that media corporations have bitten into a bitter fruit. They have been stampeded into acquiring properties that they have little experience managing, are trying to integrate their ventures with the Internet, a medium that is still in its infancy, and are finding out that bigger is not necessarily better or more profitable. As the media system tilts to accommodate the needs of large corporations, the system seems to be becoming more Americanized. His conclusion is that "Canadian consumers have, in effect, voted for large doses of American product on their screens but allowed the creation of a system that benefits a few wealthy Canadian individuals and corporations."

Frits Pannekoek's extraordinary article on Canada's memory institutions deals with how technological changes and the new global marketplace threaten to limit Canadian cultural space. While he commends the innovative work being done by libraries, archives, and museums, Pannekoek reminds us of two overarching realities: that "the Internet has inspired a degree of chaos" and that "the best information will always require payment." The "creation and repurposing of Canadian cultural memory" will take considerable expertise, a commitment of resources, and political will. At the very least, search engines will have to be developed that will allow Canadians to find Canadian materials. In the meantime, memory institutions are caught between traditional mandates and the need to look to and invest in the future.

Christopher Dornan's article on Canadian newspapers is the lead article in the next section on Canadian media and Canadian identity. Dornan, who is the director of the School of Journalism and Mass Communication at Carleton University and who is an astute observer of developments in the newspaper industry in Canada and worldwide, chronicles the extraordinary developments that took place in the Canadian newspaper industry in 2001. He describes the battles that were waged among various newspaper groups and over editorial independence and reminds readers that newspapers play a special role in shaping Canadian life and society. Unlike the music, book publishing, or film industries, where foreign content dominates to the point where Canadian voices, images, and stories are in the minority, newspapers focus primarily on local and national events and personalities. They remain the linchpin of the Canadian communications system.

The articles on publishing, television, film, and music deal with similar themes and can be seen as part of the collective *cri de coeur* that emanates from this volume. Aritha van Herk, Rebecca Sullivan and Bart Beaty, Malek Khouri, and Will Straw describe the power of North American and global economic forces and the inability of government policies to offer tangible resistance. Audiences are attuned to Hollywood, and, while there are populist responses and evidence of a vital energy that is seeking new outlets and means of expression, something has gone wrong. It is, in fact, the best of times and the worst of times. Good music, television, books, and music are all available in great abundance – but what is available is less and less our music, television, books, and music. While much is gained as a result of the abundance provided by the global entertainment industry and by new technologies, much is also lost. Sullivan and Beaty have summarized what they see as the dilemmas that confront Canadian television in the new digital age: "The dream of national television produced by and for Canadians forming the cornerstone of the industry is drifting away. There's a new dream now of unlimited viewer choice, but it cloaks a nightmarish vision of media monopolies and limited opportunities for Canadian voices to find an audience."

One scholar with a more optimistic message is Cora Voyageur. Voyageur teaches in the Department of Sociology at the University of Calgary and specializes in the study of Canadian Aboriginal life. She begins by reminding readers of the demeaning and insulting "Tonto" images that have dominated the mass media's portrayal of Natives for so long. These painful and disfiguring images not only influenced how other Canadians saw Aboriginal Canadians but also how Aboriginals had come to see themselves. Voyageur believes that the emergence of a distinct Aboriginal media system in Canada will help erase the distortions and injustices of the past. Her article focuses on four institutions: the Aboriginal People's Television Network (APTN), CFWE radio, *Windspeaker*, and *Aboriginal Times* magazine. The value of these new ventures is that "they present Aboriginal views in a way that mainstream media cannot." This is of enormous benefit to Aboriginal communities and to those Canadians who wish to learn more about Aboriginal experiences.

The last section of the book describes the impact being made in the home, in workplaces, and in public institutions by the Internet and the new digital technologies. Maria Bakardjieva, a pioneer in the study of how the Internet is being used in the home, describes the often-complex relationship that people have with their home computers. To some degree, the sanctuary of the home is being invaded by a device that links people to the workplace and brings stress, responsibility, and forms of both oppression and empowerment. It also links people with new and extraordinary forms of entertainment. These include playing computer games and being able to tour art galleries or museums online and being able to participate in discussions in chat rooms occupied by people who share their hobbies or interests. For some people, however, the computer has clearly invaded their time and space. They are unable to free themselves from the torrents of work-related e-mail messages that descend on them at night and on weekends. They find themselves always on call, always within reach of their bosses, clients, or co-workers. Of course, for some people, the ability to work at home is a blessing. The power of Bakardjieva's contribution lies to some degree in the portraits that she draws of the people she studied and how they are trying in their own ways to adapt to the new technology, balance their roles as mothers, fathers and workers, and separate their work from their home life.

For the parents of school-age children, the computer is both a critical window for education and learning and a dangerous labyrinth of consumer traps and no-go zones where pornography and violent games are found in abundance. Bakardjieva calls for "a new branch of education" that will help parents to manage their children's use of the Internet.

In the next article, three respected medical researchers at the University of Calgary offer their perspectives on the developments that are taking place in the telehealth sector. They explore the new relationships that have developed between health care providers and patients from whom they are separated by considerable distances. Remote screening, electronic visits, teleconferencing, the development of software that can store and transmit vital information, and the use of websites for patient information are just some of the advances being made in e-health. Although there have been successes — and each life that is saved or made better represents a triumph — serious problems remain, particularly with regard to the lack of training and standardization. Marilynne Hebert and her colleagues provide readers with a glimpse of a future that holds considerable promise.

The last article, by Graham Longford and Barbara Crow, is a devastating critique of the employment practices that prevail among teleworkers.

This is an article that needed to be written and needs to be read. It sounds an alarm bell about shabby working conditions and the possible deskilling of much of the Canadian work force. While there has been a great deal of hype about the employment opportunities that will supposedly be generated by the new economy, Longford and Crow paint a much different portrait. They describe workplaces that are the modern equivalent of sweatshops and where the old wounds of social inequality based on gender, class, and region are kept open. They conclude with a series of recommendations for reform and a call for action.

★ ★ ★

Whether or not we have entered a new world of Canadian communications, a world sharply different from anything that we have previously known, is open to debate. Some believe that we are at an important crossroads. New technologies and global arrangements have created different economic and cultural rules. Governments are unwilling or unable to step into the breach to the extent that they once did. In the age of e-health, video games, e-mail, and digital technology, it is not clear that the past is a reasonable guide to the future. As Frits Pannekoek told the symposium meeting in Banff:

> Library use in Canada is decreasing at the rate of 10 per cent per year and that is something to factor and what does that mean? We are not quite sure, but it is decreasing.... I have my own assumptions about what it means, but there is a considerable shift happening for the first time in how people access, use and deliberate over information, where they get it from and what they consider authentic sources. I think something subtle is happening, something dramatic is happening, we don't know exactly yet, whether it will persist, whether when people turn a certain age they are going to change. I suspect they won't.

But interestingly, Bart Beaty gives this a different interpretation:

> We are seeing an overthrowing of old norms, old forms of contemplation ... that there is some kind of radical transformation taking place in the change from analog to digital. We're still fixed with the model of an individual user or consumer who is facing a large unseen hidden media conglomerate that is controlling the

choice and controlling the opportunities. I don't think that that is fundamentally different from what happened in preceding generations. (Banff symposium, November, 2001)

The message from the contributors to this volume is that Canadians need to take decisive action in order to understand and master these new technologies so that our homes, our workplaces, our cultural life, and our public places can become more open, democratic, and humane. This is not easily accomplished, given that states have ceded much of their power to international trade regimes and power blocs and to giant conglomerates. What is called for are acts of will, acts of inventiveness and resistance, that will allow Canadians to again hear their own voices. There is also the need to produce music and TV programs and books that are truly compelling – that touch people's hearts and reflect their lives. If we can do this then we have nothing to fear.

References

Cameron, David, and Janice Stein. 2002. "The State as Place Amid Shifting Places." In *Street Protests and Fantasy Parks: Globalization, Culture and the State*, ed. David Cameron and Janice Stein. Vancouver: University of British Columbia Press.

Communications Management. 2002. *Fragmentation, Consolidation and the Canadian Consumer.* January.

Gitlin, Todd. 1980. *The Whole World is Watching.* Berkeley, CA: University of California Press.

——. 2002. *Media Unlimited.* New York: Metropolitan Books.

Harmon, Amy. 2002. "Digital Video Recorders Give Advertisers Pause." *New York Times*, online edition, May 5.

Kushner, David. 2002. "Sports Fantasy is Catching Up with Reality." *New York Times*, 25 July.

MacAfee, Michelle. 2002. "Canucks Threatened by U.S. Culture, Poll Results." *Calgary Herald*, 1 July, p. A3.

Meisel, John. 1996. "Extinction Revisited: Culture and Class in Canada." In *Seeing Ourselves: Media Power and Policy in Canada*, ed. Helen Holmes and David Taras, 249–56. Toronto: Harcourt Brace & Co.

Pal, Leslie. 1999. "Shape Shifting: Canadian Governance toward the 21st Century." In *How Ottawa Spends 1999–2000*, ed. Leslie Pal, 1–35. Toronto: Oxford University Press.

Raboy, Marc. 2002. "Communication and Globalization: A Challenge for Public Policy." In *Street Protests and Fantasy Parks: Globalization, Culture and the State*, ed. David Cameron and Janice Stein, 109–140. Vancouver: University of British Columbia Press.

GOVERNMENT *and* CORPORATE POLICIES

FROM MASTER TO PARTNER TO BIT PLAYER

The diminishing capacity of government policy

Richard Schultz

[T]his country must be assured of complete control of broadcasting from Canadian sources, free from foreign interference or influence. – R. B. Bennett, 1932[1]

The difference between what may and what can happen [in telecommunications] will be decided by political will. – Eric Kierans, Minister of Communications, 1969[2]

Canada's response to the information revolution will be 10 percent technology and 90 percent government policy and regulation. – Perrin Beatty, Minister of Communications, 1993[3]

Viewed from one perspective, the last few years have witnessed little change in terms of governmental communications policy developments. While there has been one substantial policy initiative and several other issues emerging onto the policy agenda, for the most part, these years are notable for the paucity of new policy developments. From another, more macro, perspective, however, they were years of profound, corrosive change, in which the diminished capacity for a systemic steering or directing role for government policy-makers in the communications sector became more and more apparent. In this article, I propose to review the one major initiative as well as three other issues demanding attention on the communications policy agenda. More importantly, I want to discuss and explain why I think government policy-makers, and consequently government policies, particularly those policies which rely on command and control, are losing their influence in the Canadian communications sector. In the first section of the paper, I describe the major changes that I believe are profoundly altering the traditional Canadian approach to communications policy. In the second section, I will link those changes first to the one specific policy initiative undertaken by the federal government in the past two years and then to the major issues that I see emerging on the government's radar screen.

Part 1: From Control at the Centre to Influence on the Margins

In the 1995 final report of the Information Highway Advisory Council, there is the remarkable statement that "[w]hile the government has found it advisable to regulate cultural and intellectual content, neither the intent nor the effect of such regulation has been to limit consumer choice" (Information Highway Advisory Council 1995, 25). While the statement is correct with respect to the *effect* of such regulation, a point to which I shall return, insofar as governmental *intent* is concerned, this statement reflects either a wilful misreading or an appalling ignorance of the history of Canadian communications policy from the onset of mass communications some seventy years or so ago. The unifying thread of a series of policy undertakings since the creation of the CRBC in 1932 has been an explicit attempt by governments to control, to a significant degree, what Canadians can receive through various broadcasting media. By control, I am not suggesting that successive Canadian governments have attempted to censor what Canadians can receive. My point is simply that it is incontestable that the core objective has been to restrict or constrain the choices Canadians have had in their access to broadcasting, and to a less extent other media, outlets. The following are the major examples of actions taken by governmental authorities to exercise control over the media to restrict Canadians' choices:

- Private radio networks were prohibited for several decades;
- The introduction of television was delayed and, when finally authorized, was subject to significant geographical and networking constraints;
- The number of American channels authorized on cable systems was severely restricted;
- An attempt was made to restrict the geographical reach of cable television by prohibiting the use of microwave to distribute signals;
- The licensing of pay television was delayed for almost a decade;
- Individual Canadians initially could not own satellite television receivers, and then, after a few years of relaxed requirements, more rigid rules were instituted, rules which, in effect, criminalized Canadians who sought direct access to American systems; and
- Punitive tariffs, ownership controls, and restrictive tax deductibility provisions were imposed to discourage the availability of American magazines.

In its attempts to control "consumer choice" (the Advisory Council's term), successive governments have employed every single policy instrument in their extensive tool-kit, from public ownership and spending, to tax restrictions and tariffs, to regulatory prohibitions and constraints, and, most recently, the criminal law. So intent have governments been to pursue such control that they have normally used individual instruments in multiple combinations.

It is indisputably the case, however, that, notwithstanding the intent and the deployment of the tools, Canadian governments have had extremely limited success in satisfying their objective of controlling consumer choice. Indeed, it is rather ironic that defenders of the limited effect often cite the fact of limited success as if it mitigates the intent. On the other hand, in one of the few serious attempts (particularly among those sympathetic to the effort) to explain its shortcomings, John Meisel (1989) has noted that, throughout the history of Canadian broadcasting policy, there has been a profound "performance gap" between public objectives and attainment. Moreover, the gap extends beyond the broadcasting sector to encompass

Table 1 Foreign Share of Canadian Cultural Markets

Percent Foreign:	In these Canadian Markets:
95	Feature-films screened in theatres
70	Music on radio stations
84	Retail sales of sound recordings
69	French-language retail sale of sound recordings
60	English-language television programming
33	French-language television programming
85	Prime-time drama on English-language television
75	Prime-time drama on French-language television
70	Book market
83	Newsstand market for magazines
81	English-language consumer magazines

Source: Mulcahy (2000, 184) and sources cited therein

almost every field of cultural policy. The most obvious measure of that gap is the dominance of foreign, especially American, imports in the individual cultural markets. Table 1, tabulated by Kevin V. Mulcahy, shows how vast the gap is.

For purposes of this paper, which has as its central argument that the long-standing governmental inability to control consumer choice has grown and can only continue to grow, it is imperative to identify the primary reasons for this communications policy "performance gap." In part, such a significant gap suggests either that the policy intent was simply symbolic, *à la* Edelman (1964), or reflects a congenital absence of political or regulatory will to take enforcement seriously. Acheson and Maule contend, for example, that for years *Time* effectively flouted the relevant income-tax provisions by sending editorial content first on microfilm and then via the telephone lines to a Canadian printer and did so with impunity (1999, 198–99). Similarly, with respect to content quotas, the CRTC's performance has routinely been found wanting (Ellis 1992; Stanbury 1998; Hardin 1985; Caplan–Sauvageau 1986). From this perspective, it would not be unfair, nor inaccurate, to describe political and regulatory efforts in the communications sector, to employ Krasner's phrase, as displaying a large component of "organized hypocrisy" (Krasner 1999).

Meisel, who focused solely on the broadcasting, especially the television, sector, sought to answer his own question as to why "a large majority of Canadians is locked into a television regime dominated by the conventions, styles, and content of the American television industry" (1989, 195). More pointedly, and plaintively, he asked, after surveying the extensive record of public investigations, "why the perpetual charade of inquiries, recommendations, failure, more inquiries, more recommendations, more failures, and so on and so on" (1989, 193). His answer, which I think is compelling, is "the dominant value system of Canadians ... [and their assumption] that their basic rights give them access to any television signal that modern technology makes available." He concluded that there is "widespread and vociferous insistence by Canadians that no one, the government included, is going to tell them what programs they are going to bring to their magic screens" (194).

One qualification I would make to Meisel's highly persuasive analysis is to emphasize that this situation predates television. Notwithstanding Prime Minister R. B. Bennett's conceit about "complete control ... free from foreign ... influence," Canada and Canadian governments have never possessed such control. Canada did not have that control before 1932 and did not attain it after the creation of the CBC or its predecessor agency. Canadians who could afford the expensive radio sets in the early days of radio broadcasting had become as devoted to American programming as subsequent generations were to American television. As the cost of radio sets decreased, direct access to American signals expanded among Canadian listeners.[4] Similarly, notwithstanding the rigid controls on the development of Canadian television announced in 1952, hundreds of thousands of Canadians had already established direct access to American signals. As many commentators have noted, such was the powerful attraction of American programming for Canadians that both public and private broadcasters, radio (Filion 1996) and television (Rutherford 1990), had to respond by including a significant proportion of American programs in their own schedules.

A second qualification, directly relevant to our contemporary concerns, is that the tradition of limited control over Canadian audiences was a consequence not simply of Canadian mass tastes but of the relative ease of technological exit from the grips of would-be Canadian controllers. As I have argued elsewhere (Schultz 1995), if state authorities, regulatory or otherwise, cannot enforce their restricted choices to impose a preferred pattern of behaviour on consumers, as opposed to the producers of regulated services, such as railroads, airlines, etc., then the power of any regulatory regime is not only significantly diluted but probably non-sustainable. Certainly, the ready availability of radio receivers and the television sets that could, by the simplest of devices – in-set and roof-top antennae – directly access American signals, argues for both an appreciation of the permeability of the Canadian broadcasting sector and its consequences for Canadian broadcasting production and regulation.

The current controversy over Canadian access to American direct-to-home satellite services (of which more shortly) is only the most recent manifestation of the problems Canadian authorities face today in seeking to restrict, by "political will," to invoke Kierans' phrase, Canadian communications consumers' choices. More importantly, the best, or worst, depending on one's viewpoint, is yet to come. Notwithstanding the demise of ICraveTV.Com, that victory for Canadian, and American, broadcasters will surely be short-lived. It will be cited in textbooks as an historical example of a technological Canute unable to stop the waves. The potentialities, increasingly the actualities, of the Internet and especially what George Gilder calls the "telecosm," or infinite bandwidth, will erode the last strands of any pretensions to sovereignty, and particularly that undefined, probably indefinable Canadian variant, cultural sovereignty.[5] In Gilder's telecosm, the "customer is sovereign," something which has never been envisaged, albeit it has been practised, even if in a diluted form, in Canadian communications. The listener or viewer in the future, with the aid of devices such as MP3, Napster-like alternatives, CD burners, digital television recorders, and free video downloading software such as Morpheus – all of which are currently possible – and the Internet, will be her own broadcaster, radio station, and recording library. The delivery systems, whether fibre-optic cable, wireless, or satellite, will be, in terms of content carried, largely, if not completely, beyond regulation (Globerman and Hagen 1998). The notion that an "act of political will" by a player of such evidently limited capacity as Canada, or alternatively, that the development of such a cornucopia of alternatives will be overwhelmingly shaped by "government policy and regulation," i.e., the 90 percent solution preferred by Perrin Beatty, is monumental hubris or chutzpah or a mixture of both.[6]

The Canadian government has also accepted self-imposed limits on that capacity through its adoption of international trade agreements that have increasing relevance for communications policy. Canada was one of the original signatories to the General Agreement on Trade and Tariffs (GATT), although for most of the history of that agreement the presumption was that cultural concerns were beyond its scope. As we shall see in the next section, this presumption has been shattered in recent years.

Canada has been at the forefront of efforts to expand the scope of trade agreements to include services, particularly telecommunications. The Canada–U.S. Free Trade Agreement included a provision, albeit one highly limited, that established an international precedent for a constraint on national sovereignty over domestic telecommunications regulation (Schultz

1990; Globerman et al. 1992). Subsequent negotiations, first in the North American Free Trade Agreement (NAFTA) and then particularly in the General Agreement on Trades in Services (GATS), radically expanded the scope of the binding constraints on governments in the telecommunications sector (Janisch 1998; Trebilcock and Howse 1999).

Of course, the conventional argument is that the FTA and NAFTA do not encompass cultural policy because of the so-called cultural exemption clause. Moreover, Canada has taken the view that GATS does not apply to cultural industries because it made no commitments regarding them when it signed the agreement (Browne 1999b). There are, however, several problems with both of these arguments relevant to the presumed continuing control capacity of government policy-makers. The first is that both the FTA and NAFTA permit retaliation by an affected government were the cultural exemption clause to be invoked, making the latter far less significant than is commonly assumed.[7] The second is that Canada learned in the magazine dispute, discussed below, how fragile its presumed cultural policy protections in fact were. Third, and potentially far more corrosive, is that, with the convergence of telecommunications and broadcasting media, Canada's trade obligations for telecommunications are far more stringent than hitherto was the case. The problem for Canada, in the case of future challenges, will be to persuade our international competitors and their home governments that cultural policy concerns and, where pertinent, trade exemptions trump our telecommunications trade obligations.

Part 2: Cases in Current Communications Policy

Having sketched out the historical and contemporary constraints on governmental policy in the communications sector, and consequently what we believe to be the fundamentally diminished capacity of governmental policy-makers, we now turn to four cases illustrating and supporting these arguments. The cases are:

- magazine policy;
- broadband access policy;
- foreign ownership restrictions; and
- direct access to American DTH satellite services.

The first of these involved the one major policy development, while the remaining three are issues or initiatives now, or soon to be, on the governmental agenda.

Canadian Magazine Policy

In 2000, the Canadian government undertook a new policy initiative, the Canadian Magazine Fund, described as "a key element of the Government's comprehensive policy in support of the Canadian magazine industry" (Canadian Heritage 2001). The background to the development of this magazine policy represents all that Canadian policy-makers should fear about the potent admixture of popular Canadian tastes, technology, and trade obligations.

The issue of the sale in Canada of American magazines, particularly split-runs and regional variations, and their presumed impact on the Canadian magazine industry because of the competition posed for advertising revenues, goes back to at least the O'Leary Royal Commission on Publications established in 1960. Two central recommendations emanating from that commission were: first, that advertising from Canadian sources in magazines directed at the Canadian market should not be deductible for Canadian tax purposes, and secondly, that foreign – read American – magazines with advertising directed at Canadian readers should not be permitted into Canada. When the federal government acted on the recommendations, it surprisingly (or not, depending on one's theory of political influence) exempted the two largest of such magazines, *Time* and *Reader's Digest*.

In 1976, the federal government amended the *Income Tax Act* to remove the grandfather clause exempting *Time* and *Reader's Digest*. As a result, the latter decided to "Canadianize" itself so as to be exempt from the non-deductibility provisions, while the former closed its Canadian version. Acheson and Maule report, however, that *Time*'s real strategy was to lower its advertising rates for Canadian advertisers and to flout the law by sending editorial copy first by microfilm and then by telephone lines to printers in Canada for production and distribution.[8]

For more than fifteen years after the presumed punitive tax measures in 1976, it appears that *Time* flouted the law, becoming as profitable if not more so than it had been before the measures were introduced, and did so with complete impunity. The relative quiet life of the Canadian magazine policy charade, however, was disrupted in 1993 when Time Warner announced that it would publish a split-run edition of *Sports Illustrated* in Canada. It proposed to avoid the tax regulations by sending American editorial copy via satellite for printing in Canada. As there was no actual physical object involved, Canadian tariffs and tax regulations to prevent such magazines were not applicable.

The government's response, after the obligatory task force which, not surprisingly, confirmed that the health of the Canadian magazine industry was indeed threatened, was to introduce a new tax measure that imposed an 80 percent tax on each issue of a split-run magazine based on the value of all the advertising in the Canadian edition (Acheson and Maule 1999, 191–205; Browne 1999). Time Warner, obviously assuming that the prior policy of non-enforcement of the regulation was not an option, instead enlisted the United States to appeal the tax to the World Trade Organization. The United States did so, but not on the grounds that it violated Canada's obligations under NAFTA or the newly minted GATS, but instead under the GATT. According to Acheson and Maule (1999, 201), the United States chose not to challenge the tax under the provisions of the former "perhaps because it did not want to test the meaning of the cultural exemption." In any event, the WTO, after appeals from both parties, ultimately ruled that Canada's excise tax was prohibited because it was found to restrict trade in periodical goods and as such was disallowed.

Canada's initial response was to attempt to make the tax non-discriminatory in order to conform to its international trade obligations. After the United States threatened to retaliate, a negotiated settlement was agreed upon, which largely amounted to a complete retreat by the Canadian government. The centrepiece of the agreement was the creation of the Canada Magazine Fund. The public explanation for the fund makes no reference to the trade conflicts, the WTO decision, or the Canadian–U.S. negotiated settlement. Instead, there is simply an anodyne statement that "[r]apid change and globalization make it more important than ever to preserve and strengthen the bonds of citizenship and promote cultural diversity. Canadian magazines play a significant role in the cultural life of Canadians" (Canadian Heritage 2001, 1).

The fund consists of three elements: support for business development for small magazines; support for infrastructure development; and most importantly, support for editorial content. The last element amounted to $25 million and was distributed to 402 publishers across Canada. The creation of this fund and the extensive nature of the recipients demonstrate why governments would normally prefer regulatory measures as a means to provide hidden subsidies to more explicit forms of subsidization (Posner 1971; Stanbury and Lermer 1983). Whereas under the former tax regime, the direct cost to the Government of Canada was minimal, although we can never know the extent to which Canadian firms ignored the non-deductibility provision, now Canada must provide a $25 million subsidy, and that subsidy could grow to close to $100 million (Chilton 1999, 4). Moreover, where, under the former regime, the ostensible objective was to protect perhaps a handful of Canadian magazines threatened by the loss of advertising, now at least four hundred magazines are receiving grants. Given that the stated purpose of the program is to "strengthen the bonds of citizenship and promote cultural diversity," the list of recipients, available at the Canadian Heritage website, running to thirteen pages, is a fascinating mix of magazines including *Aggregates and Roadbuilding Magazine, Canola Digest, Hazardous Materials Management, Perspectives in Cardiology, Structured Cabling,* and *Dental Practice Management.* I leave it to other students of Canadian cultural policy more competent than I to undertake a content analysis of the cultural role of these magazines in strengthening our bonds of citizenship, however worthy they may otherwise be. Of course, the usual suspects are also on the list: for the fiscal year 2002–2003, *Maclean's* receives almost $1.15 million, *L'Actualité* $288,000, and *Toronto Life* $208,000. In the interests of balance, *Report: BC Edition* receives $64,000.

I would make two final comments about this policy initiative. The first is a query. Am I the only one concerned by the fact that the Canadian government is subsidizing "editorial content" for Canadian newsmagazines? Would there be an equal amount of equanimity if, or is it *when*, Canadian newspapers started putting their collective hands out? The second point is to suggest that the development of Canadian magazine policy has only reached a new stage, not its endgame. I understand that American magazines, probably the now-legal split-runs, are contemplating a request to be eligible for the editorial support funds. Who among us is the one to make the Solomon-like decision of choosing between the American *Sports Illustrated* or *Time* and Canada's *Today's Trucking* or *Stitches: The Journal of Medical Humour*?

36

Richard Schultz

Broadband Access Policy

In June, 2001, the National Broadband Task Force released its report recommending a comprehensive program estimated to cost between $2.75 and $4.6 billion to bring broadband access by 2004 to public institutions and individual residences and businesses in remote and rural communities in Canada (National Broadband Task Force 2001). The task force was appointed to develop a plan to implement the government's commitment made in the last election, and reiterated in the subsequent Speech from the Throne, to provide such access, although the original commitment was to provide access to unserved communities, not individual residences or businesses. This commitment reflected prior concerns, arising from the development of competition in telecommunications, that not all regions or areas were benefiting from such competition and the adequacy of the CRTC's attempts to redress the problem (CRTC 1999). In addition, it was an extension of Industry Canada's earlier program to connect all Canadian schools and libraries to the Internet.[9]

The report estimated that it would cost between $1.3 and $1.9 billion to bring broadband access to remote and rural communities that would not apparently be served by the private sector because of the presumption that the market could not bear the cost. The cost of connecting public institutions in those communities was estimated to be between $500 to $600 million, depending on the technology deployed. The final component of the plan, connecting individual residences and businesses in the remote areas, was estimated to cost between $900 million and $2 billion.

It is doubtful whether a public report has ever been greeted with more hostile and negative reactions. The extent and nature of the critical responses provoked the now-former Industry Canada minister, Brian Tobin, to lash out, calling the criticisms "pompous, arrogant, misguided, [and] short-sighted" (Bryden 2001). For his part, David Johnston, the chair of the task force, criticized the media reports for demonstrating "an urban–centric bias and a limited understanding of the problems faced by rural and remote communities across Canada" (Johnston 2001).

The criticisms admittedly were probably overstated because of a focus on the high-end figure of $4.6 billion to connect not only remote communities but also individual residents and businesses in those communities. It could be argued, however, that the task force provoked the criticisms by addressing an issue that its mandate did not include. Indeed, even the minister of Industry Canada acknowledged that the projected total cost was far too expensive and that government policy would concentrate on the cost of providing access to public institutions in remote communities (Whittington 2001). It is also possible that industry participants were successful in persuading the full task force to endorse a strategy of making a $1.5 billion subsidy program more palatable by getting them to undertake a more comprehensive analysis with a commensurately much greater cost.

The task force report may be flawed as the basis for the development of a broadband access policy because it appears to favour contemporary technologies for delivering remote access. This is probably not surprising because the task force was heavily weighted toward representation of incumbent firms in the telecommunications and cable sectors. There is, however, no extended discussion of alternative delivery systems, especially satellites, which may in the future provide a less expensive option. Moreover, the report also appears to favour current technology and its providers by defining broadband as a service capable of running at 1.5 megabits per second (Mbps). According to one report, the International Telecommunications Union defines broadband as a service capable of running at 10 Mbps. The former standard may have been endorsed by the task force, according to one neutral industry source, "in order not to embarrass the telephone and cable companies that advertise their residential high-speed services as broadband services" (Aiken 2001).

A further problem with the task force report is its injunction that the CRTC "should ensure that its decisions, in matters which affect revenues, reflect the particularly heavy demands and challenges facing facilities providers in terms of capital generation and capital recovery" (National Broadband Task Force 2001, 14). This would appear to encourage the CRTC to develop a subsidy system in its pricing decisions to support private industry contributions to the broadband access goals. The problem with this is that the reduction, not to mention the removal, of hidden cross-subsidies has been the most intractable problem for both the regulator and new entrants in making the transformation of the telecommunications sector, at all levels, local and long distance, from a monopoly to a competitive market (Schultz 1995; 1998; Crandall and Waverman 2000). Furthermore, it ignores the precedent of the rather dismal effort made by the cable industry to develop and deploy digital technology in response to the presumed threat from American direct-to-home satellite services when the CRTC provided the industry comparable pricing relief in the first half of the 1990s.

A larger question perhaps goes beyond the task force's mandate, although, as noted, this did not seem to restrict the task force. At the risk of being condemned as "pompous, arrogant, short-sighted, or urban-centric," surely it is a legitimate question to ask what is the specific principle of equity that justifies a concentration on remote or rural communities for subsidization. Why subsidize individuals or businesses in those areas regardless of specific need, rather than the poor or other disadvantaged groups in urban or suburban areas? Regardless of where one stands on the merits of addressing the so-called digital divide that may or may not be emerging, if there is such a divide, surely it is more pressing in urban areas.

A recent report, for example, by the Public Interest Advocacy Centre, commissioned, interestingly enough, by Industry Canada and Human Resources Development Canada, contends that there is a "dual digital divide" in Canada (Reddick et al. 2000). The report noted that, while two-thirds of high-income Canadians had household Internet access in 1999, less than 25 per cent of low-income Canadians did. The "dual divide" consists of "near-users, those of varying degrees of interest in being connected" but who lack the means, including funds and requisite literacy skills, and those "who have little or no interest … and perceive no value in the Internet to meet their everyday and online services" (Reddick et al. 2000, 2). Their figures correspond to recent American studies that suggest there is a credit/income gap as well as a resistance, especially among the elderly, to the Internet (Angwin 2001).

The lack of a discussion by the task force of the principled reasons for addressing, at substantial cost, the needs of remote communities as opposed to what would appear to be equally needy, and more numerous, urban and suburban citizens is a major shortcoming of its report. It may also account for the skepticism that greeted the publication of its report. Seen from this perspective, the task force, however well-intentioned some of its members may have been, may have been exploited by its industrial participants more as a vehicle to gain legitimacy for a demand for a much-needed corporate subsidy than as a plea to aid remote communities. Wrapping oneself collectively in a blanket of concern for "First Nation, Inuit, rural and remote communities (including Metis communities)" is probably more palatable than a simple Dickensian request for "more."

As 2001 ended, former Industry Canada minister Brian Tobin undertook a rather exceptional public lobbying effort to persuade his Cabinet colleague, the minister of finance, Paul Martin, or alternatively the prime minister, to include $1.5 billion in the upcoming budget to fund the construction of the infrastructure to provide access for remote communities (Scoffield 2001b). The effort was largely unsuccessful, however, for the

December federal budget only included less than 10 per cent of what Tobin had sought, and even that amount was spread out over three years (Vardy 2001). Moreover, according to some reports, Tobin took the decision personally, which, it was claimed, contributed to his decision to resign from federal politics early in January 2002 (Fife 2002; Fife and Taber 2002; Schultz forthcoming)

Foreign Ownership Restrictions

Regardless of the government's actions on the task force's recommendations on broadband access, one major consequence of its report is to bring to centre stage the policy issue of foreign ownership in Canadian telecommunications, and, I would suggest, by implication, in Canadian communications generally. Undoubtedly as a tradeoff for accepting the task force's major subsidy proposal that would largely benefit the incumbent telephone firms and cable companies, the new entrants were able to persuade the task force to recommend a review of the existing foreign ownership restrictions. The following is the full text of the recommendation:

> To ensure that a maximum amount of capital is made available to finance the expansion of broadband access and to ensure that all industry participants are in a position to partner with government in facilitating broadband deployment, the federal government should conduct an urgent review of foreign investment restrictions for telecommunications common carriers and distribution undertakings with a view to determining whether they are currently restricting or likely to restrict increased industry participation in the competitive deployment of broadband infrastructure in Canada. This review is only intended to include restrictions on foreign investment in telecommunications common carriers and distribution undertakings (National Broadband Task Force 2001, 13–14).

The restrictions now in place that limit the amount of foreign voting capital in operating telecommunications carriers and broadcasting distribution undertakings to 20 per cent, and to 33.3 per cent in holding companies, subject to the overriding requirement that both be Canadian controlled, are of relatively recent origin. The first restrictions were announced by the federal government in 1987, just before the negotiations leading to the Canada–U.S. Free Trade Agreement, but were only legislated in 1993 with the enactment of the Telecommunications Act.[10] It is important to note that, at the time of the legislative imposition of the restrictions, BC Tel, then the second largest telephone company in Canada, was foreign-controlled and had been so for almost seventy years. There has never been any evidence, to the best of my knowledge, it merits stating, that such foreign control had a negative impact on either regulatory control or the behaviour of BC Tel.[11] In 1993, BC Tel was grandfathered from the legislative restrictions; subsequently, it and AGT merged and now operate as Telus, which is now fully compliant with the regulations.

Although the predecessor to the broadband access task force, the Information Highway Advisory Council, had also recommended in 1995 that the foreign ownership restrictions be reviewed (Information Highway Advisory Council 1995, 18), the government had taken no action. Moreover, during the negotiations that led to the General Agreement on Trade in Services and the creation of the World Trade Organization, the Canadian government specifically refused to make any commitments to liberalize the foreign ownership restrictions for telecommunications. Subsequently, it linked any relaxation with future trade negotiations and was opposed to any unilateral action. The initial reaction of the industry minister upon receipt of the task force's report was sympathetic to undertaking the review (Scoffield 2001a). As discussed below, however, it would take more than a year before the review was initiated.

Although the foreign ownership issue is linked to broadband deployment, that link is somewhat tenuous. The real problem is that competition in the telecommunications markets, long distance and local, which the CRTC permitted in 1992 and 1994 respectively, has been rather fragile, and indeed a number of new entrants have gone bankrupt. Indeed, the company that put long distance competition on the regulatory agenda, Unitel Canada, failed to survive and had to be taken over by several banks in collaboration with AT&T.

In December, 2002, the minister of Industry Canada, Alan Rock, announced that the Government had requested the House of Commons Industry, Science and Technology Committee to undertake a review of the current investment policy, which it did between January and February, 2003. It has not yet reported. Not surprisingly a wide range of views were presented favouring and opposing changes. One important aspect of the review was that cable companies intervened to argue that the current restrictions applicable to them should also be lessened if not removed in their entirety. Some broadcasting companies also made presentations, even though broadcasting was originally excluded from the terms of reference of the committee, urging no changes in the rules.

If the Committee recommends that the restrictions should be removed but only for the smaller telecommunications companies currently facing difficulties raising capital, the consequences for the telecommunications sector, or more generally for the communications sector, will not be all that significant. If, however, the Committee recommends larger changes, and the Government agrees, two very important "ifs," the implications for the communications sector, generally, and for the role of government policy-makers could be far-reaching, and far more so than appeared to be initially acknowledged by industry participants. As indicated in the recommendation from the Broadband Task Force cited above, there is a central assumption that any review can make and defend as tenable a distinction between restrictions for telecommunications common carriers and distribution undertakings such as cable systems, and content providers.

In an age not only of convergence of services but of corporate convergence, where a company such as BCE provides telecommunications services (Bell Canada), distribution (ExpressVu), and content (CTV television and *The Globe and Mail*), it is extremely problematic that the telecommunications and distribution sectors could have one set of rules, presumably liberalized, while the content providers would be governed by a more stringent set of ownership restrictions. The precedent supporting this argument is the government exemption of BC Tel, while still foreign-controlled, from the ownership restrictions governing broadcasting distribution undertakings in order to put it on a level playing field with the other domestic telephone companies to engage in trials to distribute video-on-demand. If convergence of carriage and content does lead to synergies, as its corporate defenders such as BCE insist it does, then surely non-Canadian firms will have a strong case that Canada is violating its WTO obligations by giving domestic firms a competitive advantage. The international trade agreements to which Canada is party, and specifically the WTO decision on magazines, thus may cast a far larger footprint on both the substance of communications policies and the capacity for independent action by governmental policy-makers than hitherto has been acknowledged.

Access to American DTH Satellite Services

The final issue we wish to discuss is one that reflects the twin issues for Canadian policy-makers of technological change, namely the development of high-powered digital satellite television delivery systems and what Meisel described as the "dominant value system of Canadians [and their assumption] that their basic rights give them access to any television signal that modern technology makes available" (1989, 194). This is an issue that the federal government presumed that it had clearly addressed and resolved. It appears, however, that the policy involved is under severe challenge and may have to be revisited in the very near future.

The issue goes back to the 1970s, when large satellite dishes increasingly became popular for people in remote areas as the price of the equipment decreased and the range of programming increased. Canada's initial response was to prohibit individual ownership of such equipment. A number of Canadians ignored the prohibition, and, consequently, in large part because of the cost of enforcement, the federal government removed the prohibition against individual ownership. The minister of communications defended this action, claiming that his new policy "should create a rapidly growing market for earth stations, thereby lowering their cost substantially, and bringing them within the price range of Canadians who cannot be served in any other way" (Government of Canada 1983, 11). As a result, by the early 1990s, it was estimated that between 300,000 and 400,000 Canadians owned satellite dishes (Ellis 1992, 161). Around this time, the third generation of satellite delivery systems and of dishes, so-called pizza-size dishes, was being developed and licensed in the United States.

The third generation of Canadian public policy on satellite delivery systems began just before the introduction of the third generation of satellites.[12] In 1988, the government introduced amendments to the *Radiocommunications Act* that were ultimately passed in 1991. The major purpose of the amendments was to prohibit both ownership and sale of equipment used for decoding "an encrypted subscription programming signal or encrypted network feed, otherwise than under and in accordance with authorization from the lawful distributor of the signal or feed."[13]

Both government and opposition members of parliament made two major arguments during the debates on these amendments. The first was that they were being enacted to provide the owners of copyrighted signals with the right to take private action regarding so-called signal piracy. As the parliamentary secretary to the minister of communications stated in the House of Commons on December 4, 1990, "the private right of action for theft of signal is a very important aspect of this bill" (Edwards 1990). Secondly, as a government backbencher noted when the amendments were introduced: "The indication I have been able to receive, both from the Minister's Office and from CRTC officials, is that the Government does not intend to become involved in any such prosecutions in that area, leaving it in essence to a matter of private law between the creators of the intellectual property and those who are infringing it to be remedied by the courts" (Boyer 1988).

Of course, that is not what happened. Over the years, as the new American dish systems became more and more popular – one estimate is that by 1996 there were over 500,000 dishes receiving American systems – public prosecutions were undertaken as the Mounties seized the equipment, especially from those selling it to Canadians. (Attallah 1996). It is in fact almost impossible to keep track of the number of cases that have been or are currently before the courts across Canada. While the government has won a number of these cases, it has also lost a number. One of the major points raised by those charged is that the prohibitions violate their right to free speech, as provided for by the *Charter of Rights and Freedoms.*

What has put the issue of Canadian policy on access to American satellite systems back on the agenda of the government was a series of conflicting judicial decisions and especially a decision in April, 2001, by the Ontario Court of Appeal that effectively eviscerates the existing prohibitions. The court ruled that the relevant section was ambiguous. It then went on to state:

> Parliament's intention is not sufficiently clear to warrant the use of the coercive powers of the criminal law to punish individuals and companies engaged in the reception of DTH satellite programming signals from foreign countries. The content of foreign programming is not prohibited. It is the decoding of the signal that is of concern.[14]

It will be recalled that the government and its supporters during the parliamentary debates declared that they had no intention of criminalizing Canadians but were only providing for a private right of action.

In part because of the rash of conflicting decisions taken by courts across Canada on the legality of the prohibitions, the Supreme Court of Canada issued a ruling in April, 2002, that only partially clarified the situation.[15] Bell ExpressVu had earlier been denied by the B.C. Supreme Court an injunction prohibiting a B.C. company from assisting Canadian residents in gaining access to and decoding American DTH programming signals. The B.C. Court of Appeal had upheld this decision. The Supreme Court of Canada reversed the lower courts and ruled that the law was not, contrary to a wide range of lower court decisions, ambiguous in its prohibition against decoding encrypted satellite signals.

This decision, however, does not resolve the conflict because the Supreme Court expressly ruled that it had not addressed the claims that the prohibitions were unconstitutional inasmuch as they were in conflict with the freedom of speech provisions of the *Charter of Rights and Freedoms*. It stated in its decision that, when the issue returned to court, parties could apply to have the provisions declared unconstitutional for violating the *Charter*. That issue has been joined, as there are currently appeals before the courts in British Columbia and Ontario to accomplish this objective.

If the current appeals are successful, policy-makers will face limited choices. One is to let the amendments lapse, which will effectively end domestic restrictions on accessing American DTH systems. Alternatively, new amendments can be introduced to correct the judicial problems. If it is the former, then Canadians' insistence on their rights of access will win out once again; if the government chooses the latter, it faces an acrimonious debate, one that assuredly will be far more public than that which accompanied the original amendments.

Conclusion

We have argued that Canadian public policy has been characterized by two extremes. On the one hand, for most of the last eighty years, successive governments have sought to control so as to restrict (or at least have claimed that was their intention) Canadians' media choices. At the other extreme is the reality that such control has been largely ineffectual because of the combination of popular tastes, the permeability of the Canadian communications sector, and the relative ease of technological exit from it. In addition, the lassitude displayed by government, and its agents such as the CRTC, particularly in enforcing its magazine policy and its Canadian content requirements, suggests at best a rhetorical commitment to announced policy.

Whatever the prior record or contemporary governmental intentions, our claim is that government policy is increasingly a diminished, if not a spent, force insofar as the stated purpose is to control the communications choices that Canadians make. The past few years signals that, in addition to the traditional constraints government policy-makers face, which themselves show no sign of abating, new constraints have emerged. To the traditionally powerful combination of mass tastes and technological ease of exit has been added the potent force of international trade commitments that Canada has willingly embraced. Intermingled as the forces undoubtedly are, the one sure conclusion to draw from the four case studies discussed in this paper is that they have further eroded any governmental power to attain objectives by controlling the Canadian communications sector.

Of course, this should not lead to the conclusion that such developments demonstrate that there is no, or at best only a minimal, role for government policy in Canadian communications. The continued erosion of its control capabilities only suggests that Canadian governmental policy-makers must attempt to exploit other instruments in their policy tool-kit if they wish to be a significant player in communications. The development of the new magazine policy demonstrates both the potential for new approaches and their limitations as well. The only definitive conclusion is that "command and control," for too long the preferred alternative, is largely, if not completely, undermined as the primary tool for the attainment of Canadian communications policy. Whether Canadian policy-makers will both accept the new realities and, more importantly, imaginatively and creatively respond to the dominant trends shaping their environment must be a subject for a future analysis.

References

Acheson, Keith, and Christopher Maule. 1999. *Much Ado About Culture*. Ann Arbor: University of Michigan Press.

Aiken, David. 2001. "Task Force misses the mark on technological, investment issues." *Financial Post*, June 20.

Angwin, Julia. 2001. "Internet adoption hits the wall." *Globe and Mail*, July 16, B8.

Attallah, Paul. 1996. "Narrowcasting: Home Video and DBS." In *The Cultural Industries in Canada*, ed. Michael Dorland. Toronto: James Lorimer.

Beatty, Perrin. 1994. *Globe and Mail*, February 24, B23.

Bennett, R.B. 1932. House of Commons, *Debates*, May 18.

Boyer, Patrick. 1988. House of Commons. *Debates*. September 14, p. 19251.

Browne, D. 1999a. "Our Flawed New Magazine Policy." *Policy Options* (January–February): 49–55.

Browne, D. 1999b. "Canada's Culture Trade Quandary: How Do We Resolve the Impasse?" *International Journal* (Summer).

Bryden, Joan. 2001. "Minister defends Internet access plan." *Ottawa Citizen*, June 26.

Canadian Heritage. 2001. "Canadian Magazine Fund." Available: http://www.canadianheritage. gc.ca/progs/ac-ca/progs/fcm-cmf/

Caplan-Sauvageau. 1986. *Report of the Task Force on Broadcasting Policy*. Ottawa: Ministry of Supply and Services.

Chilton, D. 1999. "Publishers Mull Split Run Partners." *Marketing*, 7 June, 4.

Crandall, Robert W., and Leonard Waverman. 2000. *Who Pays for Universal Service: When Telephone Subsidies Become Transparent*. Washington: Brookings Institution.

CRTC. 1999. "Telephone Service to High Cost Service Areas." Telecom Decision CRTC 99–16. Ottawa, 19 October.

Department of Foreign Affairs and International Trade. 1999. Cultural Industries Sectoral Advisory Group on International Trade, "Canadian Culture in a Global World: New Strategies for Culture and Trade." February.

Edelman, Murray. 1964. *The Symbolic Use of Politics*. Urbana: University of Illinois Press.

Edwards, James. 1990. House of Commons. *Debates*. December 4, p. 16258.

Ellis, David. 1992. *Split Screen: Home Entertainment and the New Technologies*. Toronto: Friends of Canadian Broadcasting.

Fife, Robert . 2002. "Insiders say Tobin quit after snub by Chrétien." *National Post*, January 17.

Fife, Robert, and Jane Taber. 2002. "Tobin says PM betrayed him, friends say." *National Post*, January 19.

Filion, Michel. 1996. "Broadcasting and Cultural Identity: the Canadian Experience." *Media, Culture and Society* 18: 447–67.

Gilder, George. 2000. *Telecosm*. New York: The Free Press.

Globerman, Steven, Hudson Janisch, Richard Schultz, and W. T. Stanbury 1992. "Canada and the Movement Towards Liberalization of the International Telecommunications Regime." In *Canadian Foreign Policy and International Economic Regimes*, ed. A. Claire Cutler and Mark W. Zacher, 237–85. Vancouver: University of British Columbia Press.

Globerman, Steven, and Daniel Hagen. 1998. "The Impacts of Technological Change and Globalization on Cultural Content in Broadcasting." In *Adapting to New Realities: Canadian Telecommunications Policy Conference*, ed. David Conklin, 113-132. London: Richard Ivey School of Business, University of Western Ontario.

Government of Canada. 1983. "Towards a New National Broadcasting Policy." Minister of Communications.

Hardin, Herschel. 1985. *Closed Circuits: The Sellout of Canadian Television*. Vancouver: Douglas and McIntyre.

Information Highway Advisory Council. 1995. *Final Report: Connection, Community, Content: The Challenge of the Information Highway*.Ottawa: Industry Canada.

Janisch, Hudson. 1998. "International Influences on Communications Policy in Canada." In *The Electronic Village*, ed. Dale Orr and Thomas A. Wilson. Toronto: C. D. Howe Institute.

Johnston, David. 2001. "Broadband critics are short-sighted." *Globe and Mail*, June 27.

Krasner, Stephen. 1999. *Sovereignty: Organized Hypocrisy*. Princeton: Princeton University Press.

Meisel, John. 1989. "Fanning the Air: The Canadian State and Broadcasting." *Transactions of the Royal Society of Canada*, Series 5, 4.

Miller, Barbara. 2000. "Foreign Ownership in Canadian Telecommunications: Can an Explosion be Regulated?" Paper presented to the conference, Breaking the Mould: Reconceiving Telecommunications Regulation. Organized by the Faculty of Law, University of Toronto and Fasken Martineau DuMoulin. Toronto, February 17–18.

Mulcahy, Kevin V. 2000. "Cultural Imperialism and Cultural Sovereignty: U.S.-Canadian Cultural Relations." *American Review of Canadian Studies* (Summer).

Mussio, Lawrence. 2001. *Telecom Nation: Telecommunications, Computers, and Government in Canada*. Montreal: McGill-Queen's University Press.

National Broadband Task Force. 2001. *The New National Dream: Networking the Nation for Broadband Access*. Ottawa: Industry Canada, June.

Pitts, Gordon. 2001. "Monty supports relaxing foreign ownership rules." *Globe and Mail*, October 5, B6.

Posner, Richard A. 1971. "Taxation by Regulation." *Bell Journal of Economics and Management Sciences* 2 (Spring): 22–50.

Reddick, Andrew, Christian Boucher, and Manon Groseilliers. 2000. *The Dual Digital Divide: The Information Highway in Canada*. Ottawa: Public Interest Advocacy Centre.

Rutherford, Paul. 1990. *When Television was Young: Prime Time Canada, 1952–1967.* Toronto: University of Toronto Press.

Schultz, Richard. 1990. "New Domestic and International Bedfellows in Telecommunications." *Media and Communications Law Review* 1.

——. 1995. "Old Whine in New Bottle: The Politics of Cross-Subsidization in Canadian Telecommunications." In *The Future of Telecommunications Policy in Canada*, ed. Steven Globerman, W. T. Stanbury, and Thomas A. Wilson, 271–88. Toronto: Institute for Policy Analysis.

——. 1995a. "Paradigm Lost: Explaining the Canadian Politics of Deregulation." In *Governance in a Mature Society: Essays in Honour of John Meisel*, ed. C.E.S. Franks et al., 259–77. Montreal: McGill-Queen's University Press.

——. 1998. "Universal Service/ Universal Subsidies: The Tangled Web." In *Adapting to New Realities: Canadian Telecommunications Policy Conference*, ed. David Conklin, 139–52. London: Richard Ivey School of Business, University of Western Ontario.

Schultz, Richard. Forthcoming. "Dancing around the Digital Divide: The Broadband Access Debate." In *How Ottawa Spends 2003–2004*, ed. G. Bruce Doern. Toronto: Oxford University Press.

Scoffield, Heather. 2001a. "Ottawa to review telecom restrictions." *Globe and Mail*, June 19.

Scoffield, Heather. 2001b. "Tobin to seek $1.5-billion for Net." *Globe and Mail*, October 13.

Stanbury, W.T., and George Lermer. 1983. "Regulation and the Redistribution of Wealth." *Canadian Public Administration* 26; 378–401.

Stanbury. W.T. 1998. "Canadian Content Requirements: Description, Rational, Politics and Critique." *Fraser Forum*, Special Issue, August.

Stentor. 1993. "Appendix 3, Written Submissions to the CRTC in accordance with Public Notice CRTC 1994–130, January 16, 1993."

Trebilcock, Michael J., and Robert Howse. 1999. *The Regulation of International Trade.* 2nd ed. New York: Routledge.

Vardy, Jill. 2001. "A secure visionless future: Funding for high-speed Internet program has been delayed for a year." *National Post*, December 11.

Wernick, Michael. 2000. "Impact of the Internet on Cultural Policy." In *The Canadian Telecommunications Policy Forum: Strategies for the 21st Century*, ed. David Conklin. London: Richard Ivey School of Business, University of Western Ontario.

Whittington, Les. 2001. "Internet promise too costly." *Ottawa Citizen*, June 20.

Notes

1   R. B. Bennett, House of Commons, *Debates*, May 18, 1932.

2   Eric Kierans, *Montreal Star,* Sept. 9, 1969, quoted in Mussio (2001, 92).

3   Perrin Beatty, *Globe and Mail*, February 24, 1994, B23.

4   For an excellent review of the early history of access to and popularity of American signals for both radio and television, see Filion (1996).

5   Gilder (2000). For a relevant, albeit more focused, earlier Canadian discussion, see Ellis (1992).

6   For an example that suggests an appreciation of these developments and an emerging "new realism" in Ottawa, see Wernick (2000). See also Department of Foreign Affairs and International Trade (1999).

7   The relevant clauses of the FTA, which were carried over to NAFTA, are Articles 2005 (1) and (2).

8   Acheson and Maule (1999, 189–90). Much of the detail in the next few paragraphs is taken from this source.

9   For information, see the Industry Canada website, http://www.ic.gc.ca, specifically "Connecting Canadians."

10 The legislative provisions were spelled out in greater detail in the "Canadian Telecommunications Common Carrier Ownership and Control Regulations," which came into force in 1994. For a detailed and critical review of the restrictions and the regulations see Miller (2000).

11 For a more positive assertion to this effect, see Stentor (1993).

12 In the interests of full disclosure, I should note that I appeared as a witness for the defence in one of the court cases involving charges under the *Radiocommunications Act*. Much of what immediately follows is drawn from my legislative history of the amendments prepared for the trial.

13 *Statutes of Canada, Radiocommunications Act*, s. 9(1)(c).

14 *R. v. Branton*, April 20, 2001, 53 *O.R.* (3d) 737 at 751 (C.A.).

15 *Bell ExpressVu Limited Partnership v. Rex*, 2002 SCC 42.

NO CLEAR CHANNEL
The Rise and Possible Fall of Media Convergence

Vincent A. Carlin

Business strategies used to be discussed in the back pages of the business sections of newspapers. But today, strategies in the communications field can affect us all right in our homes. So they have become front-page news and the stuff of popular culture.

In recent months, two popular songs have taken business strategy as their theme: Tom Petty's song "The Last DJ" is a comment on the virtual disappearance of truly local radio in North America. He laments the disappearance of the independent record spinner, free to explore different musical tastes ("… there goes your free-dom of choice; there goes the last human voice …"). He may be lamenting something that never existed, but clearly he is voicing an unease that many people feel about the massive concentra-tion of ownership that has taken place in the United States and Canada.

Two U.S. companies (Infinity and Clear Channel) now control a healthy plurality of radio stations there. And in Canada, Corus Entertainment and Standard Broadcasting together control over a hundred stations.

Long-time rocker Peter Gabriel satirizes the "trash" TV phenomenon, which is the hallmark of turn-of-this-century television. His "Barry Williams Show" mocks the eclipse of one trash talker by a younger, prettier trash talker.

The trash TV craze symbolizes the frenzy of the exploding number of services competing for the same audiences. Anything that attracts a few extra viewers in certain key demographic groups is instantly copied by other programmers.

It is, perhaps, beyond irony that Petty's song is produced by Warner/Reprise, part of the gigantic communications monolith AOL Time Warner. And that Gabriel is partner with Warner Records in a digital music distribution company. As we will see, AOL-TW and its copycats are largely responsible for the concentration of ownership which leads to the loss of DJs and to trash television.

Of even greater importance to how we live and communicate is the fact that more and more information services are controlled by fewer and fewer companies. Despite the plethora of services, we may actually be hearing a narrower range of views from fewer people.

The Urge to Converge

At the very start of the twenty-first century, "convergence" was the touchstone word. No one seemed quite sure what it meant, but no one wanted to miss out on whatever opportunities it might provide.

It was the time of "Nerd Nirvana," epitomized by the stereotypical lads with sallow complexions and bad haircuts who could spin software dreams of incredible grandeur only occasionally buttressed by some passing connection to the laws of economics. Eventually, things have to be paid for. A company's value cannot be based solely on "street cred," but must have some tangible product or service that people are willing to spend money on; a "cool" idea still needs to be marketed. There was a sense that things were "converging," but it turned out few knew how to make those dreams a reality.

It is sadly ironic now to read the stories dismissing old-style value investors like Warren Buffett as past their prime, unable to deal with the new "reality" of the high tech world: that value can attach to an idea, not a balance sheet. In the midst of the white-hot market for "tech" stocks, the *Financial Post* (Hanley 1999) reflected on this:

> As a result, even some of the Buffett faithful are growing uneasy, questioning the oracular powers of the great man and his steadfast decision to avoid the very hot-growth technology issues, which have powered the stock market to new heights and probably will be the most popular equity segment in the early years of the new millennium.

But through the late 1990s and into the early days of this century, the talk was of competition and convergence. New and various companies were trying to find ways to combine sources of information and entertainment through the use of digital technology – words, pictures, sounds all translated to ones and zeros and delivered by new devices, or over the Internet.

Convergence can be defined in a number of different ways:

- The convergence of content: adapting material gathered for one medium for use in another (putting newspaper stories on the Internet);
- The convergence of technology: using the digital media in combinations that extend the use of each (using new technology to combine and extend, for instance, the experience of watching TV news by accessing additional material from a library and having the ability to pause a live program while doing so).
- The convergence of ownership: control of different types of media coming under one owner.

The last is what has become common in Canada, with only hints of the other two. And that trend of ownership convergence has been fostered by the fashion of deregulation sweeping across North America, led by the United States, but with Canada not too far behind.

For example, as Ben Bagdikian noted in his book "The Media Monopoly" (Bagdikian 2000), in 1983 there were fifty companies dominating the media business of the United States. By 1996, the number was down to ten. But now, only six years later, another four have disappeared. No more than a mere handful of companies are dominant – AOL Time Warner, Disney (ABC), Viacom (CBS), General Electric (NBC), Rupert Murdoch's News Corporation (Fox, newspapers and local broadcasting), Gannett (newspapers) and Tribune Corp. (newspapers) (Forbes, 2002).

In Canada, the situation is somewhat different, with CanWest Global and CTV dominating the private English broadcast television market, and CHUM-CITY nipping at their heels. But Canada has a public player of size, the CBC. There is no equivalent in the United States.

In this country, the regulators were supposed to see that in broadcasting, at least, appropriate competition took place. Companies large and small talked of the benefits to consumers of new technologies and new competition. Instead, deregulation, supposedly to achieve greater competition, resulted in the opposite: competition has been endangered in the media sectors of both the United States and Canada.

Looking South

The broadcast regulator in the United States, the Federal Communications Commission (FCC), appears to be speeding plans to deregulate the industry. The Chair of the FCC, Michael Powell (son of U.S. Secretary of State Colin Powell) has called regulation itself "oppressive." He goes on to say: "The public interest at its core is the same thing as my oath of office: a commitment to making sure the American *consuming* [italics added] public is benefited" (Powell, M. 2001). Powell sees his job as taking care of consumers, not citizens. "I try to make the best judgment I can in a way that I think will optimize and provide the greatest benefits to consumers" (Powell, M.).

Those who favour more stringent regulation see it as a method of expressing the public interest rather than supporting private profit. But in fact, the greatest support appears to be flowing to owners, although some of them are having a hard time realizing those benefits.

The biggest single communications deal in the United States was the AOL purchase of Time Warner. It would be hard to underestimate the influence that single deal had on business people around the globe – especially in Canada. In his book on convergence, "Kings of Convergence," author Gordon Pittes quotes the then-CEO of BCE, Jean Monty: "The AOL-Time Warner deal forced us to react faster.... It didn't tell us what the strategy should be – it pushed us to move faster" (Pitts 2002, 116). BCE's target would be the CTV television network.

Companies in the United States and Canada reached out almost obsessively to acquire anything which could be trumpeted as a convergence buy. Very few of these deals are standing up to later scrutiny.

For instance, Robert Pittman, the Chief Operating Officer of AOL Time Warner, was forced to resign in 2002 as the price of the combined company's stock declined by 75 per cent. The vaunted convergence of content and delivery has not happened. This is a company that owns the world's largest Internet portal (AOL), the landmark cable news network (CNN), some of the most recognizable brand names in the magazine business (TIME, Sport Illustrated, People, Fortune) as well as extensive cable operations and the premier cable movie outlet (HBO). And, of course, the Warner Brothers movie company.

Executives who tried to follow AOL Time Warner's example have been left to wonder how the deal could possibly have failed. One needs only to look at the beginning of the twentieth century to note that similar pre-Internet convergence was attempted by William Randolph Hearst. He owned newspapers, magazines, newsreel companies, radio stations and a movie studio. He thought he could leverage all those properties into even larger profits. It didn't work. (Olive 2000).

The Canadian Way

Through the first years of the new century in Canada, we have seen the clash of corporate might, played out in boardrooms and, most especially, in hearing rooms of the Canadian Radio-Television and Telecommunications Commission (CRTC), the body charged with regulating the public airwaves. It has been pointed out that the communications field does not readily lend itself to competition. In *The Death of Distance*, her book on the communications "revolution," Frances Caincross (1997, 155) observes: "Competition does not come easily in communications. The opportunities to restrict access and build monopolies have been greater in communications than in many other businesses."

The truth of this observation has been made evident by the events of 2001 in Canada. We will return to this at the end of the chapter.

When the corporate feeding frenzy of the late 1990s ended, ultimately endorsed by those regulators who had to have a say (primarily the Competition Bureau and the CRTC), it became clear that the universe had changed, but not in the way that many thought. The prospect of widespread competition between new and varied players in the information field had dimmed. In fact, the end result was the growth of fewer, more bloated and debt-ridden conglomerates, reducing choice and placing communications power in fewer and fewer hands. In the words of one close observer: "Canada has the dubious honour of being home to one of the planet's most concentrated media and telecommunications markets" (Reguly 2002).

Convergence has been largely confined to ownership, and competition has proved a chimera, observable only if you are a close student of marketing, the only departments in some of the new companies in which things seemed to have actually converged.

We have been left with two companies dominating the newspaper business in most cities in the country: CanWest and the Sun Media Newspapers; two-plus in private English television: CanWest again, along with BCE, which controls CTV, and CHUM–CITY and some smaller players; a handful in radio: Corus, Standard and CHUM; and in English language cable: Rogers, Shaw and Astral . Even those numbers may be revised downward in the not-too-distant future if Canada follows the lead of the United States in removing restrictions on ownership concentration *within* most sectors and ownership *across* sectors. While corporate strategies have been cloaked in the language of innovation and consumer choice, the results so far have been the restriction of choice and the postponement of innovation.

It is worth noting that Canada was a world leader in the spread of cable technology, becoming fully wired well before the United States. This country also was a pioneer in the domestic use of satellites. Both of those leads were lost when policy and regulation inhibited the growth of satellite service providers and when cable companies decided to protect high profits instead of meeting possible competition (Fraser 1999).

Canadian companies looked to the United States for inspiration, but managed to devise their own unique solutions to the problems of regulation and agglomeration. When the smoke had cleared here, we were left with fewer but larger companies that, theoretically, should have been making bigger profits. But citizens also faced a possible constriction on the flow of information previously unthinkable in a democratic society.

BCE, CanWest Global and Rogers Communications are the exemplars of the new reality in Canadian communications.

Suspending the Laws of Economics

Through the end of the 1990s, it appeared that our economy was infected by the delusion that parts of the information world could function outside the normal rules of economics. Buzzwords and phrases proliferated to underline how things had changed. According to Michael Kinsley, the founder of *Slate* magazine, one of the only successful Internet magazines (thanks to its corporate owner, Microsoft Corp.):

> The first great cliché of the Internet, carbon-dated back to the mid-1990s, was "information wants to be free." the notion, purged of poetry, was that no one should have to pay for "content" – words and pictures and stuff like that – and, in the friction free world of cyberspace, no one should have to." (Kinsley 2001, ¶1)

Kinsley (2001) goes on to point out that the "laws of economics are not suspended in cyberspace like the laws of gravity in outer space" and that content needs to be paid for (¶3).

If something is in demand, someone or some institution will find a mechanism to sell it – for want of a better word, to "monetarize" that bit of information.

In the last five years, the big entities that control large pools of information have ransacked that "free" bazaar of information on the Web and absorbed many of those "free" bits into databases for which we now have to pay. Increasingly, the information displayed is designed to enhance a marketing strategy, rather than increase the sum of human knowledge.

An interesting example of this occurred at Sympatico, the Web portal owned by BCE. In the late 1990s, Sympatico set up a site that provided new journalistic content, a clear alternative to the marketing-driven content of such services as America OnLine (AOL) which was making substantial inroads into Canada. Most of the material on the AOL site was, and is, commercial material: someone paid to have it on the site, either through cash or barter. These were not independent sources of information being written for AOL subscribers, but information designed to market a product or service. It did not take the people running Sympatico long to see the commercial value in that kind of arrangement. It is better to receive free material from marketers than to pay for independent and original material. The experiment in original content was sharply curtailed and the marketers took over.

As the new century dawned, economic gravity asserted itself on the dot-coms, those hustling and often creative companies trying to take advantage of the Internet boom. These companies were often valued at many times the actual strength of their earnings. When the economy weakened, and economic reality took hold, they either failed or were absorbed by large corporate entities.

In the regulated communications sector in Canada, the giant cable companies maintained their monopoly positions through the beneficence of the regulator. Rogers' CEO, Edward S. (Ted) Rogers, would periodically drape the flag of cultural nationalism around himself while appearing before the commission, but the results have proved to be good business rather than good culture (Fraser 1999, esp. p. 81).

At the same time, the regulator protected the cable companies from competition. For years, the CTRC prevented satellite services from competing directly with the cable monopolies. Only at the turn of the century have those services been allowed to compete more aggressively, and they have been successful. Even so, only two large companies are in the field, BCE's Bell ExpressVu and Shaw Communications' Star Choice. Only one of them may survive. BCE has the deeper pockets, but is re-thinking its corporate strategy. How the satellite business plays out will be one of the hallmarks of this decade in Canadian communications.

Appetite Comes through Eating

For companies that had resources to expend, the beginning of the century was a time to acquire, but it was not always clear what the right price was for the acquisition nor whether the acquisition actually fit into the corporate empire. With "convergence" as the mantra, companies in the United States and Canada bought up as much as they could in sectors which might, conceivably, be "converged," if only someone could figure out what the end result was supposed to look like.

In the United States, the key was supposed to be cable television: by the 1990s, close to fifty-five million American households were wired for cable, providing ready streams of transmission for information, now more "monetarized" than ever. AOL's takeover of Time Warner has often been presented as an acquisition by the "New Media" of the "Old Media" – AOL's cyber-kingdom engulfing Time Warner's magazine empire. However, the move can also be judged in the light of Time Warner's cable assets: AOL coveting those as the best vehicles for varied and high-speed access to and from subscribers' homes. But the cable operators in the United States faced aggressive competition from satellite providers.

In Canada, the cable operators had been well protected from unwanted competition by the regulator, the Canadian Radio-Television and Telecommunications Commission. The operators had managed to stifle satellite competition and failed to provide high-speed access to the Internet for its subscribers. The door was left open for an aggressive move by one of the country's most powerful corporations, BCE Ltd. It jumped into high-speed Internet access and into satellite program distribution. When it subsequently added programming elements with its purchase of CTV, the stage was set for some elements of convergence.

Surprisingly, the major competition did not come from the cable operators, but from a broadcaster – CanWest Global.

The Global Phenomenon

Starting with a single TV station in Winnipeg, CanWest, with what some may see as less-than-aggressive regulation by the CRTC, built itself into Canada's most profitable network. Its formula for success: American programming, aggressive cost control, and minimal investment in Canadian programming. Matthew Fraser (1999), in his book about Canadian communications policy, reviews the CRTC's naïve belief that CanWest would actually produce significant Canadian programming: "The CRTC failed to understand that Izzy Asper (the Chairman of CanWest Global) was above all a shrewd tax lawyer. Patriotism came after profits. Asper saw in Global TV not a showcase for Canadian dramas, but the first piece in a national television system that would serve as a low-cost, high-profit conduit for American television shows" (141).

Asper wanted to keep his company out from under the expensive obligations that the CRTC imposed on "networks," e.g., more stringent foreign content rules, tougher rules for investing in Canadian programming.

Those are the rules which applied to CTV and CBC. But Asper carefully billed his company as a "system" rather than a network, and claimed he did not have to endure the same restrictions since his "system" did not go coast-to-coast. The regulator endorsed this strategy that critics said was nothing but a bit of sophistry.

CanWest succeeded in becoming the most profitable Canadian television network, thanks in no small part to the immensely favourable rulings of the CRTC, protecting Canadian television networks from U.S. competition while allowing them to run U.S. programming.

With that base and convergence as their touchstone, the one-time, small-time TV operators went on to acquire the dominant newspaper chain in the country (Southam) and one of the two national newspapers, the *National Post*. However, analysts pointed out that CanWest had gone into debt to finance the purchases and that the benefits were not obvious. Company share prices declined sharply.

The company's leaders say they will stay the course. They even use the "c" word, which many of their competitors have dropped. CanWest CEO Leonard Asper spoke to the Canadian Club of Ottawa in December of 2002:

> We use a word called convergence, and despite the denigration of that word by the doubting Thomases, or the merely impatient, the fact is that companies, consumers and advertisers love it, as do most but admittedly not all of their employees. (Asper, L. 2002)

Leonard, Israel's son and the company's day-to-day leader, lashes out at critics of media concentration and of his company's practices. He pictures it as a struggle between the outsiders (CanWest) and the "insiders" – journalists, academics, political and business competitors. "The elite, discomfited by the presence of a new voice, not part of their club, their geography or their ideology, can continue their bleating into their self-contained sound chamber." (Asper, L.)

Of course, these "outsiders" control the major newspapers in most major cities outside Toronto, a national newspaper and the most profitable television network. It appears that over the years they have also had the ear of those who are supposed to be regulating them.

Deregulating the Regulator

Now, one might wonder how we have ended up with our consumer screens dominated by so few companies despite what is supposed to be a vigilant and public-oriented regulator.

In Canada, we have had a regulator that supposedly maintained an interest in "citizens" as opposed to consumers. With the presence of a huge public broadcaster like the CBC (huge as compared to public broadcasting in the United States, which is vestigial, at best), there are many opportunities to discuss and make obeisance to the public interest. What has evolved is a particularly Canadian approach: citizens if necessary, but preferably consumers.

Through both regulation and government policy there has been a transfer of substantial sums of money from the public to the private sector (Friends of Canadian Broadcasting 2001, 30). It is ironic that the private broadcasters, having spent decades criticizing the CBC's public subsidy, should now be lining up eagerly to have their operations subsidized by taxpayers, despite their healthy profit margins throughout the 1990s. In addition, CanWest wants to remove even more competition; witness Izzie Asper's recent call for virtually dismantling the CBC, which actually produces successful Canadian programming. In a speech to the Canadian Club in Toronto in 1999, he said:

> In my view, the CBC should not be state-owned, but most Canadians might be prepared to pay, on a privately funded basis, for a real public broadcaster, much as PBS is supported, but not owned, by the U.S. government … CBC should ultimately get out of the [sic] national news programming. (Asper, I. 1999)

What Izzy Asper wants to eliminate would appear to many to be exactly what makes the Canadian broadcast environment uniquely Canadian.

Ironically, Matthew Fraser, the clear-eyed analyst of the Canadian industry, is now in the employ of CanWest as a columnist for the *Financial Post*. He recently conducted an interview with Asper on IChannel, a digital specialty service. Asper was asked about regulation and complained about having to justify himself when he wanted a licence renewal. But when asked if he wanted the regulator abolished, Asper said no. Fraser, who had earlier suggested that CanWest Global's success was a result of favourable rulings from the regulator, did not pursue the point further (Fraser 2002).

CanWest is seeking more favourable rulings, both from the Commission and from Parliament. As this is being written, the Heritage Committee of the House of Commons is holding hearings on possible revisions to the Broadcasting Act. CanWest is asking the Committee to ease restrictions on foreign ownership in broadcasting. The main result would be an increase in the value of Canadian properties as U.S. investors entered the market.

But CanWest will also be arguing for continued regulation by the CRTC, as long as the regulations are not too onerous.

The tone was probably set by Canada's Commissioner of Competition, Konrad von Finckenstein. In his testimony, he called for the CRTC to get out of the business of regulating the business activities of broadcast enterprises. The CRTC's job, he said, should be "the attainment of core cultural objectives: the production and distribution of Canadian content and the promotion and maintenance of a diversity of voices" (von Finckenstein 2002, ¶23). He calls for a more market-driven broadcast environment and suggests that the CRTC shift from a "supply push" strategy for Canadian content to a "demand pull" strategy. Up to now, the CRTC has encouraged networks and other programming services to produce Canadian programming. It would then be available for viewing and, it is hoped, viewers will find it and enjoy it – the supply would "push" the level of demand.

The other view, the one the Commissioner is recommending, is to look at ratings and other measures, determine what Canadians want (what they "demand") and let the programming enterprises give them that. This is based on the theory that Canadian audiences have free choice of programming and that all producers, U.S. and Canadian, are on equal footing. However, since U.S. programming can be acquired for Canadian broadcast at a fraction of the cost of producing Canadian content, this argument is not persuasive to supporters of Canadian production.

Interestingly, the Commissioner makes his recommendations after acknowledging that Canada has one of the most successful broadcasting systems in the world thanks in no small part to regulation. (von Finckenstein 2002, ¶39).

And that regulation does not just protect public broadcasters like the CBC. A group called the Friends of Public Broadcasting (Friends of Canadian Broadcasting 2001) has done a study of how Canadian television is paid for. This study shows that the public funds that have flowed to the private conventional broadcasters have, in fact, helped subsidize spending on U.S. programs.

Vincent A. Carlin

Meanwhile, the CBC, with a mandate to treat listeners and viewers as citizens rather than consumers, saw its Parliamentary allocation slashed by one-third. It is forced to rely more on commercial activity and professional sports in order to generate sufficient revenues to produce Canadian programming.

The CBC was also a pioneer in programming convergence before the phenomenon had acquired the name. Increasingly in recent years, the publicly funded corporation shared content across "platforms": television content on radio, radio reporters on television, material from both media on the CBC website. No one called it "convergence": it was most often done in the name of economy, cutting back on the number of reporters and using all available material in multiple formats.

But as this century began, we saw in English Canada two large private agglomerations of information, CanWest and BCE, both now encompassing broadcasting and newspapers, with only the next step to cable to ensure a completely integrated communications duopoly.

Bell, Book and Cable

While Global had been building itself up from a modest station in Winnipeg, the other big convergence player, Bell Canada Enterprises (BCE), already had deep pockets and a long reach: Bell started life as a regulated monopoly – a phone company, particularly in Quebec and Ontario. Its monopoly position enabled it to pile up large reserves of cash.

Bell Canada has traditionally had the image of what is called a "value" company – a conservatively managed enterprise that is dominant in its field and possessing a large cash flow. By 2000, its CEO, Jean Monty, obviously saw a different future for his company than lines and circuits. He had seen some of his Bell cousins in the United States move aggressively into both the content and content distribution business. (Fraser 1999, esp. 78–79). As we have seen, he was also very impressed with the AOL–Time Warner merger.

Monty realized that, like the cable companies, he had wires running into almost everyone's home. The fight would be over who controlled what went over the wires and which company would survive the battle. The technology already existed to bring telephone and high-speed Internet access to TV broadcast cable, but work still needed to be done on bringing TV and radio through phone wires.

In the last decade of the last century, Bell, the erstwhile phone company, refashioned itself as an entrepreneurial communications company. It was split into separate companies to concentrate on specialized activities. Its highly successful research division, Northern Electric, eventually was spun off into the even more successful high-tech company Nortel. In recent times, Nortel has faced a profound struggle to survive, much less regain its former success. Other divisions of the company have also had some difficulties. But as it evolved its strategy, the new holding company, Bell Canada Enterprises, bet on convergence as a cornerstone of its corporate philosophy.

Clearly, BCE's strategy was based on a "brand name" play. It acquired as many of the "names" within program and content production as were available: CTV (which brings TSN and a raft of other specialty channels), the *Globe and Mail* and Sympatico/Lycos. In the release announcing the creation of its new subsidiary, Bell Globemedia, BCE made this clear, quoting its then-CEO Jean Monty: "BCE's content strategy is to assemble the leading Canadian content brands and leverage them with connectivity and commerce." (Bell Globemedia 2001a, ¶3). The company said its new subsidiary will "grow these properties through continued investment in content for new and traditional media, thus creating a strong, competitive multi-media company." (Bell Globemedia 2001a, ¶2).

But in the short term, the benefits appeared to be few. The convergence visionary, Jean Monty, resigned amid a chorus of negative commentary about the company's prospects. Its new CEO, Michael Sabia has called for a reconsideration of the Monty strategy. In a speech to the Canadian Club of Toronto in November, 2002, Sabia said: "What we saw was the vulnerability of business models driven by unbridled exuberance, with too little financial discipline. Too much capital chasing far too few true business opportunities" (Sabia 2002, 3). While it will be some time before the new strategy takes shape, there are signs that BCE may be wondering whether television and newspapers are an essential part of it. Sabia's speech was titled "From Here to Simplicity," and it seems to be a call for BCE to return to the core businesses that historically brought it such success.

In a subsequent announcement, Sabia clearly raised the question as to whether Bell Globemedia was one of those core businesses: "The underlying promise, the underlying hope or drama of a convergence view of the world is probably something that is not intrinsically in the genes...for a connectivity company and a content company" (Damsell 2002). Jean Monty said that convergence was the key, but his successor has changed the locks on the executive suite.

It appears that even large, sophisticated companies can be misled by hype or self-delusion into thinking that something which is "cool" will automatically be profitable.

Strength through Debt

Some small dot-com entrepreneurs made fortunes, selling out before the gap between capitalization and results became all-too-obvious. Many rode the wave all the way down and wiped out in the crash of the technology markets.

Our big communications companies went into debt to try to pry value out of the tech boom and convergence.

CanWest paid more than $3 billion for Southam and half of the *National Post*. It subsequently announced that it would acquire the rest of the Post, but no figures were announced.

BCE paid over $2 billion for CTV. The year 2001 was not a banner one for communications companies generally. Revenues were basically flat; shareholders lost money for the first time in memory.

Meanwhile, Rogers Communications consolidated its position as the largest cable operator in the country, while expanding its reach into other areas, even some previously prohibited by regulation, such as program production. Rogers and the other main cable player, Shaw, have both become quite active in owning program-producing companies, signalling another area of concentration as we move further into the new century. For example, besides its cable franchises, Shaw has interests in such producers as YTV, Nelvana Studios, and Treehouse Television. Rogers has stakes in the Canadian Sportsnet, the Shopping Channel, and CFMT Toronto (Omni 1 and 2).

All of these communications companies trumpeted the virtues of convergence. In his annual report for the year 2000, Ted Rogers said that "convergence continued to define the future and we continued to define convergence" (p. 1), although few examples were actually offered.

Bell Globemedia boasted: "With Bell Globemedia, we're fulfilling the promise of convergence – the experiences you want, when and where you want them" (Bell Globemedia 2001b).

CanWest Global's Annual Report for 2001 is entitled "Convergence at Work," although the main effect at that company seemed to be having journalists from Southam papers appearing on local Global television news shows.

However, there have been only a few other signs of the kind of convergence that was being forecast. One notable one is "State of the Nation," a joint project of Global Television, the *National Post*, Southam Newspapers and CanWest Internet properties. Based on a series of polls and other studies, the programs were a marriage of editorial and marketing strategies. "State of the Nation" is probably what some of the business dreamers are thinking about when the word "convergence" is uttered: a twelve-page supplement examining the differences between Canada and the United States, appearing in the *National Post* and distributed throughout the Southam chain; highlights from that study on Global's evening newscasts; a special anchored by Peter Kent, other coverage in the *National Post* business magazine and other publications of the group as well as supplementary material on CanWest's Canada.com and *National Post* websites. All this was topped off with extensive interviews with Gordon Nixon, the President and CEO of the Royal Bank. Why him? Well, the Royal Bank Financial Group happened to be the sponsor of the whole enterprise. Skeptics might see it as less a journalistic enterprise than a multi-platform marketing campaign. But those in the marketing world see it as a breakthrough (Powell, C. 2001, 17–18).

Even more recently, CanWest announced yet another "convergence" campaign, supposedly in support of International Women's Day, but which is a promotional vehicle for a large cosmetics company, L'OREAL.

For BCE, the main elements of its convergence strategy appear to be similar: joint projects, both journalistic and marketing, of CTV, the *Globe and Mail* and its Internet affiliates.

In another irony, the public corporation, the CBC, again showed what convergence of content could mean with a week of programming and public events about the health care system. The corporation marshalled its radio, television and online outlets to present material and discussion in anticipation of the Romanow Report on the future of Medicare in Canada. The multi-format exercise was not part of a marketing plan, but a journalistic one.

When Do We Get a Say?

Looking down the road of the new century, it is not at all clear that "convergence" will prove profitable as a business strategy. There have been few successes in turning convergence into positive cash flow. Only large and previously profitable enterprises like BCE and CanWest have been able to afford to ride out the initial reverses.

As we have seen, BCE may be reconsidering its place in the world of convergence. CanWest appears ready to maintain its commitment to the strategy, at least publicly, although a continued slough in the economic climate may lead them to shed some of the properties outside their core business, which is television.

At the same time, in both the United States and Canada, government bodies are holding hearings on major aspects of convergence. The Heritage Committee of the Canadian House of Commons is looking into broadcasting, while in the United States the Federal Communications Commission is having hearings about further deregulation.

In both countries, politicians and citizens will be contemplating the benefits and deficits of concentration and of "cross-ownership" – companies like CanWest, like Rupert Murdoch's News Corp., which have extensive holdings across media lines within the same city.

Owners like Leonard Asper argue that the synergy created by owning television and newspapers in the same city is both a benefit to his company, and also to "consumers" (Asper, L. 2002).

The trends in communication at the beginning of this century also do not augur well for choice or input by citizens. The policy fashion continues to be deregulation which, if recent history is a guide, will lead to even larger corporate concentrations, certainly in the United States and, it would appear, in Canada.

We have fashioned for ourselves a framework that tries to mix public and private, citizen and consumer, with the result that few of the elements thrive.

Canadian consumers have, in effect, voted for large doses of American product on their screens but allowed the creation of a system that benefits a few wealthy Canadian individuals and corporations. The public sector, the CBC in particular, but other public broadcasters as well, has seen their finances sharply curtailed. Regulation has produced protection and profits for the increasingly few who have now used those profits to control the print media in this country: Rogers has its large publications division, led by *Maclean's* magazine; BCE owns the largest national newspaper, the *Globe and Mail*; and CanWest controls the major daily paper in virtually every Canadian city outside Toronto and has the *National Post* as well.

The landscape is now dominated by private leviathans that, while constantly paying lip service to competition and innovation, work to preserve a system that has rewarded concentrated ownership.

As citizens we will face choices on how we want our communications environment to develop. Broadcasting is regulated, and there are legislated restrictions on the ownership of Canadian newspapers. Since those businesses have come together, we will have to decide how we want them to develop.

If there is a desire to have a diversity of ownership in the newspaper business, we may have to contemplate a major policy shift to allow non-Canadians to control newspaper properties, something that is currently prohibited. The owners would welcome that change, since rich U.S. and other owners would bid up the price of scarce Canadian assets. We would be faced with a decision: maintain concentration in the hands of few Canadian owners, or open up the playing field to be potentially dominated by foreign corporations.

If there is a desire to limit cross-ownership, what regulations can be brought in which would not prevent companies from making legitimate profits sufficient to sustain full-service operations. Arguably, Canada has benefited from having a few major players with the resources to mount sophisticated news operations as well as produce Canadian entertainment and sports programming. Should we move to a system that has a greater number of players with fewer resources, it may not prove to be of benefit to Canadian culture.

As the new millennium unfolds, we will be watching to see if a converged system can produce both healthy profits for the companies and satisfying choice for the citizens/consumers.

References

Asper, Israel. 1999. "Canadian Broadcasting into the Millennium." Speech to the Canadian Club. Toronto, May 17.
Asper, Leonard. 2002. "Inventing the Future." Speech to the Canadian Club. Ottawa, December 17.
Bagdikian, B. 2002. *The Media Monopoly*. 6th ed. Boston: Beacon Press.

Vincent A. Carlin

Bell Globemedia. 2001a. *News releases/Bell Globemedia launched* [Online]. Available: http://www.bce.ca/en/news/releases/bce/2001/01/09/5580.html.

Bell Globemedia. 2001b. *Bell Canada Enterprises 2000 Annual Report*. Montreal: Arthurs-Jones Clarke.

Caincross, F. 1997. *The Death of Distance: How the Communications Revolution Will Change our Lives*. Cambridge, MA: Harvard University Business School Press.

CanWest Global. 2002. *Annual Report 2001: Convergence at Work*. Winnipeg: Gordon Fisher.

Damsell, Keith. 2002. "Sabia Questions Convergence." Report on Business. *Globe and Mail*, December 19, B4.

Forbes Magazine. 2002. Forbes 500s/Entertainment and Information List. March 26. Available: http://www.Forbes.com/2002/03127/Forbes500.html (see under "Entertainment and Information.")

Fraser, M. 1999. *Free for All: The struggle for Dominance on the Digital Frontier*. Toronto: Stoddart.

——. 2001. *I on Media with Matthew Fraser/Izzy Asper interview*. Toronto: Stornoway Communications, February 13.

Friends of Canadian Broadcasting. 2001. *Who Paid for Canadian Television, 1990–2000*. Toronto, August.

FAIR-L. 2001. *FCC moves to intensify media consolidation*, April 20 [Online]. Available: http://www.fair.org/activism/cross-ownership.html.

von Finkenstein, Konrad. 2002. Comments of the Commissioner of Competition to the Standing Committee on Canadian Heritage on the Study of the State of the Canadian Broadcasting System [on-line] (May 6). Available: http: strategis.ic.ca/ssgi/et02358e.html

Hanley, W. 1999. "Berkshire coming back to earth?" *Financial Post*, September 9, C1, C3.

Kinsley, M. 2001. "It's not just the Internet: Almost no one pays for content in any medium" [10 paragraphs]. *Slate* , May 10 [Online serial]. Available: http://slate.msn.com/default.aspx?id=105903

Olive, D. 2000. "Crazy, hazy days of convergence: U.S. experience exposes some flaws in media marriages." *Financial Post*, September 16, D1.

Pitts, G. 2002. *Kings of Convergence*. Toronto: Doubleday Canada.

Powell, C. 2001. "Banking on convergence: despite all the hype about media convergence, it's tough to find actual examples of it." *Marketing, 106* (30): 17–18.

Powell, M. 2001. Chairman Powell's Press Briefing, February 6 [Online]. Available: http://ftp.fcc.gov/realaudio/pressconfs.html.

Reguly, E. 2002. "Consumers beware: Canada is a haven for media oligopolies." *Globe and Mail*, February 28, B17.

Rogers Communications Inc. 2001. *2000 Annual Report*. Toronto.

Sabia, M. 2002. "From Here to Simplicity." Speech to the Canadian Club of Toronto. Toronto, November 4.

CANADIAN MEMORY INSTITUTIONS AND THE DIGITAL REVOLUTION

The Last Five Years

Frits Pannekoek

Introduction

Three American companies carry 80 per cent of Internet traffic. America Online has a large financial interest in two of these companies. Today there are about 1.5 million connections to the Internet; by 2010 there will be 1.5 billion. From 1993 to 1997 graphic content moved from zero per cent to 14 per cent; by 2010 it will dominate. The average capital cost to access the Internet is about $3,000, with an annual operating cost of $400 – enough in most of the world to support a family of four for a year. Over 90 per cent of all communication on the Internet is in English, and most activity on the Internet is commercial. In 1980 there were 411 digital databases; in 1997 there are over 10,000. Over 57 per cent of University of Calgary undergraduates prefer to access information in digital form. Only two to three universities in Canada can afford all the available databases and full text materials. A 2000 University of Calgary study for the Social

Science and Humanities Federation indicates that there are only two hundred Canadian sites that meet basic scholarly standards. Six vendors control most of the key academic databases. Fifty-seven per cent of Canadian scholars who identified a reason for not using electronic resources indicated that they were not credible (Archer 2000, Table 6).[1]

What sense can be made of these apparently random numbers and events? Castells (1997) has offered a profound analysis. He argues that we are in the midst of an "information technology revolution" that is "pervasive" and which is influencing social and economic interactions. He would argue further that the adaptations of the new technologies depend very much on national identities and cultures. It should be noted, however, that in his approximately fifteen hundred pages he does not mention libraries, archives or museums even once.

If one acknowledges these memory institutions as players in the new information age, however, several conclusions become apparent. First, the "cultural democracy" of the Internet is at the moment an illusion. Content creation and access still rests with a few Western, English-speaking information aggregators who have their roots in commerce rather than in intellectual pursuits or culture. Second, there is an even more concentrated control over the best Web content than there ever was over print. This is in part because the technical capacities of the digital environment allow for the perfect commodification and control of information. Third, the early stages of content and technology development were undertaken by American government agencies, for example the National Science Foundation. Leadership has now been handed off to the private sector. Sprint, Ameritech, and Microsoft now dominate technology, and Thomson[2] and Elsevier high-end content. And the library world's OCLC (Online Computer Library Center), the American-based information collaborative, is beginning to dominate the English-speaking post-secondary world.

The new Web world can marginalize fragile cultures like Canada's (Pannekoek 2000). Most cultures fall prey to analyzing themselves on the Web through the "tourism" filters encouraged by Western commercial interests. Sardar and Ravet (1996, 19) offer a biting insight which has some resonance.

> Once a culture has been "stored" and "preserved" in digital forms,
> opened up to anybody who wants to explore it from the comfort
> of their armchairs, then it becomes more real than the real thing.
> Who needs the arcane and esoteric real thing anyway? In the post

modern world where things have systematically become memen-
tos, nature has been transformed into "reserve," knowledge is
giving way to information and data, it is only a matter of time
before other people and their cultures become "models," so many
zeros and ones in cyberspace, exotic examples for scholars, voyeurs
and other interested parties to loan on their machines and look at.
Cyberspace is a giant step towards museumisation of the world.

Indeed, Canada's library, museum, and archive websites have both demonstrated and contributed to this tendency during the last five years.[3]

The Canadian Context

An analysis of the digital communication practices of Canada's memory
institutions – its archives, libraries, and museums – illustrates that the country is verging on descending into the abyss of being such an "information"
deficit nation. Canada's ability to communicate and to control its memory
both now and in the future is in serious jeopardy. Our cultures are marginalized on the Web, and our university and public libraries cannot afford the
costs of retrospective digitization to ensure that Canada's memory has an
internationally competitive presence. What sites we do possess have fallen
prey to the process of "museumisation" mentioned above. Our citizens are
increasingly finding that the best information they need in order to contribute to or to challenge commercial, economic, and government interests is no
longer readily available to them. And the provinces and federal government
have still to determine a strategy to address the cultural issues posed by the
Web, although signs exist that governments are beginning to shift themselves. There is a real and present crisis, particularly in the communication
of cultural memory.

On the surface, Canada's museums, libraries, and to a lesser degree its
archives, appear to have embraced the new digital communication technology of the last decade with eagerness and with success.[4] And compared to
the nations of Africa or Eastern Europe, this may be true. But our embrace
of the Web in these institutions seems to have been with great celebration,
but little reflection and understanding of its cultural impact.[5]

Canada's libraries, archives, and museums appear to have participated in the nation's descent into despair over the lack of digital Canadian

cultural content. To be is to be on the Web – and, if that is the only definition, Canada would appear to have resuscitated itself. However, in the environment of fiscal impossibility and policy angst, real success has been marginal. Our memory institutions are hardly able to meet their current mandates, much less those imposed by the new technologies. Canada's National
Library and National Archives have fallen into an appalling state. Perhaps
it was in part because decision-makers believed that libraries and archives
were simply outdated – mere holders of antique print? Who wants to invest
in yesterday?! Miraculously everything worthwhile would be reborn digitally – and available with little effort and for free (English n.d.). And it was
often Industry Canada, not the Department of Canadian Heritage, who led
the cultural charge. Culture mattered insofar as it tied into our economic
infrastructure.

I. Museums

Some national memory institutions, realizing opportunity, did seize a
role as cultural validators by creating a digital presence. Museums had the
most aggressive public presence on the new communication instrument.
Canadian museums have not lost their popularity and are visited by over
54.9 million people each year. These visitors have become critical bastions
in the funding defence. At the same time that museums had to increase their
paying visitation, they attempted to redefine themselves from being places of
validation and celebration to places of discourse and challenge. And museums
were the most aggressive of all memory institutions in the use of the Web to
advance their causes. No major museum is without a Web presence.[6]

Unfortunately this presence is variable, and for the most part, information is "dumbed" down. Whatever culture is offered is generally through
the "tourism" lens. Most museum websites do not reveal their intellectual
antecedents and offer little meaningful intellectual sustenance. At best they
validate peoples and cultures as being relevant simply by being present in the
new environment; at worst they act as shills for cultural tourism. And they
are almost without exception in English, and in Quebec in French, although
other languages are sometimes offered as a choice. Museum websites have
created the illusion of cultural access, but access to mediocrity is no access
at all.

What is as important to note is that there are no museum or archives
websites that are at the moment "pay for view." Digital library materials, on
the other hand, almost uniformly are, although patrons may not realize this.

Is this because museums and archives see the Web as a marketing mechanism to increase their gate and the sales in their gift shops?[7] Is it because museum collections have never been widely used for research in the first place? Is it because the public values the museums for the spirit of the "real" which cannot be adequately captured digitally?

II. Archives

The National Archives was also an early adopter. However, the best that a few of the provincial archives managed was the automation of their catalogues, and the establishment of national rules for archival description.[8] If the provincial archives of Alberta and Manitoba resisted the new technologies, the Provincial Archives of British Columbia and the Archives of the North West Territories managed a smattering of online content.[9] But even their samples are so limited and the criteria for selection so vague that few scholars would ever seriously use this material in isolation from the rest of the archival documents in the collection. So, to date, archives have done little but advertise or experiment with technology.[10] The next few years may see radical change. With most archives having converted their inventories to a common national format, Canadian archives are now poised to place all of these online. In western Canada this has already happened. Whether the rest of Canada's archives have the imagination and, as important, the resources to do so remains to be seen.

III. Libraries

While the majority of public libraries could not afford to be early adopters of the opportunities that the new technologies offered, they saw themselves, as eventually did governments, as the window to digital content for the community at large. Industry Canada, through its "Connecting Canadians" initiatives, as well as more modest efforts on the part of the Bill and Melinda Gates Foundation, were instrumental in providing the resources to ensure that every Canadian community would have access to digital content.[11] In Alberta, Supernet, the $1-billion fibre-optic high-speed connectivity project, will ensure that every community and library has high-speed Internet capacity. Whether there will be any sustainable worthwhile content has yet to be determined.

Academic libraries became Canada's most aggressive entry point into the digital age partially because the best digital information required the kind of buying power that only the larger academic libraries had.[12] Whether they liked it or not, Canadian academic libraries found themselves at the forefront of the true digital revolution in the communication of information. Pressed by their academic users who had no choice but to follow international information trends, Canadian academic libraries had to assume leadership of the digital revolution, particularly in acquiring content and in copyright management. It was also in the academy that the full impact of the digital revolution was being explored.

Three Trends in Canadian Memory Institutions

Three trends emerge from this revolution in communication that is impacting libraries, archives, and museums – all a direct result of the new digital structures. First, there is convergence. While in the past information and its communication had been controlled by three professions – librarians, curators, and archivists – often in separate locations and separate formats, a single point of intersection, the Web, has increasingly blurred the boundaries among the disciplines and their institutions. This is very much apparent in, for example, the twenty-seven history exhibitions that are part of the Virtual Museum of Canada, and in Industry Canada's School Net projects.

Second, information can now be more effectively commodified than it ever could in the analog world. As Canada moved into the knowledge economy, information became of increasing value. But who should pay? Should information be seen as a public utility or should it be subject to the competition of the marketplace? The old model of libraries, archives, and museums being there for the common good is being seriously challenged in the age of digital commodification. Their primary purpose is now to support the new knowledge economy! This would explain the key role of Industry Canada.

Third, memory institutions have yet to come to grips with their archival and memory roles in the new digital age. To what degree are they responsible for the preservation of memory in digital format? Are they responsible for the preservation of increasingly complex social and economic data to ensure that society's memory remains intact? If they do preserve memory of a nation's data, who has the right of access? Just the servants of the nation-state – just academics – or everyone? For the first time, the Web offers the opportunity for complete control of information. In the past,

Frits Pannekoek

memory institutions, particularly libraries and archives, facilitated access to their collections generally regardless of status; now they can *completely* control digital access through pin and identity numbers. What is the role of the state in the regulation of the memory institution? Increasingly users get what memory institutions and their governments feel they can have – not necessarily what users need. The next decades must see the reinvention of memory institutions and their role in civil society. The debate is just beginning.

I. Convergence

The Web has impacted the collection and exhibition habits of most memory institutions and their users. In the past, memory institutions were driven by different professional traditions developed in part because each required different types of collection spaces and had different users and different methods of communication. In the Web's virtual space, the elimination of physical constraints, the inability to segregate user types, determined that there would be a convergence in collection organization and in exhibition/ communication with respect to the collections. At the same time that free Web information began to create the myth that "information was free" and that it was readily available, or ought to be, users began to ignore – and perhaps they always had – the boundaries among libraries, archives, and museums. Does it really matter whether an information resource is an archival document, a library book, or a museum object? In the past, users would often have to go to three different institutions to secure the information they needed. It became apparent from the various search engines, which now number several hundred, that this distinction was no longer relevant.

In the first years of the new cyber-millennium, Canadian memory institutions all tended to use the Web as an advertising medium for their middle-class publics. There was no evidence that anyone actually visited a memory institution because of a previous cyber-visit, so it was really an attempt by all to validate themselves as "modern," essential in a society that seemed enthralled with the Web. What is peculiar is that Canadian institutions rarely used the same intellectual rigour on the websites as they did in the more traditional pursuits of their own professions. Authorship, sources, and perspectives were hardly transparent or known, and on-site self-censorship was not unknown.[13] It is almost as if the memory institutions thought of the Web as a "television without credits," or that the Web would expose the fragility of any singe memory profession. In Canada's national institutions the professions continue to try to define their roles with little success, often abandoning their own professional conventions and acting increasingly like amateur publishers.

It can be argued that what has happened is the McDonaldization of digital cultural information. Users seemed to want more information faster and faster and in smaller, instantly consumable quantities. The Web both created and then reinforced that tendency. Information was in screen segments, and quickly digestible. There was always the faint hunger for more and more – faster and faster. In a 2000 survey done for the Social Sciences and Humanities Federation, the University of Calgary could find only two hundred refereed sites with Canadian content on the Web that met minimal scholarly criteria. This dumbing down of cultural content on the new medium is evident in the examination of the websites of some of Canada's key memory institutions.

The key federal memory agencies have in fact used the Web as an instrument of national policy rather than education. The National Museums website, for example, highlights the Aboriginal past, women, and Canada's military past. The discomforts of racism, class, and marginalization are not topics encouraged.

Canadian museums are often thought to be at the forefront of the information revolution. The Department of Canadian Heritage, through the Canadian Information Network, has been aggressive in its interest and in exploring the topic. If in 1995 the primary interest was in encouraging museums to put their collections on the Web, by 2001 museums were encouraged and indeed active in putting up exhibitions through the Virtual Museum of Canada project. Some have also attempted to put up illustrated inventories of their collections; however, only a few are currently available.[14]

At best, the Canadian Heritage Information Network, through its new initiative the Virtual Museum of Canada, has provided a location from which Canadians can enter their virtual galleries. These galleries are for the most part those that were produced by SchoolNet, the digital content initiative of Industry Canada, or by the Millennium Bureau. They have become the standards to which museums generally work, although because of lack of concern over intellectual ownership it is difficult to determine which websites served as models.

By January 2002 there were a total of fifty-two exhibitions, although not all were on Canadian subjects. One of the most prominent exhibitors is the British Columbia Heritage Branch, whose materials are worth looking at because they embody so many of the problems. Their Yale exhibit, like most on the Web, evidence a "team" approach to production. Responsibility is, however, so devolved that responsibility for content is muddied. Second, the site no longer focuses on "object" or "structure" but rather on "context." The curator appears no longer interested in material culture and how it can be used to create new understanding. Rather the curator is interested primarily in the broad historical context of the events. While some will argue that there is nothing wrong with this approach, curators are not historians. Their focus has been material culture and its context. More often than not they are not aware of the intricacies of the shifting interpretations of the historical narrative. If curators shift away from a focus on the understanding of material culture, who will assume that role?

The Point Ellice House virtual exhibit is a case in point.[15] Point Ellice House is the restored nineteenth-century Victoria, British Columbia, home of Gold Rush Magistrate and Commissioner Peter O'Reilly. On the website the traditional approach to the house museum is reinforced, with much focus on individual artifacts, including the accession records. But the interpretation is shocking. The vehicle for interpretation are a group of "gossipy" and "oppressive" women. It would seem that those responsible for the site were ignorant of recent historiographical trends and chose to reinforce old stereotypes.

Has the site, last updated in 1996, used the new technology to improve communication? Hardly! At best, if the "Well, hello there! I hope you are enjoying your stay at Point Ellice. It's just about teatime – the perfect time to trade GOSSIP! So pull up a chair" approach does not work, an alternative tour is offered by a Chinese houseboy introducing his replacement to the house. He does so in exceptional English, with minimal rancour at all at the inhumane treatment of his people. There is considerable focus on the obvious material wealth of the European culture of the home, but little on the life of its Chinese servant. There is no real interaction, and the technical abilities of new softwares are not used at all. It would be interesting to measure the impact of this site on community understanding and on the school curriculum.

The National Archives emulated the leadership of the National Museums, but only in 2001. In its budget submission to Parliament that year, the National Archives promised the following:

Using the Internet as its primary vehicle of service delivery, the National Archive of Canada will increase Canadians' access to the sources of their history, to unique, authentic and reliable, timely and easy-to-access information about Canada. The Archives will develop quality Canadian digital content based on its vast multimedia holdings. Its expanded digitization program will connect Canadians, particularly youth and lifelong learners, with the riches of Canada's archival heritage on line and in both official languages (National Archives of Canada 2001, 12).

The National Archives is now a "publisher" responsible for creating new content as well as collecting, and organizing. Its website now has sections on publications, exhibitions, and "Virtual Memory Exhibitions." As far as can be determined, publications are full text with authorship, exhibitions are physical exhibitions on-site, and virtual exhibits are just that. There is a credits page, but the team is so diffuse that it is difficult to determine who is responsible for historiographical thrusts. It is interesting, however, to note that the production needed as many experts as a Hollywood spectacle.[16]

The National Archives, given its critical leadership and financial role and its stature as a national body, will ensure that national rather than regional agendas are met in its projects. Its "The Canadian West" would seem an exception, but much of the interpretation is from a centralist perspective. Generally its new creations are in politically appropriate subject areas like living memory, Aboriginals, women, war, and other current items of political correctness high on the current ruling party's agenda.[17] The theme of "Pride and Dignity" on the website hardly conjures up the oppression that was the reality for so many new Canadians.[18] Historica, Canada's not-for-profit foundation, not the National Archives, has put up a unit on the First World War internment of Canada's Ukrainians.[19] But Historica, like the National Archives, has no transparent criteria for inclusion or non-inclusion of material in its websites.[20]

What has the National Archives really accomplished in the area of full text, or complete fonds? They have the military attestation papers, their much-appreciated fond-level descriptions, and a few unique collections. No one would argue that they should digitize all of their collections – only that they should be thoughtful and transparent about why they are doing what they are doing. But perhaps those that are the most used, and those that are most critical to national identity – like the prime minister's papers – might be placed on the Web first. What the National Archives has been most successful at has been providing a platform from which the great full text collections can be digitized and placed on the Web.

Regional archives have also been active, although there are few total fonds. The Archives Society of Alberta, an unlikely leader in "sex memory," has attempted to sell archives with exactly that. In 2000 they created a site, "Passion Preserved."[21] It offered single images from archival collections around the province, each of which illustrated a single passion: lust, love, pique, obsession, loyalty, mania, yearning, wrath, desire, and agitation. The "tongue-in-cheek" approach to political as well as sexual passions was appreciated, but who was responsible for the selection, if anyone? The Moshie Shafdie Hypermedia Archives at McGill, while an apparent example of the riches that can happen, is also a cyber-exhibition rather than an archives.[22] The site, however, does provide a single intellectual authority – Irena Murray, Curator-in-Chief, Canadian Architecture Collection.[23] The role of the librarian is also noted. It is interesting that in this case professionals called "curators" and "librarians" do digital exhibits, not those with the title "archivist."

The Glenbow Archives has only a few of its hundreds of thousands of photographs on the Web.[24] The Canadian Women's Archives, founded in 1977 at the University of Ottawa, offers the least of any archives regardless of format.[25] In 2001 its site contained no listing of the collections. The Canadian North West Archives database is an excellent project, which now includes most western archival descriptions at the fond level. Keyword and Boolean searches are both possible.[26]

If archives have been quick to recreate the "virtual exhibits" of museums, they are ultimately further ahead in making their collections accessible because of their commitment to CAIN (Canadian Archival Information Network) and RAD (Rules for Archival Description). In the coming years, scholars in particular hope that they will tie full text to their catalogues. That will begin to test the full power of the digital environment. Canadians can then interpret their own past rather than relying on the guiding hand of memory professionals.

The most profound contribution has been by Canada's libraries. Individually and as members of large collectives, libraries have done a great deal to develop digital information bases and to connect Canadians to information. First, through their commitment to MARC[27] catalogue records, and then to Dublin core metadata, libraries had developed standards as early as 1995. These ensured that, as the Web became more robust, individual library catalogues could be combined into "union" catalogues, and most important, that there were common searching protocols.[28] The National Library's Amicus bilingual database, which was first conceived in 1993 and made available last year on a no-fee basis to Canadians, contains over twenty-four million bibliographic records of Canadiana, including books, magazines, government documents, theses, sound recordings, and maps. It makes accessible forty million holdings from over thirteen hundred Canadian libraries through interlibrary loan, allows the display of full bibliographic records from five hundred Canadian libraries, and, most important, allows the downloading of these records, making cataloguing for Canadian libraries a much less costly task. The National Library would also like to create a "virtual Canadian union catalogue," and this remains very high on its agenda.

The importance of machine readable cataloguing should not be underestimated in the communication of digital cultural memory. If all catalogues were on the Web and if all new digital material and all repurposed material were made available through direct links from existing cataloguing records – not an impossible task – there would be structured access to digital information, with potential for full-text searching across data sets.

Currently, however, the initiative to link Web-based catalogues to full text materials is centred in the United States in Dublin, Ohio, at OCLC (Online Computer Library Center) through Worldcat, with its over forty-seven million unique records. If OCLC were to offer to all libraries the opportunity to deposit their digital content at no cost and link it to their cataloguing records, they would become the single most powerful memory repository in the world. The assumption will likely be that your own records will be freely accessible to you, but that there will be a charge for accessing those of other depositors. While libraries could link directly to other digital content providers, it would be easier and more cost-effective to link for a fee to assured records with constantly updated links. The implications of having all of the world's memory managed by one institution is something that is both exhilarating and frightening. What would be the implications for Canada's cultural sovereignty, if any? While some would argue that this is evidence of the real erosion of national boundaries, others would argue that it only increases the influence of wealthy nation states through their corporate expressions. What would happen should the American government, for example, refuse the export of deposited data for reasons of national security?

But rather than focus on being the repository for Canada's digital information, the National Library chose to display its technological prowess in another way – the digitization of sample collections. The National Library intends to continue (with Industry Canada money) the development of the Glenn Gould site, to digitize selected rare book illustrations, information about selected Governor General's Literary Awards recipients, and a bibliography of doctoral research on Canada. It is interesting to note that, except for a handful of libraries like the City of Calgary Public Library and the Toronto Public Library, few have chosen to copy the National Library and aggressively participate in the "creation" of new Web resources in the form of "cyber" exhibitions.

In March, 1997, however, the National Library did take an initiative in digital libraries, consulting with libraries on the state of their digital collections. Now the nation has a collaborative of twenty-two libraries largely from the academic sector, the Canadian Initiative on Digital Libraries (CIDL).[29] With funding from the Department of Canadian Heritage, in late 2001 it spearheaded through the University of Calgary Press and the University of Laval library the digitization of all of Canada's local histories.

But for the most part Canada's libraries, archives, and museums have yet to pull together a concerted vision of communication of information in the new digital age. At best, libraries, archives, and museums and their professions acknowledge responsibility for collections whose primary common characteristic is that they contain memory information. All acknowledge an equal interest in making these collections available and interpreting them to a larger audience. What does this mean? Whether a curator developed a Web tour, an archivist an exhibition, or a librarian an online bibliography – all had become "e-publishers." All have abandoned their more traditional focus of providing access to collections in favour of becoming Web-based publishers of mediated, selected, and interpreted materials, with context being more important than the information inherent in the object itself. But were they effective in their new role as publishers?

In fact, in this natural movement toward convergence, the coordinating discipline – that of the publisher – is absent. The Canadian literary and academic presses and their distributors, with few exceptions, have not participated in the digital age. Canada's large commercial houses, like Thomson-Gale, however, did, and became internationally successful giants.

II. Commodification

In the 1990s, the word's best digital information became commodified and its access controlled. Medium-sized Canadian universities each host approximately eight thousand digital journals. All of Canada's public and academic libraries found increasing difficulty with the new digital databases. This was not only because of cost. They found that the restrictions on who could have access to these data sets flew in the face of their own traditions of ensuring access. Within five years, print information that had once been public was now for the most part restricted to a clientele defined by licence. When you log onto any Canadian library site, minimally you have to have your library card number for remote entry. It can be argued that this is no different than it has always been when any visitor to the library could access information and with a card take it home. However, the technology demands and at the same time allows more. No Canadian library, for example, allows the acquisition of a library card through the Web, which might permit immediate access to digital full text.

In university libraries the situation can be even more serious. Model licences do suggest that "walk in" traffic be allowed (Yale University Library 2001). However, many academic library catalogues indicate that the material is available to "faculty and students" only, discouraging all but the most persistent "walk in" user. The licences present further challenges. They often limit location of access, and many do not allow the library to keep a copy of the full-text materials when the licence expires. Some libraries are refusing to sign licences that preclude archiving rights. With print, the issues never arose.

Licences also attempt to limit the number of hard copies and the transmission of full-text digital articles to other users. Community borrower cards at university libraries, by no means inexpensive, do not usually provide remote, or indeed in some cases any, access to electronic data where institutions have decided to restrict access through pins and ID's. So if libraries in the past were the points of access to the information needs of society, insuring that everyone at least had access to material, that is no longer true. The situation is likely to become more complex.

With the increasing possibility of revenue through controlled access, copyright issues also became of greater concern. The Canadian Association of Academic Libraries has enunciated a strong digital copyright policy which would protect intellectual property rights while favouring clearer education uses, but Canada as a nation has yet to define its digital copyright position.

To date, the law is decidedly on the side of the creator, with little concession to the needs of learners.

The increase in costs that came with change in form has not been understood by decision-makers. The myth remains that the cost of information on the Web is "free" – just as libraries are "free." Yet this is far from the truth; retrospective digitization and creating new digital information involve incredible intellectual and capital costs, just as the traditional library did. Most of the electronic product, which has taken an incredible amount of capital to develop, costs well into the tens of thousands of dollars, a price beyond the reach of any but the wealthiest Canadian libraries. Indeed, probably only three Canadian libraries can afford all of the digital information that is currently available. It is not an accident that cultural materials have almost entirely been subsidized by governments or foundations.

Is there an alternative to the traditional models of funding? Libraries and their users want to have access to information in perpetuity. The tradition of paying for information on a per-view basis or leasing information on an annual basis is alien. The 1990s have seen experimentation, but few successful options, particularly for cultural materials. One model supported by libraries was that offered by Colorado-based netLibrary.[30] It sold individual titles and collections to public, academic, or corporate libraries and allowed individual library patrons to borrow an e-book for a specific time period. Libraries also had perpetual archiving rights to the e-books they purchased. But in the dot com shakedown of 2002, the company failed and accepted an offer by OCLC. While this model of commodifiction proved acceptable to many American publishers, Canadian publishers were late participants. Many thought the e-world would disappear, and those who did not participated in netLibrary. Questia,[31] another model, aimed to sell directly to undergraduate students or faculty at approximately US$20 per month or US$150 per year for access to the entire collection of ultimately some forty thousand volumes. Publishers were paid, not by individual title, but by the number of hits their titles received. Some Canadian publishers have made their backlists available to Questia, but there have been few Canadian student subscribers. Compared to netLibrary, revenues were minimal for most Canadian publishers. And Questia, like netLibrary, also faced financial uncertainty in 2002. Other models that are being offered are publishing collaboratives. In these, universities would become members of an e-publishing co-operative through annual payments based on the number of scholars in their institutions. The e-publishing co-operative would then referee and make the publication available at no cost to anyone who wanted it. Those scholars who wanted to submit a manuscript, but whose university did not subscribe, would have to pay a page fee of several hundred dollars. Whether this model is sustainable or could work in Canada remains to be seen. It would seem on the surface that the digital future for Canadian libraries will be confined to full-text government material, retrospective material for which copyright has expired, and journal literature at exorbitant cost.

Large collections of current Canadian monograph materials will likely continue to have to search for a model that will meet market conditions. And given the traditional government funding sources for Canadian publishers, it is unlikely that, without change to these programs, there will be the fountain of innovation. For example, while early on, netLibrary digitized retrospective content for free, now it cost-shares only those items it feels essential to its collection – i.e., those that have market appeal. If a publisher insists on inclusion – and netLibrary agrees to list the book – the publishers will have to pay the full cost. Since Canadian studies is not of burning interest internationally, and the Canadian market is very small, Canadian titles are not frequently requested. So Canadian students pursuing digital information by key aggregators may not find themselves or the memory of their country in international digital collections.

One of the responses to the commodification of information and the rising costs of information has been the formation of Canadian consortia, themselves co-operating again through the newly formed Consortia Canada. Their effort has been to begin licensing electronic resources at regional and at national levels. Contributing consortia include: the Alberta Library, the Council of Atlantic Librarians, the Consortium of Ontario Libraries, the Council of Federal Libraries, the Council of Prairie and Pacific University Libraries, La Conférence des recteurs et des principaux des universités du Québec, the BC Electronic Library Network , the Manitoba Library Consortium, the NEOS Library Consortium, Novanet, the Ontario Council of University Libraries, and Saskatchewan's Province-wide Library Electronic Information System. Their priority has been and continues to be to acquire broad-based full-text content, databases, and electronic resources. Canada's sixty-four senior universities and colleges have themselves been successful in accessing $20 million over a three-year period to support a $50 million project to acquire high-end scientific material.[32] Even then, a research-intensive university like the University of Calgary, reputedly the fifth largest in Canada, can only afford 25 per cent of all the digital material a research university ought to have. Yet how successful these will be in an international information marketplace that sees Canada as a smaller version of California is yet to be determined. Some information providers are indicating that in the future they may deal only with individual institutions. Consortial buying was costing them too much.

The commodification of information will continue to be the single most important problem for Canada's publishers, Canada's creators, and Canada's libraries. The formula for success which will allow creators and publishers to make a living while ensuring that libraries can preserve their access principles continues to elude. Solutions seem to rely on state intervention of one kind or another. Several initiatives are underway in Canada. School Net, the National Library-sponsored Canadian Initiative on Digital Libraries, and Early Canadiana on Line all rely on Canadian government or foundation funding. It is interesting to note that much of the foundation funding for Early Canadiana on Line was from the Pittsburgh-based Mellon Foundation. More recently, Historica, the Bronfman family initiative, seems to be offering hope. But it survives with government support as well. Most important of all, it exhibits all of the same tendencies as the senior memory institutions, with too often marginal, dumbed-down, celebratory content.

If Canada is to be an active participant in the information age, a new national information policy must be aggressively developed. In October, 2001, the University of Calgary and the University of Montreal held a conference in Calgary entitled "The Information Deficit: Canadian Solutions" to attempt to address these issues. While the issues were identified, and recommendations made, no strong future directions were offered. We don't yet know how we will communicate our cultural memories to the next, the digital generation.

III. Controlled Access

Even as digitally published information becomes increasingly restricted to those who can pay, other restrictions were also being placed on information, particularly primary information that is critical to the production of new knowledge. In 1983, Canada passed its Freedom of Information legislation, and a number of provinces soon followed suit — without much thought as to its implications for libraries, archives, and their community and scholarly users. These Acts, while seeming to advocate access to information that had been previously closed, did the opposite. For the first time, severe restrictions were placed on a citizen's access to information collected by the government.

While the notion of restricting a person's private information was sound, it created a situation which left archives unable to provide scholars with the information they needed to undertake even aggregated social science research. In a democratic environment, this is particularly dangerous. Civil servants will have access to the information they need to develop programs and policies, but those who should be testing these assumptions will not always get access to the same data. The recent initiative on the part of Statistics Canada to provide to approved scholars on a need-to-know basis access to raw unaggregated data through the Canadian Foundation for Innovation-funded Research Data Centres in Canada's regions is a first step to allowing the use of previously confidential data.[33] However, few provinces show an inclination to follow the lead. The anecdotal evidence continues to suggest that Canadian scholars are continuing to use European and American data to test their theories because Canadian material remains too restrictive. The cost of Freedom of Information and Privacy (FOIP) compliance alone remains a major hindrance.

One of the key issues for Canada has been the inability of Canada and its archives or libraries to archive the digital data sets created at considerable expense by Canada's scholars, its public affairs institutes, and its statistical agencies. It has been estimated, for example, that there has been over $1 billion worth of quantitative data alone generated by scholars in this country and only perhaps at best $10 million has been archived for future use. Although the Social Science and Humanities Research Council has urged scholars to deposit their data sets with their respective universities, virtually none have done so. The loss of these unique data sets to archives and libraries not only prevents future scholars from generating new knowledge, it also prevents the testing of previous hypotheses without very expensive replication. It is a major impediment to scholarly communication, to testing social assumptions, and to accountable government. Canada remains the only G8 nation without a national data archiving policy. What is important is that Canadian agencies, particularly the National Archives, the National Library, university libraries, Statistics Canada, and the Social Science and Humanities Research Council have realized that the issue is a serious one and are exploring solutions. These cannot be implemented too quickly before another generation of national digital memory is lost.[34]

Equally important, Canada has not yet developed policies which would ensure that digitally created or repurposed material will be appropriately maintained by its memory institutions. In its 2001 brief to the federal government, the Canadian Library Association carefully outlined the problem:

> ... those electronic documents which are continually "updated" can also create a serious issue – publications which are always "current" cannot show how they have changed over time. The result is that previous editions of publications run the risk of disappearing altogether if they are not archived before the next changes occur. Thus, enhancements and improvements to equipment and software need to be accompanied with a commitment to ensuring ongoing access by archiving information produced by the Canadian Government. (Canadian Library Association 2001)

If Canada does not soon come to grips with the implications of having no digital archive strategy, the nation will be unable to maintain its national memory and the viability of its national memory institutions and professions.

Conclusion

Libraries, archives, and museums, Canada's chief memory institutions, have been taking a leadership role in shaping the future of Canada's cultural communications. While there is convergence among the three, it is worthwhile noting that Canadian publishers are not in the mix. It may be that publishers are "middlemen" who don't add value to the process of communication. If memory institutions can validate the quality of information and deal directly with "creators" or become "creators" themselves, then perhaps Canada is witnessing a revolution in communication. However, if this is the case, why are we not seeing a serious fall in Canadian publishing output? What the memory professionals have been the best at is the creation of the tools to find the new information. What they have an increasing responsibility for is "information literacy." The Internet has inspired a degree of chaos. Everyone, whether government, memory institution, scientist, or crackpot, can be their own publisher. And that information can be available from a library terminal, from the office desktop, or from the home. While the best information will always require payment, likely from a consortia source, and in rare cases by the individual, the bulk of citizen information will come from the "free" alternatives. This will require judgment and the highest information literacy skills. Memory institutions will start to develop search engines that are designed to find and rank Canadian materials. They will begin to develop information standards, to teach information and media literacy. As information becomes more chaotic and as the number of websites relating to Canada increases exponentially in the next five years, the organizational and validation efforts by Canadian libraries, archives, and museums will become of paramount importance. But funding will remain a key issue and the cyber-objectives will increasingly conflict with traditional mandates. Those institutions that represent mainstream Canada with their significant budgets will have to ensure that those on the margins continue to be involved in the dialogue.

Meanwhile, six key questions will have to be appropriately and imaginatively addressed by Canada's memory professionals if the nation's cultural memory is not only to survive but flourish in an increasingly converged and internationalized environment.

First, audience behaviour and user needs will have to be understood. Canadian memory institutions have little information on the needs of clients – most is intuition. The most serious research deficit has been knowledge about users. What do users want in repurposed material? How do users use repurposed cultural material? Are repurposed materials reconstituted in new data forms? How do different age and societal groups use repurposed cultural materials?

Second, the professions will have to resolve issues surrounding archiving. Canada has no provincial or national protocols, strategies or mechanisms to ensure that the considerable investment in repurposing will be available to users even five years from now. The development of strategies for archiving at a national level that are transportable and scalable to an international level is critical. The information base of the new knowledge economy is not sustainable without such a strategy. How much repurposed or digitally created material should be preserved? What is the role of memory institutions? How does convergence among libraries, archives, and museums impact the decisions?

Third, the professions will have to begin to evaluate technical standards for creation, communication, and preservation. There are a number of national and international protocols by memory institutions for the preservation and repurposing of materials. There has been, however, no investigation as to whether these standards are being applied and, more important, whether the standards are reasonable.

Fourth, a model for the creation and repurposing of Canadian cultural memory that is sustainable will have to be developed. There has as yet been little discussion in Canada as to the appropriate economic models to ensure sustainability for digital cultural memory. Is a model that encouraged the commodification of information in the public domain possible? What role do cultural memory institutions have in making materials available? What responsibilities do they have toward archiving? What new public policy models might be needed? What should be the role of the marketplace? What new models can be created? Research is required to determine alternatives within the Canadian cultural context that might work.

Fifth, the various digital activities of memory institutions should be interoperable. That is, it should be possible to harvest data from a number of national memory projects. At the moment, that may or may not be possible. There have been some attempts through the Open Archives Initiative toward an interoperable model that could harvest across national barriers (Shearer 2002). Results of these have been variable at best. For repurposed memories to add value, particularly to the research community, it is critical that there be linkages among databases. An important data set that would be worth examining and determining protocols for linkages would be European, American, and Canadian records and data relating to immigration and emigration.

Sixth, and most important, memory institutions and professionals will have to come to grips with their role in creating new knowledge from digital information. The assumption is that repurposed and reborn digital information is more complex and has more opportunities for innovative curricula and research use than analogue material, and that memory professionals must "digest" the material and design a new curriculum for its use. But who is responsible for taking, for example, the Alberta Heritage Digitization Project and determining the new questions, or the new interactive curricula? Perhaps it is time that educators, publishers, and those involved in other presentation become involved in the debates.

Selected Bibliography

Anon. "Surfing! Who's putting what on the Web." *Muse* 19(1): 58.

Archer, Keith. 2000. "Electronic Publishing in the Humanities and Social Sciences: a Preliminary Report on Survey Findings." Unpublished report prepared for the Humanities and Social Sciences Federation of Canada, 1–25.

Barkley, and John R. Porter. "Considering Blockbusters." *Muse* 18(1): 26–30.

Canadian Library Association. 2001. CLA Submission to the Access to Information Review Task Force. June 1. Available: http://www.cla.ca/issues/airtf.htm#4.

Castells, Manuel. 1997. *The Information Age: Economy, Society and Culture*. 3 vols. London: Blackwell.

Diaz, Luis Alfredo Baratas, and Angeles del Egido. 1999. "Science Museums on the Internet." *Museum International* 51(4): 35–41.

Duff, Wendy, and Stoyanova Penka. 1998. "Transforming the Crazy Quilt: Archival Displays from a Users' Point of View." *Archivaria* 45 (Spring): 44–79.

English, John, and Consultants Jane Beaumont and Dr. Marcel Caya. n.d. "The Role of the National Archives of Canada and the National Library of Canada." Report submitted to the Honourable Sheila Copps.

EVA 2001 Montreal. 2001. "Conference Proceedings: Helping Improve Canadian-European Union Cooperation." *'Culture x Technology' in the Next Decade*. Montreal: MIM.

Gilbert, Jay. 2000. "Access Denied: the Access to Information Act and its Effect on Public Records Creators." *Archivaria* 49, (Spring): 84–123.

Hawisher, Gail E., and Cynthia Selfe, eds. 2000. *Global Literacies and the World-Wide Web*. London: Routledge.

Hooper-Greenhill, Eilean. 2000. "Changing Values in the Art Museum: rethinking communication and learning." *International Journal of Heritage Studies* 6(1) (March): 9–31.

Katz, James E. 1998. "Struggle in Cyberspace: Fact and Friction on the World Wide Web." *Annals of the American Academy of Political and Social Science* 560(98): 194–99.

Kitalong, Saari, and Tino Kitalong. 2000. "Complicating the tourist gaze: literacy and the Internet as catalysts for articularing a postcolonial Palauan identity." In *Global Literacies and the World-Wide Web*, ed. Gail E. Hawisher and Cynthia L. Selfe, 95ff. London: Routledge.

Koltun, Lilly. 1999. "The Promise and Threat of Digital Options in an Archival Age." *Archivaria* 47 (Spring): 114–35.

Lucas, Catrina. 2000. "Exploring the Digital Frontiers." *Museums Journal* (May): 47.

Luska, Jane. 2000. "Digital Visionary George F. MacDonald and the World's First Museum of the Internet Century." *Museum News* (March/April): 35–39, 41, 72–74.

Macneil, Heather. 2000. "Providing Grounds for Trust: Developing Conceptual Requirements for the Long Term Preservation of Authentic Electronic Records." *Archivaria* 50 (Fall): 52–78.

Millar, Laura. 1998. "Discharging our Debt: The Evolution of the Total Archives Concept in English Canada." *Archivaria* 46 (Fall): 103–46.

Muise, Del. "Celebrating Milestones at Canada's Museums." *Muse* 18(4): 55–56.

National Archives of Canada. 2001. 2001–2002 Estimates – Report on Plans and Priorities. Available: http://www.archives.ca/04/042809_e.html.

Outsell. 2000. "Today's Student's Tomorrow's FGUs." *Information about Information* 3(24) (October 16): 1–25.

Pannekoek, Frits. 2000. "Information Technology and the Marginalization of Regional Cultures." Paper delivered to the TEND Conference, Abu Dhabi. April.

Sardar, Ziauddin, and Jerone R. Ravet. 1996. *Cyber futures, Culture and Politics on the Information Superhighway*. Washington: New York University Press, 1996).

Shearer, Kathleen. 2002. "The Open Archives Initiative Developing an Interoperability Framework for Scholarly Publishing." *CARL/ABRC Backgrounder* Series 5 (March).

Starrs, Paul F. 1997. "The Sacred, the Regional and the Digital." *Geographical Review* 87(2) (April): 193–218.

Tuer, Dot. "On Questions of Museum Practices and New Technologies: Reading Walter Benjamin through the Digital Lens." *Muse* 18(2): 20–24.

University of Calgary and the University of New Brunswick. 2001. "Scholarly Electronic Publishing in the humanities and social sciences in Canada: a Study of the Transformation of Knowledge Communication." Unpublished report. Calgary. Full text available: http://ahdp.lib.ucalgary.ca/e-pub/.

University of Calgary and University of Montreal. 2002. "The Internet as a Site of Citizenship." Final Report of the Information Deficit: Canadian Solutions Conference. University of Calgary. Available: http://www.ucalgary.ca/idcs-disc.

Vaughan, Jason. 2001. "Three Iterations of an Academic Library Web Site." *Information Technology and Libraries* 20(2): 81–92.

Yale University Library. 2001. Liblicense Licensing Digital Information (July). Available: http://www.library.yale.edu/~llicense/national-license-init.shtml [August 4, 2001].

Notes

1 See also http://ahdp.lib.ucalgary.ca/hssfc/ [accessed August 18, 2000].
2 See http://www.galegroup.com/
3 See, for example, the essays on Pacific cultures and the WWW in Hawisher Selfe (2000). Particularly interesting is Kitalong Kitalong, 95ff.
4 See http://icom.museum/vlmp/canada.html
5 Ibid. But for the rest of the world, it is worth noting that where "hits" are recorded, they are few. For example, the Bahrain national museum at http://www.bnmuseum.com/English.htm has 201 hits. (The number of hits includes the Arabic version.)
6 See the Canadian Information Heritage Network at http://www.chin.gc.ca/ For the virtual exhibit collection see http://www.virtualmuseum.ca/English/Exhibits/index.html
7 The Royal British Columbia Museum site at http://rbcm1.rbcm.gov.bc.ca/index_rc.html is the exception to the rule in providing full text of selected research papers by the staff.
8 Canadian Council for Archives, "Rules for Archival Description," available at http://www.cdncouncilarchives.ca/archdesrules.html
9 See http://pwnhc.learnnet.nt.ca/databases/index.htm
10 See http://pwnhc.learnnet.nt.ca/exhibits/teadance/teadance.html The tea dance exhibition is replete with the marvels of technology, including full sound, textual additions, and the biographies of American anthropological authorities.
11 See http://www.connect.gc.ca/
12 Canadian Association for Research Libraries, "Copyright Forum Discussion Paper on Digital Copyright Issues," available at http://www.uottawa.ca/library/carl/frames_index.htm
13 In the Virtual Canadian Museum site, for example, institutions rather than individuals are cited as "authors." The credibility of the institution rather than the intellectual prowess of the individual seems to matter most.
14 For sample online inventories see http://www.chin.gc.ca/English/Artefacts_Canada/index.html. The humanities database has about 2.5 million objects, the natural science base about 1 million objects, and the archaeological inventory about seventy thousand sites. There are, however, few entries with images, and the very generality of the descriptions will make most of little use to the citizen at large.
15 See http://collections.ic.gc.ca/peh/
16 See http://www.archives.ca/05/0529/052902/05290299_e.html
17 See http://www.archives.ca/08/08_e.html
18 See http://209.82.14.226/history/internment/
19 Historica was founded by the Hon. Charles R Bronfman and is best known for its Heritage Minutes, its Heritage Fairs and its involvement in education. See http://www.histori.ca/historica/eng_site/index.html#
20 See the credits for the Western Canadian exhibit at http://www.archives.ca/05/0529/052930_e.html#030 It is impossible to determine who is responsible.
21 See http://www.archivesalberta.org/passion/passion.htm
22 See http://cac.mcgill.ca/safdie/
23 See http://cac.mcgill.ca/home/about2.htm
24 See, for example, the lantern slide show at http://www.glenbow.org/lantern/lantern.htm
25 See http://www.uottawa.ca/library/archives/cwma-acmf-e.html
26 See http://aabc.bc.ca/aabc/icaul.html
27 Machine Readable Cataloguing (MARC) is the standard for library cataloguing managed by the Library of Congress. Canadian MARC standards are modified by the National Library of Canada.

28   The history of the Dublin Core Metadata Initiative can be found at http://
     dublincore.org/about/history/
29   See http://www.nlc-bnc.ca/cidl/
30   See http://www.netLibrary.com/index.asp
31   See https://www.questia.com/LoginMediator.qst?action=displayLoginForm
32   See http://www.uottawa.ca/library/cnslp/
33   A good summary for the Research Data Centres exists at http://
     www.stats.uwaterloo.ca/Stats_Dept/SWORDC/history.html
34   For a report on the consultations on a National Data Archives to date, see http://
     mmsd1.mms.nrcan.gc.ca/archives/

CANADIAN MEDIA *and* CANADIAN IDENTITY

Over the course of the twentieth century, however, economic imperatives in the newspaper industry all but eradicated the independent and locally owned title, as proprietors recognized that profits are increased by sharing the costs of news-gathering and production among a number of papers, and that financial stability comes with owning multiple holdings in a variety of markets. Hence, what became the Southam newspaper chain began with one title, the *Hamilton Spectator*, but as early as 1923 the company also owned the *Ottawa Citizen*, the *Calgary Herald*, the *Edmonton Journal*, the *Winnipeg Tribune* and the *Vancouver Province*. Over the rest of the century, the trend moved inexorably toward chain ownership; corporate control; proprietorship by companies with cross-media holdings; market rationalization in which newspapers no longer competed head-to-head for the same readers, but carved up urban markets between them; and a concentration of ownership in which fewer and fewer companies came to acquire more and more of the nation's outlets of print journalism.

It is this feature of the newspaper industry — in which local titles with near-monopolies in local demographic communities are the properties of national corporate entities — that has most commonly excited concern among critics. Bluntly, the fear is that when members of a local demographic market have no alternative but to depend on a single title as a source of social intelligence, and when a small number of corporations owns these agencies of public address, corporate owners may be in a position to use their holdings to promote a particular view of political and economic affairs at the expense of alternative perspectives. The worry is that proprietors might restrict the range of debate within newspapers and skew news coverage so as to favour select interests, thus propagandizing the population. Were this to happen, it would be anathema to democracy, which requires that citizens be fully and fairly informed on the issues of the day so as to be able to come to sound decisions on how they wish to be governed. Partisan control over public expression would amount to control over public opinion, and therefore to control over the political process itself.

The Changing Face of Canadian Newspapers

Canadian newspaper publishing has long been accompanied by anxiety over the extent of corporate concentration of ownership. Typically, these worries

PRIN
MATT
Canadian New

Christophei

With the obvious exceptions of those that carry
themselves as "national" titles in their respective
linguistic communities – the *Globe and Mail*, the
National Post and *Le Devoir* – Canadian newspapers are typically parochial undertakings, serving
an urban or local constituency. This is as true of
a circulation giant such as the *Toronto Star* as it is
of the *Hill Times*, a weekly tabloid catering to a
readership of politicians and staffers on Ottawa's
Parliament Hill. A century ago, this meant that
newspapers serving different markets were independently owned by proprietors who themselves
resided in those markets.

have waxed and waned in light of developments in the industry, spiking with each new consolidation of corporate control and receding in moments of expansion or quiescence. Concentration of newspaper ownership was a principal concern of the Special Senate Committee on Mass Media (the Davey Committee) in 1970. The simultaneous closings of the *Winnipeg Tribune* and the *Ottawa Journal* in 1980 – which left the Thomson corporation's *Free Press* with a monopoly in Winnipeg and Southam's *Citizen* with a monopoly in Ottawa – prompted an official inquiry into the state of the industry, the 1981 Royal Commission on Newspapers (the Kent Commission). From the early 1980s until the mid-1990s, however, the issue of press concentration abated as a matter of policy concern. In part, this was because the period was marked by relative stability in the industry, and indeed expansion, as the *Sun* chain of tabloids entered various Southam-dominated markets, the *Globe and Mail* launched a satellite-printed national edition, one by one the urban broadsheets began to publish on Sundays, and the *Financial Post* turned from a weekly into a daily in direct competition with the *Globe and Mail*'s Report on Business (Dornan 2000, 54). In the latter half of the 1990s, however, concern over consolidated control of the Canadian newspaper industry was rekindled as a consequence of the actions of a single company: Conrad Black's Hollinger Inc., which emerged as the dominant newspaper proprietor in the country. With the departure of Black from the Canadian newspaper scene in 2001, debate over concentration and control in the newspaper industry became if anything more inflamed, as all but a few of the major titles are now in the hands of companies that also own broadcast networks, Internet portals, and cable and telecommunication distribution systems.

On November 1, 2001, in the wake of the events of September 11 and in the midst of the U.S. bombing campaign in Afghanistan, the front-page photograph in the *Globe and Mail* was notable. For days, the front pages of the nation's newspapers had shown F-18 fighters roaring off the decks of American aircraft carriers, Northern Alliance soldiers pointing shoulder-launched rockets at distant Taliban positions, street demonstrations in Pakistan, and violent confrontations between Palestinians and Israeli Defence Forces. This day, the *Globe* chose to feature above the fold a full-colour portrait of Conrad Black, resplendent in his red ermine robes, on the occasion of his investiture in the British House of Lords as Lord Black of Crossharbour. By devoting such prominent attention to the man and the occasion, the *Globe* was acknowledging the influence its great rival had wielded in the country in the previous five years through his actions in the newspaper industry, while simultaneously marking the end of that influence and hence the end of a tumultuous chapter in Canadian newspaper publishing. The period ahead for the industry promises to be no less turbulent, but the year 2001 likely marks a fault line between two moments in its history.

In 1996, Black took control of the Southam chain of broadsheets in urban markets from Montreal to Vancouver, and ignited a remarkable interlude of activity in a media industry that had long been unremarkable in its stolid performance (see Table 1). Once dismissed as yesterday's medium – an obsolescent cultural form catering to an aging and dwindling readership, and slowly but surely losing its prominence in the social and economic life of the nation – the newspaper was suddenly a hot property. There was the birth of a new national daily in Anglophone Canada, a full-blown newspaper war in the largest city in the country, and a flurry of changes in ownership as the country's largest communication corporations sought either to acquire or divest themselves of newspaper properties according to their respective strategies of how best to position themselves for the multimedia future. In the space of four years, for example, the *Guelph Mercury* changed proprietorship five times. Originally owned by the Thomson corporation, it was purchased by Conrad Black's Hollinger Inc. in 1995 when Thomson sold a raft of its smaller Canadian papers so as to concentrate on electronic publishing ventures. In 1998, Hollinger included it in a package acquired by Sun Media in exchange for the *Financial Post*, an acquisition essential to Hollinger's plans to launch a national political- and business-oriented daily. Sun Media was then bought by Quebecor, which in turn sold the *Mercury* in 1999 to the Toronto *Star.*

The result is that, by 2002, with only a handful of exceptions, every major Canadian daily newspaper was the property of a parent owner with interests that extend far beyond newspaper publishing. The *Sun* chain of tabloids is owned by Quebecor, which also owns, in addition to its Quebec newspaper titles, Quebecor World printing, the Videotron cable company, and the TVA network. The Southam dailies, including the *National Post*, are owned by CanWest Global Communications Corp., a broadcasting company. And the *Globe and Mail* is a property of Bell Globemedia, which also owns the CTV network and the Bell Sympatico Internet service provider, which in turn is owned by Bell Canada Enterprises (BCE), the telecommunications giant – all of which invites the question of what these corporations intend for the newspaper properties they now control, what this portends for the practice of journalism in Canada, and what it may mean for the publics these newspapers serve.

Table 1 Timeline of Ownership Changes in the Canadian Media Industry

1994

Conrad Black's Hollinger Inc. purchases the Regina *Leader-Post* and the Saskatoon *Star-Phoenix* from Saskatchewan's Armadale Co.

1995

Hollinger purchases a raft of papers from Thomson corp.

1996

Hollinger acquires control of Southam corp.

1997

The London Free Press is purchased by Sun Media from the Blackburn family.

1998

Hollinger acquires the Financial Post from Sun Media in exchange for the Hamilton Spectator, the Kitchener-Waterloo Record, the Guelph Mercury, and the Cambridge Reporter.

October 27, 1998

Hollinger/Southam launches the National Post.

December 1998

The Toronto Star acquires the Hamilton Spectator, the Kitchener-Waterloo Record, the Guelph Mercury, and the Cambridge Reporter from Sun Media; Quebecor purchases Sun Media.

April 2000

Hollinger announces its Canadian newspapers are for sale, excluding its major urban dailies.

July 2000

In a transaction worth some $3.5 billion, CanWest Global agrees to purchase most of Hollinger's daily and weekly newspapers, including thirteen of Southam's major urban dailies and a 50 per cent interest in the National Post.

September 2000

BCE Inc. buys majority control of the Globe and Mail. Its subsidiary, Bell Globemedia, comes to include CTV, Bell Sympatico, ExpressVu, and the Globe and Mail.

November 2000

A sudden downturn in the bond market restructures the CanWest Global/Hollinger deal, shaving some titles from the package. The deal proceeds, valued at $3.2 billion.

2000

Thomson sells the Lethbridge Herald and the Medicine Hat News to Horizon Operations Ltd. of B.C. Osprey Media Group, headed by Michael Sifton, whose family had owned Armadale in 1994, purchases sixteen smaller Ontario dailies from Hollinger.

August 2001

Conrad Black sells his remaining interest in the National Post to CanWest Global.

November 2001

Thomson sells its last remaining daily newspapers, the Winnipeg Free Press and the Brandon Sun, to Canadian Newspapers Company, a company formed by Ron Stern and Bob Silver, partners in the Winnipeg-based textile manufacturer Western Glove Works. Hollinger sells its last two Ontario dailies, the Chatham Daily News and the Sarnia Observer, to Osprey Media.

Make no mistake: even in an expanding media environment marked by the advent of entirely new concourses of communication, newspapers remain vital to social, political and economic affairs, from the local to the national. In a nation of some thirty million, Canadian Newspaper Association (CNA) data show that in 2001, Canada's 104 daily papers sold an average combined total of 5,184,571 copies per day, and these are purchased across all

Table 2 Canadian Daily Newspaper Circulation 1990–2001

YEAR	# of Dailies	Copies Mon-Fri Average	Copies/ Saturday	Copies/ Sunday	Total Copies/ Weekly	Average Sold Per Publishing Day
1990	108	5,638,729	5,894,245	3,227,134	37,315,025	5,814,510
1991	108	5,474,027	5,733,488	3,184,431	36,288,055	5,228,124
1992	108	5,357,172	5,735,296	3,192,564	35,713,721	5,553,409
1993	108	5,340,462	5,742,539	3,271,337	35,716,186	5,517,913
1994	108	5,285,338	5,748,793	3,242,760	35,418,224	5,491,150
1995	104	5,068,068	5,813,309	3,137,573	34,291,222	5,309,600
1996	106	4,978,201	5,706,756	3,096,107	33,593,868	5,191,677
1997	105	4,780,217	5,568,377	2,986,865	32,456,325	5,108,709
1998	105	4,768,951	5,591,107	3,010,498	32,446,631	5,004,913
1999	106	4,986,095	5,711,058	3,108,606	33,750,142	5,177,072
2000	104	4,970,102	5,682,906	3,093,650	33,627,066	5,166,255
2001	104				33,710,216	5,184,571

Source: Canadian Newspaper Association, Newspaper Facts, Dec. 2001.

Table 3 2001 Canadian Daily Newspaper Circulation by Ownership*

OWNER	# OF PAPERS	WEEKLY CIRCULATION	AVE. ISSUE CIRCULATION
Southam Publications	27	11,437,605	1,792,906
Quebecor Inc.	15	6,968,043	1,019,809
Torstar	5	4,621,724	686,851
Power Corp. of Canada	7	3,049,424	458,115
Bell/Globemedia	1	2,185,663	364,277
Osprey Media	18	1,536,963	247,021
Canadian Newspapers Co.	2	1,039,837	148,548
Halifax-Herald Ltd.	2	713,870	104,731
Brunswick News Inc.	3	675,278	116,472
Horizon	5	630,319	93,232
Hollinger Cdn. N.L.P.	10	326,277	59,361
Independents	5	314,700	57,078
Black Press	1	114,388	19,065
Annex Publ.& Printing	2	94,125	17,125

*Based on 2001 ABC Fas-Fax ended March 31, 2001 or other Publisher's Statements collected by the Canadian Newspaper Association. Note: Hollinger Cdn. N.L.P. denotes Hollinger Canadian Newspapers, Limited Partnership.

social classes – though readership increases with income, education and job responsibility (see Table 2).

(In November 2001, the Saint John *Times Globe* was absorbed by the New Brunswick *Telegraph Journal*, both owned by the Irving family's Brunswick News Inc.; the *Telegraph Journal* became a two-edition paper, one serving the local market of Saint John and the other a provincial daily serving all of New Brunswick. As well, in February 2002, the Cambridge

Reporter moved from daily to twice-weekly publication. Consequently, by early 2002 there were 102 daily newspapers published in Canada, as opposed to 143 in 1911 (see Table 3).

Despite the recent newspaper war, with its aggressive circulation drives, total average circulation of all Canadian dailies is down from a peak of 5,824,736 in 1989 – a drop of 640,000 copies per day over the past twelve years, even as the population of the country has grown. Nonetheless, it remains a substantial number. And although readership is demographically uneven – older people are more attentive to newspapers than younger – nonetheless, 57 per cent of Canadians over the age of eighteen report reading a paper on an average weekday, 64 per cent read a newspaper on the weekend, and 83 per cent report having read a newspaper in the past week (Canadian Newspaper Association 2001). As has been pointed out elsewhere, this means that more people read newspapers regularly than view Canadian films, read Canadian books, patronize the Canadian arts, purchase Canadian recordings or watch Canadian television drama and light entertainment. As a fact of this country's cultural life, newspapers are rivalled only by domestic sport and by news and current affairs programming on radio and television (Dornan 1996, 60).

As an advertising vehicle, they are no less important to affairs of commerce. They are, in fact, the single largest advertising medium in the country. In 2000, according to CNA data, newspaper advertising revenue reached a historical high of just over $2.58 billion. This accounts for a quarter of the total national advertising expenditure in 2000 of some $10 billion. The private television broadcasting networks, by comparison, accounted for $1.76 billion in advertising revenue; the entire radio industry reaped just over $1 billion; the specialty TV channels $381 million; consumer magazines $434 million; outdoor ads $293 million, and so on. Internet advertising – to which we will return – amounted to only $109 million, or a mere 4 per cent of the money spent on newspaper advertising (see Table 4).

Perhaps more important, in a country in which news and journalism in their various forms are the pre-eminent domestic communication genre, newspapers are the bedrock of an information culture. It is true that Canada can point with some pride to its domestic feature film industry, its recording industry and its independent television production industry – sectors that barely existed some thirty years ago – but for the most part these entertainment enterprises remain overshadowed by the cultural exports of the juggernaut to our south. Journalism is relatively cheap to produce when compared to the per-hour production costs of programs such as *Da Vinci's*

Table 4 Advertising Revenue by Medium

Net Advertising Revenue – Millions of Dollars

	1995	1996	1997	1998	1999	2000
Daily newspapers	1,900	1,960	2,303	2,379	2,429	2,580
Television – Total	1,850	1,982	2,100	2,312	2,378	2,456
Public and non-commercial TV					n/a	*265
Specialty TV					304	381
Private TV (including infomercials)					1,759	1,763
Direct mail	991	1,110	1,168	1,251	1,190	1,200
Yellow Pages	864	892	899	935	975	1,000
Radio	758	792	849	921	954	1,002
Community newspapers	579	597	634	765	788	820
General magazines	316	318	347	381	389	434
Trade magazines	229	233	252	277	283	295
Outdoor	167	200	220	250	270	293
Other print	47	48	48	49	49	50
Internet	–	–	10	25	56	109
Total	7,700	8,132	8,829	9,543	9,759	*10,190

* estimated.

Source: Canadian Newspaper Association, Newspaper Facts December 2001.

Inquest. News is also inherently parochial. It is largely (although not exclusively) preoccupied with local, regional or national concerns. Even its attention to the world beyond our national borders is inflected with an interest in how events *there* affect us *here*, if only by touching our emotions. That is as good a definition of news as any: it is a running chronicle of what is meant to matter to us in the here and now; a means by which an agenda of concern is established. Because news is therefore unavoidably parochial, it cannot easily be provided by foreign undertakings. Hence, the distinctive Canadian communication genre is journalism. And though news and current affairs programming is a prominent feature of the television schedules, while political talk looms large on private and public sector radio, newspapers remain essential to the enterprise of Canadian journalism. In every city, the newsrooms of the local daily newspapers dwarf the staffs of the local broadcast news teams; the sheer amount and variety of information contained in the daily paper far outstrips what can be contained in a local newscast; and the morning newspaper remains for the most part the daily briefing book for the broadcast operations, cueing them as to what stories to follow. Even at the national level, the editorial staffs of the *Globe and Mail* and the *National Post* vastly outnumber the complement of personnel in the national newsrooms of the CBC, CTV or Global.

Newspapers are therefore not merely profitable ventures of manifest utility. They are essential to Canadian civic life. And yet they are constitutionally saddled with a tension – one might say an absurdity – that reveals

Table 5 2000 Top 10 Advertisers in Canadian Media

Advertiser	Total spending in all media	Total spending in dailies	% change vs 1999
General Motors Car Dealerships	$84,004,600	$76,641,300	+12.3%
Chrysler Car Dealerships	$72,932,900	$68,754,700	+21.3%
Chrysler Dodge Jeep Dealers	$82,610,800	$63,653,900	+20.8%
Wesbild Holdings Ltd.	$78,315,300	$59,458,800	+39.2%
Chevrolet Oldsmobile Dealers Association	$62,856,900	$56,315,400	+3.7%
Pontiac Buick Cadillac Dealers Association	$63,501,300	$56,315,400	+4.5%
Ford Consolidated Local Car Dealerships	$60,769,900	$55,439,300	+18.6%
Ford Dealers Association	$65,299,300	$48,314,600	+391.0%
Sears CanadaInc.	$75,156,400	$47,464,700	−7.2%
Rogers Communications Inc.	$85,879,600	$41,725,500	+15.5%

Source: Canadian Newspaper Association, Newspaper Facts December 2001/A.C. Neilsen.

itself most starkly just at those moments when the service newspapers provide is most valued and most required.

The tension resides in the following: Newspapers are the antennae of the economy. Because their advertising revenue derives from the full range of commercial announcements, a softening of newspaper advertising can be the first foreshadowing of an economic downturn. Broadly, newspapers carry three different types of advertising.

First, and the largest of the three categories, are retail ads purchased by businesses exactly like the local city newspaper itself – businesses whose trade is city-wide, but whose customers peter out just beyond the municipal boundaries: furniture outlets, electronics stores, supermarkets, franchises and auto dealerships. These account for almost 47 per cent of newspapers' advertising income. (Mom-and-Pop pizza delivery joints, for example, do not bother to advertise in the local urban daily, since they service pockets of limited circumference while the paper casts its net over the entire city. Who could find or remember an ad for a local pizza delivery business in the pages of the Toronto *Star*?)

Second are classified ads – a form of advertising almost exclusive to newspapers, since they cannot readily be accommodated by radio, television or magazines. Classifieds chart a panoply of any city's daily commerce, from help wanted to apartments for rent; from companions sought to puppies on offer; from items for sale to the birth and death announcements. Together, these account for some 34 per cent of newspaper advertising revenue.

Finally, national ads for companies such as auto manufacturers and phone companies account for the remaining 20 per cent. This is the smallest of the three categories in terms of total revenue, although companies in this category are newspapers' largest advertising clients (see Table 5).

Because newspapers therefore map the entire spectrum of legitimate trade, from the marketing efforts of the automotive giants to one's neighbour unloading a used sofa, no industry is more sensitive to fluctuations in advertising expenditure. At the same time, few industries are less able to adapt to fluctuations in advertising income.

The reason for this is twofold. First, newspapers subsist on advertising income. They do charge their readers for the purchase of their product, but only a pittance. The price of a newspaper has always been less than the price of a cup of coffee. More than 80 per cent of a typical Canadian daily newspaper's income derives from advertising. Second, the costs of producing, manufacturing and distributing a newspaper are relatively fixed. The editorial content has to be generated. The physical artifact of the paper has to roll off the presses. Copies of the paper must be delivered via fleets of trucks to carriers who then distribute them to households, offices, hotels, newsagents and vending boxes. In times of economic doldrums, other industries – the automotive manufacturers, for example – can reduce expenditures by scaling back production. If there should be less demand for their product, they can downscale production, putting less of their product on the market. They can shut down assembly lines and lay off employees. Newspapers enjoy no such latitude.

Newspapers, recall, are in two different businesses simultaneously, each utterly dependent on the other and yet catering to two different classes of customer. First, newspapers sell a cheap and instantly disposable *product* – a package of paper and ink – to a clientele of almost everyone in quantities that dwarf other businesses. Apart from industries that trade in products that are physically ingested – hamburgers, beer, cups of coffee, cigarettes – few other Canadian industries sell more than five million units of their product per day. Not the razor blade industry, not the toilet paper industry, not the toothpaste manufacturers. Second, and concurrently, newspapers sell a more expensive *service* to a customer base of companies and individuals who wish to catch the attention of as many people as possible. As agencies of public address, newspapers rent themselves out as promotional vehicles for other businesses. As the adage goes, they sell eyeballs to advertisers.

There is therefore a dislocation between the major source of the newspaper industry's revenue and the point-of-purchase demand for its product.

The fact that advertising budgets may be tight does not mean there is any less street-level demand for the physical product of the morning newspaper.

Even in periods of economic slowdown, therefore, newspapers cannot cut back on distribution costs without reducing their circulations, when size of circulation is the index by which advertising rates are set. They cannot reduce their outlay on newsprint without reducing the physical dimensions of the paper, making their very pages narrower (something Canadian broadsheets did during the recession of the early 1990s and more and more U.S. dailies resorted to in 2000–2001), printing fewer copies or whittling away the newshole – the editorial contents of the paper, the very reason customers buy the product in the first place. They cannot markedly downsize the editorial staff without compromising the editorial contents. Nor, in moments of reduced consumer confidence and disposable income, can they increase subscription and vending prices without running the risk of losing customers. Nonetheless, when advertising revenue dries up, they may attempt to do all these things in order to cut costs, balance the books, maintain the profit margin, service the corporate debt and satisfy the shareholders.

The essential tension at the heart of the newspaper industry, therefore, is that in times of economic hardship the public naturally becomes more anxious, and an anxious public is all the more hungry for information. Yet those very circumstances may undermine the newspaper's capacity to provide to the best of its capabilities the very product its customers seek.

This tension balloons into an absurdity at a moment, not simply of cyclical economic slowdown, but of perceived crisis – a moment such as that experienced in the last quarter of 2001 in the wake of September 11. Just when there was an unprecedented appetite and a manifest need for comprehensive news coverage at home and abroad, not to mention the full range of public debate that a mature democracy demands in uncertain and volatile times, newspapers found their operational budgets strained. They were well aware of their civic obligations, but they were equally confronted by financial realities.

The signs of an economic slowdown, at least as measured by newspaper revenue, were a year old by the time of September 11. Although advertising revenue in 2000 had been the highest in the industry's history, in the last quarter of 2000 it had declined by 1.1 per cent over the previous quarter. Similarly, newspaper circulation revenues – the 20 per cent source of income newspapers receive from their purchase by readers – had been running ahead of 1999 figures until the fourth quarter of 2000, when they dropped by 7.4 per cent against the last quarter of 1999. In fact, circulation revenues at the end of 2000 were the lowest they had ever been since the Canadian Newspaper Association began collecting such data in 1995. Meanwhile, in the first half of 2001, total run-of-press advertising lineage (that is, advertisements printed on the pages of newspapers, as opposed to insert advertising – flyers or brochures piggy-backing on the newspaper's city-wide distribution system) dropped by 4.6 per cent. In May 2001, Quebecor cut 302 positions at Sun Media, or 5 per cent of the workforce.

At the same time, newsprint prices dropped from US$605 a tonne in June 2001 to US$535 a tonne in October. Although this may seem to play to newspapers' advantage – lower newsprint prices presumably mean lower production costs – in fact it is an indication of diminishing demand for newsprint in light of falling advertising lineage. Normally, newspapers start building up their inventories of newsprint in September in order to prepare for larger papers bulked with advertising during the Christmas retail season. In September 2001, that did not seem to be happening. The antennae of the economy appeared to be anticipating a precipitous economic downturn. In October, almost a month after 9/11, Quebecor World, the largest commercial printer on the planet, announced that it was closing six plants and laying off 2,400 employees, or 6 per cent of its workforce.

So, just when newspapers were being compelled to boost their expenditures on news coverage by sending correspondents to Afghanistan, Pakistan and elsewhere in the Middle East with no idea how long the conflict might continue, just when circulation was soaring, and just when there was a clear demand for as much news as possible, centripetal financial pressures were insisting that newspapers reduce expenditures and cut back on production costs.

Hence, on September 17, less than a week after September 11, and in an effort to stem financial losses that had amounted to some $200 million in the three years of the paper's existence, the new outright owners of the *National Post*, CanWest Global, laid off 130 employees, including fifty journalists, and eliminated whole precincts of the paper. Gone were Sports, the Arts and Life section, local Toronto coverage, the experimental double-page Avenue spread, the Weekend Post and the Review sections. Company officials estimated this would save some $45 million a year. The idea was to concentrate on what were seen as the core strengths and selling points of the *Post* – its national news and political affairs coverage, and its business section – and to jettison supposedly peripheral content, but the move did not seem to have been thought through. Advertisers and readers reacted badly – it develops that those who follow the stock markets also follow professional

Christopher Dornan

sports – and within weeks, limited sports and arts coverage had returned to the *Post*. Quebecor, meanwhile, laid off senior Sun Media reporter Matthew Fisher while he was in northern Afghanistan, delivering the bad news via the very satellite phone he used to file his stories. And readers who purchased a copy of the *National Post* on October 8, Thanksgiving, received a paper that had two sections, both labelled A, and both devoted entirely to the air assault in Afghanistan, but with no *Financial Post*, no sports news, no entertainment coverage and no classifieds. The reason for the peculiar edition was that management, in a bid to save money on newsprint and employee overtime, had decided not to publish that holiday Monday. But on Sunday the U.S. air strikes against the Taliban began. After a series of frantic telephone calls, the decision not to publish was overturned and a skeleton staff rushed into the newsroom to produce a paper.

In a sense, the newspaper industry was lucky. Though appalling and unsettling, the events of September 11 and their aftermath – from the anthrax scare to the prospect of a protracted war in Afghanistan and a Pakistan aflame and ungovernable – fuelled a widespread appetite for news and made newspapers all the more relevant to readers. At the same time, the surprisingly speedy rout of the Taliban regime meant that the expensive proposition of full-bore coverage of events in a distant and inhospitable part of the world did not have to be sustained indefinitely. Finally, the economic downturn that many feared would simply worsen in the wake of September 11 did not, in the end, materialize. By March 2002, economic indicators appeared to suggest that in Canada recession had been weathered. Nonetheless, the fourth quarter of 2001 illustrated certain incongruities in a profit-driven news industry dependent on advertising revenue; it made evident the tension between what is required of the newspaper industry as an agency of public intelligence and the commercial realities that can mitigate against what is required.

When public anxiety over the al-Qaeda assault on the United States and the response of the Western nations was at its height, little attention was paid to what, by comparison, seemed trifling matters, such as the concentration of ownership in the domestic Canadian media. Even the dismissal of 130 *National Post* employees on September 17, though ruefully noted, caused little stir, perhaps also because it was widely recognized that the financial losses being incurred by the *Post* simply could not be sustained. By the end of 2001 and the early months of 2002, however, concern over the state and conduct of ownership in the newspaper industry had reawakened.

The Politics of Newspaper Concentration

In December 2001, CanWest Global unveiled a new corporate policy by which its urban Southam dailies would carry "national" editorials written or commissioned from within the chain by head office in Winnipeg. Initially, these would appear only once a week, rising later to a frequency of three per week. As innocuous as such an initiative may sound to non-journalists, it was greeted with alarm and dismay by many within the Southam newsrooms. Certainly, it signalled a departure from the traditional Southam practice, in which local editorial boards were generally run independently from corporate head office and were free to take editorial stands as they chose. Some saw the move as the first sign of the application of a broadcasting model to the newspaper industry, in which regional titles would be seen as mere local affiliates in a nationwide network of newspapers that would carry more and more centrally produced content.

Since no deviation from the new, nationally dispensed opinions was allowed in the editorials of the local papers, the *prima facie* worry was that the national editorials would straitjacket the local dailies, forever embalming them in agreement on issue after issue via the sedimentary deposit of company policy. The local editorial boards were invited to elaborate on the national editorials using local examples and evidence, but the sheer operational difficulties were readily apparent. Over time, a mass of editorial judgments from the executive suites would accumulate, which the local boards would be expected to keep track of and to which they would henceforth have to hew. They would be placed in the position of having to second-guess their own regional opinions in light of the views handed down from Winnipeg. More worrying to some was the prospect that the national editorials would not simply make the company's positions on national issues known to the public, but more insidiously they would serve as a vehicle whereby upper management let employees across the chain know where the papers' priorities and emphases in news coverage should lie.

Southam journalists had already seen the new proprietors, the Asper family, express exasperation with the journalistic conduct of the newsrooms under their control. In March 2001, David Asper, chair of the Southam publications committee, had written an opinion piece that ran in all the Southam dailies in which he chastised the national media, including his own papers, for unfairly hounding Jean Chrétien about financial improprieties in his home riding of Shawinigan. Mr. Asper, a lawyer, hinted that the incessant questioning of the Prime Minister's dealings amounted to a form of "public mischief," a criminal act, and argued that "our national political affairs have been hijacked by mischevious unfair scandal mongering." At the time, CanWest Global owned only 50 per cent of the *National Post*, the paper that had done more than any other to bring the allegations of impropriety to light. The *Post* ran Mr. Asper's broadside, but a day later than the other Southam papers and accompanied by vigorous rebuttals. Nonetheless, the incident suggested that the Aspers and their senior management took an interest, not merely in editorial opinion, but in the course of news coverage as well.

In an April 2001 speech to the Calgary Chamber of Commerce, David Asper made his views plain on what he thought was wrong with Canadian journalism and what issues CanWest intended to place on the national agenda through its newspapers. He complained of being "sick and tired" of the depiction of "redneck" Alberta in the national media, and of "our legitimate constitutional and national concerns being always subordinate to the interests of Ontario, and especially Quebec. We believe that the prism of how our country has been presented, in virtually all so-called 'national media,' has been viewed through Toronto and Ottawa."

He said the family was clear on the issues that should be brought before the public, including: a Triple-E Senate; parliamentary reform; one Supreme Court justice from each province; removal of the constitution's "notwithstanding" clause and constitutional vetoes; enshrinement of property rights in the constitution; the right of the electorate to recall MPs; public scrutiny of judges and other senior government officials; an end to deficits and debt-financing; lower capital-gains taxes; and a taxpayers' Bill of Rights (Haggett 2001).

The speech had the merit of being an unequivocal admission of where the family's political convictions lay. Journalists, however, worried that they were to be the instruments whereby this agenda of reform would be promoted in the public forum. They were mindful, too, of the June 2001 dismissal from the Southam chain of high-profile political columnist Lawrence Martin, who had been in the forefront of those posing questions discomfiting to the Prime Minister about financial dealings in his riding. Southam management insisted that Mr. Martin's dismissal had nothing to do with his performance and was merely a cost-saving measure to reduce duplication of material within the chain. Indeed, speaking on August 24, 2001, on taking outright control of the *National Post*, CanWest Global CEO and president Leonard Asper directly addressed the issue of Mr. Martin's removal: "No journalist in our organization," he said, "has anything to fear about what they write. Nobody will be let go because they criticized Jean Chretien or any other alleged reason that our usually nefarious and treacherous and certainly ill-intending competitors like to ascribe to us" (Lindgren 2001).

Unpersuaded, some Southam journalists believed the owners were using a heavy hand to micromanage the contents of the papers so as to suit a party line. They noted that Michael Goldbloom, the publisher of the *Montreal Gazette*, resigned shortly after CanWest Global took control of the paper, apparently unwilling to work with the Aspers. David Beers, a feature writer with the *Vancouver Sun*, was dismissed from his job – ostensibly for budgetary reasons – after he wrote a column defending left-wing feminist Sunera Thobani's views on the events of September 11. It was argued that columns had been altered or killed when they took issue with company policy or deviated from a pro-Israeli position on the Middle East. Stephen Kimber, the director of the School of Journalism at the University of King's College, Halifax, who had been a freelance columnist for twenty years for the Southam-owned *Halifax Daily News*, resigned his column when the paper refused to run a contribution in which he questioned the national editorial policy.

The imposition of the national editorials was therefore merely a flash point for the larger concern that the contents of the papers were being regimented according to a particular set of political convictions. At the *Montreal Gazette*, almost every non-management member of the newsroom eventually signed their names to an open letter of protest that ran in competing news outlets and on a website set up by the dissenters, and for two days reporters withheld bylines on their stories as a gesture of defiance. They were then ordered by management to return their bylines and to cease public criticism of the company on pain of disciplinary action.

The reaction of David Asper to the protest by the *Gazette* staffers was vehement. "They have launched a childish protest," he said in a speech to Oakville business leaders, "with all of the usual self-righteousness ... part of the ongoing pathetic politics of the Canadian left ... why don't they just quit and have the courage of their convictions?" By January 2002, CanWest's actions had been denounced in the Quebec legislature and by the Newspaper Guild, the Quebec Federation of Professional Journalists and the Canadian Association of Journalists, which called for a government inquiry into the consequences of concentration of ownership in the Canadian media. On January 30, the day of CanWest Global's annual shareholder meeting, the Southam papers carried a lengthy op-ed article by Murdoch Davis, editor-in-chief of Southam News, responding to the criticisms of the company in an infuriated tone consistent with that adopted by Mr. Asper. According to Mr. Davis, there was not a shred of truth to charges that content was being controlled by head office or by editors at the dailies so as to conform to a preferred perspective. Allegations to this effect, he insisted, were baseless conspiracy theories being spun by uninformed malcontents eager to believe the worst. He admitted that there had been isolated incidents of columns being withheld, but only because these had been factually inaccurate. "It isn't censorship to decline a column that has incorrect facts and other flaws."

Nonetheless, the controversy refused to die. In March, a reporter with the Southam-owned *Regina Leader-Post* covered a speech at the University of Regina's School of Journalism by Haroon Siddiqui, editorial page emeritus of the *Toronto Star*, in which he accused CanWest management of creeping censorship in refusing to run opinion pieces that disagreed with the company's editorial policy. The reporter's account of the speech was altered to remove any mention of censorship – thus, in one of those ironies beloved by journalists, inviting charges that management had censored the word "censorship" – and she withdrew her byline, prompting a one-day byline strike by nine of her fellow *Leader-Post* journalists in support. Other media outlets took notice and called the paper for comment. Four of the *Leader-Post*'s reporters went on record with their misgivings. Within days, all ten who had removed their bylines had received letters of censure from management, and the four who expressed their concerns to other media outlets were suspended for five days.

Then, on June 16, the day after he had been awarded an honorary doctorate from Carleton University in recognition of his thirty-one-year career in Ottawa journalism and his service to the local community, Russell Mills, publisher of the Southam-owned *Ottawa Citizen*, was dismissed by David Asper. According to Mills, he was offered a financial settlement to remain mute about the circumstances of his firing while the outside world would be told that he was merely retiring. He refused, saying "I hadn't spent a career in journalism in search of the truth to leave on a lie" (Harris-Adler 2002, 50).

The real reason for his dismissal, according to Mills, was that he, as publisher, had approved a lengthy *Citizen* article that detailed the collected "untruths" of Prime Minister Jean Chrétien, as well as an editorial arguing that the time had come for the Prime Minister to step down. If so, the clear suggestion was that the Asper family intended to orchestrate the news coverage of the Southam papers in a partisan manner beholden to a Prime Minister locked in an intra-party power struggle with a powerful rival whom the Prime Minister had himself dismissed from cabinet. Journalists across the country read the Mills firing as an unequivocal signal from CanWest/Southam's Winnipeg head office. Within the journalistic community, Russell Mills was seen as a careful company soldier, a man who had spent sixteen years as publisher of the *Ottawa Citizen* under a succession of corporate owners. If Mills could be dismissed, then presumably no one was safe. The action appeared to put the lie to Leonard Asper's earlier insistence that "No journalist in our organization has anything to fear about what they write."

The Mills incident was headline news across the country. CanWest management waited five days before responding to the furor. Eventually, Leonard Asper appeared before the media to contest Mills' version of events, arguing that Mills was dismissed because of insubordination and a lack of "diversity of sources of all opinions" in the *Citizen* under Mills' stewardship. That is, in a neat rhetorical turn, Mills was fired not in violation of journalistic principles, but because he himself had violated those principles, passing off conjecture about the Prime Minister as fact and presiding over a paper that favoured a particular political perspective at the expense of competing views. Mills, in response, launched a libel action.

The controversy generated by the Mills incident appeared to cool the more aggressive, or at least high-profile, aspects of CanWest's management of Southam editorial content. Quietly, the national editorials – once intended to run at a frequency of three per week – all but disappeared from the pages of the Southam papers. Management retained the right to issue must-run national opinion pieces to the member papers, but suddenly seemed to feel the compulsion to do so only infrequently. The sabre-rattling speeches and op-ed attacks on the company's critics dried up.

What is at issue in all this? Few, surely, would dispute the right of a newspaper proprietor to set the editorial policies of his or her holdings, even if one disagrees with these policies. Merely stating an editorial view, after all, does not amount to mind control of the masses. Far from it: those who regularly turn to the editorials (one of the least-read sections of any newspaper) tend to be contentious sorts, eager to take issue with the considered opinions of the newspaper.

However, it is one thing to set an editorial policy whose expression is confined to the editorial columns. It would be quite another were that policy extended to the opinion and op-ed sections such that demurring voices were expunged, belittled or marginalized. And it would be another matter entirely were it to be shown that news coverage was being manipulated so as to conform to an overtly ideological preference. The professional routines of "objective" journalism are in place precisely, in part, to shield journalists from the blandishments and pressures of unscrupulous publishers who would skew accounts of current events to suit their own interests. The promise made by newspapers to their readers is that the reportage offers reliable accounts rendered (to the best of reporters' abilities) with fidelity to what actually occurred.

For its part, CanWest has argued repeatedly that the mere fact of a national editorial policy does not mean that dissent and debate are to be extinguished in the pages of the Southam dailies. The *National Post* presumably spoke for CanWest's head office when it wrote in an editorial on the issue: "Editors, editorial writers and others can express differing views in signed pieces; many already have. Other views are welcome, even invited. Counter-arguments and contrary views have been published, just as with all editorials, and will continue to be. Many contrary letters are printed" (January 29, 2002). As well, in a March television interview on I-channel with the *National Post*'s Matthew Fraser, Israel Asper insisted that the new editorial policy was simply a means for the company to put forward a national viewpoint on national issues, nothing more, and that it certainly did not mean the company would brook no disagreement in the pages of its papers. "Does that mean we will hold off on dissent?" he asked. "Absolutely not. Does that mean our own writers can't say 'You're crazy' in print? Absolutely, yes they can."

If the proprietor is true to his word, then he understands that the civic value of a newspaper (not to mention its commercial viability) lies in it being a compendium not only of reportage, but of competing interpretation – a daily almanac of argument, contention and debate. Then what does it matter whether there is a centrally endorsed editorial policy? Newspapers would remain intact as a forum for the national conversation on which democracy depends.

Critics both within and outside the Southam chain, however, doubt that the upper echelons of the CanWest management will indeed be true to their word – not that they are dishonest, but that what they will recognize as legitimate dissent will be strictly circumscribed. Genuinely dissenting views, ones that take issue with the very premises of any given editorial policy, may run the risk of being dismissed as factually inaccurate and therefore unworthy of publication. As Murdoch Davis direly warned in his op-ed article of January 30, 2002: "It is a basic tenet of journalism and Canadian law that to be fair, comment must be based on the facts." Indeed, in the case of the *Regina Leader-Post*, the rationale for deleting any reference to "censorship" appeared to be the conviction that, since no censorship had actually taken place, Mr. Siddiqui's charges were factually false. In the case of Russell Mills, according to Leonard Asper, the former employee's crime had been to present as "fact" an investigation into the conduct of the Prime Minister that was merely "conjecture."

But even if it were true that the Southam owners and their agents had been covertly manipulating the contents of the papers – and as outrageous a transgression as this might seem on its face – one must recognize that all newspapers adopt a posture toward the world that is reflected in their news coverage: the choice of which stories to pursue and how these are played. As a consequence, different newspapers see the "facts" in different lights; there is no natural, obvious or neutral version of events, despite the insistence of every newspaper that its accounts are straightforwardly true. Thus, the *Toronto Star* has long carried itself as a paper with a social conscience (as opposed to the business-oriented dailies of Bay Street), which means that in practice it is a small-l liberal paper traditionally affiliated with the large-L Liberal party. The *Toronto Sun*, meanwhile, is patently coloured by a populist conservatism. The *Globe and Mail*, for its part, is a conservative journal of a different hue, capable of embracing social reforms that might ally it with elements of the left (rights for gays and lesbians, decriminalization of soft drugs). And it is no secret that the *National Post* was created by Conrad Black in large part to champion a stripe of conservatism that Mr. Black found lamentably lacking in Canadian political discourse. None of these dailies wilfully falsifies its news coverage to suit an ideological predisposition, but they do come to see events and social affairs through the lens of their respective identities (see Dornan and Pyman 2001 for an illustration of this).

In the case of the Southam papers, the controversy stems from the fact that some journalists believe they are being pressured to render accounts, not as they honestly perceive things, but in accord with how their superiors in a distant head office would prefer things to be: that a perspective not shared by newsworkers themselves is being imposed on the product they produce. This is all the more fractious given the traditional character – or lack thereof – of many of the Southam titles. In a market such as Toronto, with four paid-circulation dailies competing for different types of readers, it is no accident that each paper comes to acquire a vivid and distinctive personality. The Southam dailies, by contrast, long enjoyed near-monopoly status in their respective markets. They therefore strove for universal circulation, and in doing so they could not risk alienating potential readers. As a consequence, they avoided any overt political point-of-view in their news content. The typical blandness of most Canadian broadsheets, then, was the result of market economics. The "politicization" or "Asperation" of the Southam chain – if that is indeed what is occurring – is not, therefore, a corruption of Canadian journalistic practice as much as it is an extension (albeit a ham-fisted one) of existing practice from the largest urban centres to the regions. Ironically, for all their fulminations about Toronto-centrism in the Canadian media, CanWest management may be reforming the Southam papers according to a Toronto model.

If one believes that this is a lamentable, even a dangerous development, the culprit is presumably not so much the Asper family as the fact of concentration of ownership in the newspaper industry, which provides proprietors with the opportunity to impose their views on a large number of titles simultaneously. But a variety of studies have shown that whether newspapers value their civic responsibilities, and how they understand these responsibilities, has little to do with whether they are independently owned or part of a chain. Some corporately owned papers perform very well according to received standards of journalistic quality, just as some independent papers perform very poorly. It all depends on the owners. As has been pointed out elsewhere,

> This begs certain questions for those who would regulate the press in order to correct market dysfunction or corporate rapacity.... [I]f the performance of newspapers is ultimately a consequence of the decisions and priorities of those who own and manage them, what mechanisms might be put in place to ensure that either the "right" people occupy these decision-making positions, or, if the "wrong" people cannot be prevented from owning and operating newspapers, to constrain them to act in a way at odds with their own inclinations? Beyond that, assuming such mechanisms could be put in place, what would guarantee that they would be compatible with the imperatives of a free society? (Dornan 2000, 57–58)

Finally, one should ask what prompted the acquisition of newspaper properties by the broadcasting and telecommunications interests in the first place, and whether these new alignments of corporate ownership are stable. At the time of the merger, the *Globe and Mail* seemed on secure ground in its affiliation with CTV and its new proprietor BCE. The *Globe* is a single property with national reach and a valuable brand image, not an archipelago of local titles, and BCE is a company awash in profits, not debts. Quebecor, by comparison, spent a fortune to acquire Videotron and so far does not appear to be either comfortable or confident in its ownership of Sun Media. CanWest Global, similarly, spent $3.2 billion to acquire the Southam papers and is carrying $4 billion in debt. Nor is it clear that any great cost efficiencies are about to be realized simply because a broadcasting network, whose profits largely derive from airing popular U.S. programming, now owns a string of local newspapers and a money-losing national title with a reputation for ideological idiosyncrasy. In the case of the Bell Globemedia venture, BCE, a telecom giant whose interests are in the infrastructure of communication, wanted profitable content that might flow through that infrastructure. The *Globe and Mail* and CTV presumably were to provide that, with the paper feeding additional national content to its new broadcasting partner, while CTV and Bell Sympatico would offer a broadcasting and computer-mediated display window for the print operation. However, even this convergence strategy was thrown into doubt by the abrupt departure of BCE chief Jean Monty, the architect of the strategy, in April 2002, and the consequent immediate speculation that the new BCE management might sell off the "content provider" acquisitions. And if true corporate "synergies" – to use the industry's faddish phrase – are elusive in the case of Bell Globemedia, it is doubtful they will be realized in the case of CanWest Global or Quebecor. So what motivated the other players' aggressive newspaper-purchasing spree?

Part of the answer is to be found in the most recent trends in advertising placement and revenue (see Table 4 above). Even with a downturn in the last quarter, advertising revenue in almost all of the traditional media was up appreciably in 2000 over 1999. Newspaper ad revenue increased by 6 per cent, radio by 4.7 per cent, and outdoor advertising by 7.8 per cent. In traditional private-sector network television, by comparison, ad revenue increased by only 0.23 per cent. Meanwhile, Internet advertising increased by almost 100 per cent over the previous year. In fact, Web advertising in Canada went from $10 million in 1997 to $25 million in 1998, and from $56 million in 1999 to $109 million in 2000 – essentially doubling from one year to the next. The non-newspaper companies, then, have been buying up the newspaper companies because they are convinced that the advertising profits of the future lie in purveying Web content; because in Canada one of the few forms of homegrown content with an assured market is news; and because the major proven, available and robust sources of news are the newspapers.

As well, newspapers come with a stranglehold on a lucrative form of advertising that is simply incompatible with broadcasting: the classifieds. It accounts, though, for 34 per cent of newspapers' advertising income of $2.58 billion, or some $877 million. But while classified advertising may be impossible to accommodate via traditional broadcasting, it is perfectly suited for the Web. Imagine hunting for a new home in a city to which one is about to be transferred. Via the Web, one can search for properties with specific features and in particular price ranges. One can see pictures of the properties, even presumably take virtual tours of the premises. Not only that, but classifieds as a form of media content are ridiculously cheap to produce, since the content is generated by the very people who are paying to place the ads. For all these reasons, the media companies are convinced that spectacular profits lie in store for the enterprise that can harness Web content and computerized classifieds. And since the newspapers are not only a source of content but hold title to the classified market, they are essential to any cyberspace strategy. Yesterday's medium is the key to the future.

Nonetheless, it is not at all clear that news or journalism will be a profitable source of Web content. The Web is splendid as a delivery vehicle for what one might call tickertape journalism: the blunt announcement of breaking developments. But the Web's real forte is interactivity. As a computer-mediated matrix of interconnected participants, the strength of the Web is the traditional weakness of media such as television or newspapers. What is E-bay if not the sum total of all the contributions of all the visitors to the site, buyers and sellers? E-bay is nothing but perpetual exchange: pure interactivity. Journalism, by comparison, is by definition unidirectional. It is about a single, centralized source speaking with authority and credibility to a dispersed audience. It may be that journalism, as a genre of content, is as ill-suited to cyberspace as it was to cinema, and that it will be as vestigial to the Internet as newsreels were to the movies. In that case, the billion dollar investments of the broadcasters in the paper-and-ink newsrooms will simply have been a means to capture the classified market.

With all that in mind, the most interesting newspaper in Canada in 2002 – by circumstance rather than by deed – was the Winnipeg *Free Press*. It is not only the last remaining truly independent urban title, unaffiliated with any broadcaster, cable company, telecommunication giant or Internet provider – and therefore a throwback in the era of convergence – but it is the leading newspaper of the city in which CanWest Global's corporate headquarters reside, and therefore the paper best situated to provide close, non-partisan scrutiny of CanWest's corporate dealings. An old-fashioned newspaper is positioned to be the best source of intelligence on a new, multi-media conglomerate.

In the end, all news is local.

Bibliography

Canadian Newspaper Association. 2001. "Newspaper Facts." December.

Dornan, Christopher. 1996. "Newspaper Publishing." In *The Cultural Industries in Canada: Problems, Policies and Prospects*, ed. Michael Dorland. Toronto: James Lorimer.

———. 2000. "Newspaper Economics and Concentration: Select Problems and Complications." In *La Concentration de la Press Ecrite: Un « Vieux » Problème Non Résolu. Les Cahiers-Médias*. Numéro 11.

Dornan, Christopher, and Heather Pyman. 2001. "Facts and Arguments: Newspaper Coverage of the Campaign." In *The Canadian General Election of 2000*, ed. Jon Pammett and Christopher Dornan. Toronto: The Dundurn Group.

Haggett, Scott. 2001. *Calgary Herald*, April 21, A4.

Harris-Adler, Rosa. 2002. "The roar of the paper tiger." *Ottawa City*, August/Sept., 50–53.

Lindgren, April. 2001. *Ottawa Citizen*, August 25, D3.

PUBLISHING AND PERISHING WITH NO PARACHUTE

Once upon a time, in a recently more optimistic century, there was a large country with a small population (according to Statistics Canada, some 31,156,393 people in 2001). This is no fairy tale, although it is already an understatement, as virtually every summarizing description of Canada must be. This country is huge, geographically speaking, but miniscule in terms of population, our citizens a thin, eloquent sprinkle of people clustered mostly along the southern border, that geopolitical delineation shared with our nearest and dearest and large and noisily muscular neighbour, the United States of America. The stark contrast between our size and our population has multiple implications for how we Canadians communicate. Not easily, sometimes not well, and often locally rather than through our shared geopolitical nation. But despite being home to so few people, despite the contradiction of occupying the largest small country, we have, against all odds, developed a vibrant and determined culture.

Aritha van Herk

In the heady days around Canada's one hundredth birthday, 1967, with writers pouring out poems and novels and short stories and dramas and non-fiction renditions of travels and historical events and wild immigrations, a book publishing industry that had before that time been largely limited to subsidiaries of British and American houses, began to perform some interesting feats of yoga. When all this wonderful writing was published, voila! – people bought it and read it and taught it and talked about it. Small publishing houses, eager to expose distinctive voices, sprang up, and set about putting into print the beautiful and the dissonant. The result was tangible: books, books that explored space and region and language and even books that contained unexpected pictures or arguments. Those were heady days, and publishing houses and small presses, with the sagacious assistance and encouragement of the Canada Council, grew and flourished both in size and in numbers. Writers, responding to the interest of readers, wrote. They wrote so much that a few of them became world-renowned, and many of them, internationally known or not, produced very fine books. Bookstores and booksellers hand-sold books (the practice of a bookstore clerk personally recommending a particular book to a customer) and readers were happy to read books that were actually set in Calgary and Couchiching and Campbellton, books that reflected a Canada coming of age. So what happened? Why, now, do publishing, bookselling and writing appear to be suffering some horrific reversals? The Canadian publishing industry has encountered many gulfs and coulees since its optimistic early days, so what recent events have coloured that early positive picture and what will happen to the book industry in the near future? Are current setbacks millennium-related, or is some other unnameable malevolent force at work?

The world, at the turn of the twenty-first century, was cautiously celebrating an economic prosperity that should have spoken well for the future of writers (writing their fingers to the bone), publishers (working on a small but neither unhappy nor unreasonable margin) and booksellers (working on a larger if more unpredictable margin, given the tricks and vicissitudes of retail). So why is Canadian publishing, which enjoyed a relative prosperity that should have spoken well for the future, facing such different prospects now? Is this unease a reflection of the growling world of global communications, virtual books, corporate mergers and cutthroat financial balance sheets? Or is Canadian publishing teetering on a more precarious ledge, that of cultural suicide? The unspeakable and unspoken question that hovers in the air is whether Canada can actually sustain a publishing industry.

In June 2000, the House of Commons Standing Committee on Canadian Heritage (chaired by Clifford Lincoln) issued *The Challenge of Change: A Consideration of the Canadian Book Industry*. That report was based on a background study carried out between December 1999 and February 2000, after which it was decided that a more focused review of Canada's book industry was necessary. The subsequent review heard from publishers, writers, wholesalers, retailers, librarians, consumers, industry analysts, statisticians and other industry experts, and focused particularly on three key paradigm shifts in book industry practices. These were: innovations in information technology, which fostered the possibility of new types of computer-mediated commerce (i.e., e-commerce); the arrival of the retail superstore, which reconfigured the book retailing and distribution landscape; and new trends in book wholesaling practices and ownership, which left some industry stakeholders wondering whether such shifts represented a threat to the distribution and availability of Canadian-authored materials to Canadians (*Challenge of Change* 2000). As usual, the government was gazing at complexities that were already in play; and its report was behind rather than ahead of events. Still, it was an attempt to understand the business of books, an industry based on passion rather than profit (the profit margin before tax for this group is less than 2 per cent), an industry struggling with the size, distance and configuration of Canada (it could take up to eight weeks for a book to be delivered from a publisher's warehouse to a bookstore) along with the fact that cultural marketplaces are different from other marketplaces, driven as they are by concerns that go beyond any fiscal bottom line. Concerns were raised about books continuing to provide diverse cultural offerings, about bookselling as diverse retail ownership, and of course, about the overwhelming competition from large multinational companies working from a low cost base in the United States.

The very concept of publishing was undergoing a sea change, having to shift from its original configuration as an ink-stained gentleman's business to a technologically competitive, market-driven, even ruthless industry, interested in sound business practice and fiscal growth more than the genteel pleasures of elegant font or fine paper. But did that sea change bode a threat to the ecology of a fragile cultural constituency, one that could go extinct as easily as it could survive? Books suffer from a double identity; they are cultural artifacts as well as marketable and saleable products. And again and again, stakeholders repeated that without government support, Canadian publishing could not survive.

According to Statistics Canada, there were, in 1998–99, some 450 English-language publishing firms of Canadian location if not ownership and 193 French-language publishing firms of Canadian location (See Statistics Canada tables), up from 201 in 1992–93. In 1998–99, there were 193 French-language publishing firms, up from 122 in 1992–93.[1] These publishers publish, distribute and sell the work of writers (self-identified as numbering around 17,635, according to Statistics Canada, 1996), living and working in Canada. Just to place the economic base of writing within the Canadian context, the average income of those persons claiming to be writers in Canada was, according to the 1996 census, $27,942 per year. Bare poverty line – only comforting if one compares it to the average income of tattoo artists, who could expect to make $13,000 per year.[2] Approximately ten thousand English and French titles are published in Canada each year, of which about half are written by Canadians. In 1998–99, English language book sales totalled $1,352,383,000 and French-language book sales totalled $334,309,000.[3] Statistics, of course, contain their own deceptions, and these recent figures are already in flux; more important than this historical thumbnail sketch is the projected future of the grammar and economy of publishing. Numbers alone cannot explain the business of publishing: the publisher the investor who buys, edits, packages, prints, distributes, markets, and sells a work, whether poetry or fiction, cookbook or travel guide. Publishers are the economic engine of the printed word. But there are two tiers of publishing, and the "independence" of publishers is an uneasy fault zone, especially in this second-world small/large country, Canada.

The Big Six, which sounds something like a gang of motorcyclists, control in total some 89 per cent of book sales in the United States, and because Canada functions as a cultural mirror of our hefty neighbour, those statistics on ownership creep across the border. It is useful to outline their long reach, which goes far beyond book publishing, a mere crumb of the larger network of communication and media ownership. The fattest is Bertelsmann, a German house and the largest publisher in the world, owning the imprints of Random House, Ballantine, Crown, Doubleday, Bantam Dell, Knopf, Fodor's Travel Publications, along with some two hundred music labels, quite a few magazines and newspapers, as well as considerable television and radio holdings in Europe. Knopf (Canada) publishes between twenty-five and thirty Canadian literary fiction and non-fiction titles each year; Random House publishes some twenty-seven Canadian general trade books. Those books will have the clout of an enormous communications machine behind them. Next largest is the Pearson

Aritha van Herk

Group, which owns Penguin, Putnam, Viking, New American Library, Signet, Plume, Prentice Hall, Reader's Digest, extensive educational publishing (markedly different from trade books[4]), a couple of newspapers and extensive television and radio holdings in Europe. Within its fold, Penguin publishes some ninety-five Canadian trade books every year, and Prentice-Hall sixty to sixty-five Canadian educational, trade and reference books. Next largest of the Big Six is Viacom, owners of Simon and Schuster, Pocket Star, Washington Square Press, lots of television, including CBS and MTV, quite a few radio stations, Paramount Pictures, various movie theatres, and advertising billboards. None of these has a specifically Canadian arm. Next is News Corporation, which owns Harper Collins, Harper Perennial, Avon Books, Fox News, TV Guide, and a fair slice of what might be called sports and entertainment venues like the Los Angeles Dodgers, the New York Knicks, and Radio City Music Hall. Harper Collins publishes around fifty Canadian titles a year. Next, Time Warner, which is about the same size as News Corporation and which owns Little Brown, Warner Books, Book of the Month, other book clubs (with Bertelsmann), a good many cable channels including CNN and HBO, a raft of magazines, movie production companies, music labels, and to top it off, World Championship Wrestling and the Goodwill Games. None of these has a Canadian arm. Finally, the smallest of the Big Six, Holtzbrink, owns Farrar, Straus & Giroux, Faber and Faber, St. Martin's Press, and *Scientific American*. Their book publishing is high-end literary, but they too have no Canadian arm. Crouching under the shadow of these octopus tentacles are Canadian publishers, the largest of which is, strangely enough, Harlequin Enterprises, flooding the market with some seven hundred titles a year, of the sort we all recognize even if we do not read what are popularly configured as "bodice rippers." McClelland and Stewart, "THE CANADIAN PUBLISHER," brings out around eighty titles per year; their restructuring, in June of 2000, with controlling interest handed over to the University of Toronto, was an interesting paradigm shift in respect of what the nation had complacently come to believe would be "The Canadian Publisher" forever. But more on that later.

Canadian book publishers cover an enormous range, from university presses to small specialty presses to market-driven trade publishers. The largest of the university presses is the University of Toronto Press, which brings out around 150 titles a year, most of them academic rather than trade books, followed by McGill-Queen's University Press with eighty titles; the smallest is the University of Manitoba Press, which brings out about five titles a year. Examining the descriptions of Canadian publishers and their interests is one way to sample the culture of this diverse country. The Anglican Book Centre publishes some fifteen books a year about theology, life issues, and justice. Wolsak and Wynn Publishers Ltd. bring out some six books of poetry each year. Tundra Books publishes twenty literary children's books each year, while Blizzard Publishing brings out six to ten books related to drama and theatre. Caitlin Press publishes five or six trade books by authors from the interior of British Columbia; Catchfire Press Inc. publishes four books by "near north" Ontario writers. Rocky Mountain Books bring out six outdoor, recreational or history books related to the Rockies; Ragweed Press/gynergy books publishes eight to ten feminist and lesbian titles of fiction and mystery. Pemmican Publications bring out four Metis and Aboriginal titles; Novalis brings out fifty titles related to Christian growth. Empty Mirrors Press publishes one book per year, explicitly listed as being "of the publisher's choice." Butterworths Canada does thirty legal, business and accounting books; and Gaspereau Press does eight titles of fiction, poetry and history from Atlantic Canada. There are well-known names, like Broadview Press and Douglas and McIntyre, House of Anansi, Kids Can Press, Thistledown Press, and NeWest Press. And there are tiny, one-person presses scraping by on Canada Council grants and produce from the garden.[5] This then is the back story of publishing in Canada, although that complex mix of writers, their pages, publishers, printers, distributors, booksellers, and ultimately book readers, is far more difficult to unpack than is possible without a detailed history of every publisher and the books they midwife. We can only look at slices of what transpires and try to put them in context.

McClelland and Stewart, "The Canadian Publisher," has long been a benchmark for writerly activity and its production in this country. It has survived various challenges and permutations, the most recent seismic shiver in June 2000, when Avie Bennett, then Chairman and President of McClelland and Stewart Limited, donated 75 per cent of the shares of the company to the University of Toronto. The remaining 25 per cent of the shares were sold to Random House of Canada Ltd., part of that huge conglomerate under the Bertelsmann umbrella. The University of Toronto, it was announced, would hold five of the seven seats on the board of directors, while Random House would hold two seats.[6] The venerable McClelland and Stewart was founded in the spring of 1906 as a library supply house by John McClelland and Frederick Goodchild (who together abandoned the Methodist Book Room, later Ryerson Press). Although it began as a distributor, it soon began to publish under its first imprint, McClelland and Goodchild, which changed to McClelland, Goodchild and Stewart in 1914, when famously tenacious Bible salesman George Stewart joined the company. When Goodchild left in 1918, the company was renamed McClelland and Stewart Limited, and over the next ninety years became and is still virtually synonymous with canonical Canadian writing and reading. This is the house that published L.M. Montgomery, Stephen Leacock, Margaret Laurence, W.O. Mitchell, Hugh Maclennan, Mordecai Richler, Robertson Davies, and that still publishes Leonard Cohen, Pierre Berton, Alice Munro, Michael Ondaatje, Margaret Atwood, Guy Vanderhaege, and Rohinton Mistry.[7] It seemed a flagship that would never sink, despite the various ups and downs of an always uneasy business.

But when Bennett donated McClelland and Stewart to the University of Toronto, no one in the writing or publishing world knew quite what to make of this sudden shift in ownership if not determination. President Richard Prichard stressed that the University of Toronto would take seriously its role as trustee to perpetuate the company's venerable position in Canadian letters. He also stated explicitly that the company would be run independently of the university, and, perhaps anticipating the shudder that passed through many who feared that it would be controlled by a lugubrious academic publisher, that it would have no relationship with the University of Toronto Press, the largest university press in the country. But despite these reassurances, writers and booksellers shuffled their feet. What exactly did this turnover mean? Was it a sign of other changes in the wind, a protective strike, an pre-emptive unloading of a costly enterprise? Bennett's donation appeared to be altruistic. He stated,

> After fifteen years in the publishing business, I decided that it was time for me to find a way of ensuring McClelland & Stewart's future and preserving its past.... This is the culmination of more than five years of planning with the University of Toronto. What better way can there be to safeguard a great Canadian institution, a vital part of Canada's cultural heritage, than by giving it to the careful stewardship of another great Canadian institution?[8]

Bennett retains ownership of Stewart House, the separate (and more lucrative) business of distributing books by foreign publishers. And the quarter share that Random House now controls, along with their contribution to accounting, marketing, and sales, suggests that McClelland and Stewart is no longer "THE Canadian Publisher," but definitely a part of the Big Six, even if only by a quarter.

Then, in 2001, two small events crystallized the ripple of unease that seemed to be building in Canadian books and book publishing. The first was a letter dated October 4, 2001, from the owner of Books & Books, a small independent bookstore in Calgary, to its co-operative members, announcing that the bookstore would close its doors on October 31, 2001. One paragraph in that letter read,

> The situation in Canada's book industry has not improved, nor have the relationships between the publisher-distributor giants and the tiny clients, the small independents. If anything, things are worse. Here is just one example.... several publishers are suing General Distribution Services, one of Canada's largest book warehouses, for breach of contract: evidently GDS has been unable to pay for the books they have sold.

Word was out. General Distribution Services was facing huge returns from the big box stores, Chapters and Indigo, and was having trouble walking the tightwire of the bottom line.

The second item was a widely distributed e-mail (October 28, 2001) from Jamie Reid at dadababy@netcom.ca to writers, booksellers, and academics.

> Most of you are aware of the hardship and difficulty that have befallen the small publishers of Vancouver and the entire country in the wake of the Chapters fiasco. Our friend, Karl Siegler, the owner and publisher of Talonbooks, who has done so much for our local writers and for the development of a national Canadian literature is one of the publishers who has been hit very hard. Karen Tallman, while speaking to Karl when he was in town for the recent TISH@40 celebrations, learned that the situation has become so serious that Karl and Christy [the two owners of Talonbooks] actually don't know where their next month's groceries are coming from.

A small bookstore, a small publisher. But these two small stories compass a much larger story, a story that will continue to send shock waves through a fragile if tough cultural ecosystem into the future.

It is a given that all over the world, book publishing faces the daunting possibility that books may become obsolete, that reading is an activity fewer and fewer people have time for, and that previously sacred notions of the book and its life are changing as quickly as pages can be turned. The future of words printed on paper is now contingent on short-selling, shorter and shorter attention spans, and commercial tie-ins to larger media spin-offs. The shelf or bound life of a book is now radically different than it was at time when a tome – the book as object – contained its own potential sacredness and intrinsic value. And in a ruthless, market-driven world focused on branding and unconcerned with cultural value or virtue, a good many small Canadian publishers are teetering on the brink of financial ruin, related it seems to the mismanagement – and some publishers claim the downright villainous practices – of one big box retailer called Chapters. This part of the story might be sub-titled "Warlords and Warlocks," or "how to make money on books."

In Canadian publishing, 2001 was nothing less than *annus horriblis*. The first and worst of the scenarios affecting publishing in Canada was what has become known as the Chapters debacle, although the industry is now hopeful that the resultant uncertainty and instability is on its way to resolution by Chapters' merger/takeover by Heather Reisman's Indigo Books, Music, and More. Chapters first appeared on the book scene as an optimistic answer to the big box chain store trend markedly in evidence south of the border, and was brought about by a merger of Coles and SmithBooks. Its goal was to stop Borders (a big box American book chain) at the border, and Chapters promised to fight the good fight in getting Canadian books to Canadians. Chapters grew and grew, setting up huge stores wallpapered with books all over cities like Calgary (which has nine such stores, approximately one for every 100,000 people). Some charge that Chapters set out to drive independent booksellers out of business. And as it got bigger and more powerful, the chain manifested some nasty attitudes, actually quite commonplace in the world of retail. Chapters (by virtue of sheer volume) bullied publishers into giving them amazing price cuts, but it is conversely true that many publishers and distributors (including General Distribution Services), eager to jump on the bandwagon of big sales numbers, and reading Chapters as a retail outlet that literally bought truckloads of books, allowed Chapters to dictate terms to them, terms that ultimately cost more than they returned.

The breakdown of book costs and payments is worth laying out here. Usually, a bookstore orders books from publishers or their distributors for a 40 per cent discount, then sells the book at 100 per cent, which is, after expenses, how they make their profit. Chapters apparently began to demand deep discounts, up to 60 per cent from publishers, many of whom capitulated, thinking that the volume of sales would recompense for the decrease in revenue. Of course, those who succumbed to that theory are now feeling quite a pinch. Writers' royalties are a standard 10 per cent of the cover price, whereas bookstores take 40 per cent, with publishers getting the rest.

The battle of the books, as the press called it, was protracted, lengthy, and unhappy. In little more than five years, Chapters had expanded to some seventy-seven stores across Canada, throwing retail caution to the winds. Staggering under the burden of its own unsustainable growth, the chain started to crash and burn, but did its best to download its financial embarrassments onto the producers of the product they sold, namely publishers and their distributors, who are the food-chain producers of the products created by writers, those bum-sore few who sit at the keyboard or typewriter long enough to write and revise a bundle of pages full of words worth reading. Chapters was also very much determined to fight off the takeover bid of Heather Reisman's competitor chain Indigo Books (established in 1997), a.k.a. Trilogy Retail Enterprises LP. Who actually owns which parts of that company is also something of a mystery. Various rumours claim that Borders is still sneaking across the border, some say under Indigo's cloak. But that information is not public.

Crazily resisting its own takeover, Chapters began to engage in excessively risky retail practices. They apparently ordered books wildly, deep discounted them, did not pay their bills, and sometimes returned to source boxes of books that publishers thought had long ago been sold. Meanwhile, takeover mania ruled until finally, in February 2001, Indigo owners Heather Reisman and her husband Gerald Schwartz outbid (to the tune of $121 million) Future Shop to gain control of Chapters and Chapters Online (*Publisher's Weekly*, February 12, 2001, 82).They then set to work to merge Chapters with Indigo's smaller but possibly more muscled empire, Indigo Books, Music, and More. This merger was to combine seventy-seven Chapters stores, two hundred mall-based stores, and fifteen Indigo stores, but was subject to the approval of the Competition Bureau.

But of course, there is no merger without purger, and Reisman too purged – first in a fit a temper when in March she claimed that Larry Stevenson of Chapters had "doctored their financials" (*Globe and Mail*, March 15, 2001). Reisman claimed that returned books were not returned but were still gathering dust in warehouses, that Chapters had no clear sense of its inventory, and that Chapters had created a ruinous mess with a $50 million warehousing system that was utterly useless. She added a few choice phrases about waste and bad management, which made ex-chief Guy Dixon demand that Reisman sell the company back to him so he could show her how to run it at a profit. Which of the two was most right is moot; but Reisman purged a huge amount of book inventory (that she said was unsaleable and that Chapters had apparently accumulated), and began to close stores. Any observant person could have foreseen that action. Chapters had opened book boxes in neighbourhoods only short distances from one another. For example, in Calgary, there is one Chapters in Dalhousie Station and one in Crowfoot Centre, really only a stone's throw away in suburban vehicular distance. There were simply too many outlets too close together, although interestingly enough, the Chapters store and the Indigo store in downtown Toronto (just a few blocks apart) remain competitively open. And there were serious concerns about Reisman entering into restrictive covenant agreements relating to the leasing of space to other booksellers in the same vicinity as her stores.

In April 2001, after beard-tugging deliberation, the Competition Bureau finally green-lighted the merger of Chapters and Indigo, with the proviso that Chapters (under Indigo) sell certain large format stores, certain mall stores, and their interest in "Classic Books," "Prospero," and "Smithbooks." And they requested that Chapters (under Indigo) adopt a Code of Conduct governing its relationships with publishers (*Publisher's Weekly,* April 9, 2001, 12). (This Code of Conduct relates to the most contentious and potentially damaging fallout within this area.) Late in 2001, it became clear that nobody wanted to buy the mall and the format bookstores that were up for sale, indicating that another solution would have to be derived and leaving those stores in a version of limbo.

Other players did demonstrate an eagerness to compete with the Chapters/Indigo superpower. Bruce Barr and Anil Amlani, who head a group of Canadian investors convinced that there is room in Canada for another bookstore chain, tried to persuade the Competition Bureau that Chapters and Indigo were going to divest themselves only of stores which were already unprofitable, the duds rather than the cherries, and that they should be forced to give up at least twenty-four superstores and not the thirteen superstores and ten mall outlets that were agreed upon (*Publisher's Weekly,* May 21, 2001, 20).The Bureau wasn't prepared to accept that argument and allowed the deal to proceed, so finally, on June 18, 2001, the merger of Chapters and Indigo was completed, a negotiation that even included input from the Association of Canadian Publishers, desperate for some stability in their retail sector (*Publisher's Weekly*, June 18, 2001, 10). Small publishing houses in Canada were teetering on the edge, victims of a ruthless slash and burn practice that had resulted in enormous numbers of returns, and even more strategically, millions of dollars in unpaid bills. Unmanageable rates of returns and lengthy delays in payment of accounts were beginning to take their toll. McClelland and Stewart, Stoddart, and the University of Toronto Press were together owed more than $50 million. In what seemed almost like revenge, Chapters had cut back new orders to a trickle, and even worse, begun to return books (some $40 million worth) to distributors and publishers in lieu of payment, books that were often so damaged that they could not be resold, a legacy of those Starbucks-drinking customers leaving behind a coffee stained memento of their reading. Hell had come to Canadian publishing.

When statistics for the fiscal year were released, Chapters recorded a net loss of $84.5 million on sales of $686.5 million for the year ending March 31, 2001. Total sales were $660.3 million with a net income of $17.2 million. Except that during the year, revenues actually rose 2 per cent to $634 million, most of them in Chapters Superstores, while smaller stores recorded a loss. At the same time, sales in Chapters Online increased 32 per cent (more people are buying books at home), to $51.1 million, resulting in a loss of $33.1 million, compared to $35.2 million in the previous year (*Publisher's Weekly*, July 16, 2001, 68). The millions in losses were declining, but still, Chapters' response was to cut 172 on-line positions. The dollars are daunting, and to the writers who try to survive on a poverty level income of $28,000 a year, obscene. When Larry Stevenson, former CEO of Chapters was terminated, he left with a severance package of $855,750 on top of his yearly salary of $287,500 and a $105,750 bonus. Glen Murphy, former president and CEO of Chapters Retail, left with $1.4 million after his job was eliminated (*Calgary Herald*, July 14, 2001, E7). How many books would that publish? How many Canadian writers would that sustain?

The bottom line of those historical upheavals suggests that, in this instance at least, both publishers and writers appeared to be at the mercy of a commercial enterprise that does not seem to give one sweet damn about Canadian culture. Even Richard Segal, president of Chapters' Internet subsidiary, described the company's tactics before the takeover as nothing less than "brutal," a toxic cocktail of inventory mismanagement, gross incompetence, and downright subversive stupidity. Chapters didn't have a clue as to what was in its warehouses. Sometimes they claimed to have hundreds of copies of books, yet couldn't fill orders; other times they ordered from publishers thousands of copies of books, only to discover thousands of copies already in stock, and simply returned thousands, sending publishers, especially smaller and less financially flexible publishers, into a tailspin. No publisher can withstand a return rate of up to 50 per cent of copies that it believes it has successfully marketed and sold. It began to seem as if the Chapters gang were on a mission to destroy Canadian publishing. Douglas Gibson, the publisher of McClelland and Stewart, in an interview with the author, said, "you couldn't help but believe it was deliberate mismanagement" (October 30, 2001). Chapters demanded huge discounts, demanded payment from publishers for prime display spots or book dumps in its retail outlets (which sometimes did not materialize), delayed its payments to the absolute legal limit, and returned truckloads of books to publishers who, assuming that these books had sold, had already paid authors royalties on these copies. And in the backrooms of the big boxes were real, not metaphorical, mammoth shredders, huge teeth that ripped apart thousands of paperbacks in the unmarked graveyard of unwanted books because the Chapters warehousing system couldn't figure out how to process return orders.

It is important to understand that the basic rules about retail don't cross over into the retail book trade. Unlike any other retail business and product, bookstores can return books for full refund, at any time, if they do not sell. Can you imagine a clothing store returning soiled clothing to its distributor and demanding a full refund? And in this case, the customer is not only not right, but at the mercy of whatever product the book business wants to push. The many outstanding special orders that Chapters promised to fill and didn't fill became legend. Rumours and statistics aside, various reasons were advanced for Chapters' death spiral. Heather Reisman claimed that Chapters wanted to bury its one large competitor – her bookstore chain, Indigo. But the only sure thing is that Chapters' demise may have single-handedly brought about the demise of a good many Canadian publishers and writers, people working with budgets of far less than a million dollars, but hoping to meet that average annual income of less than $28,000. Worst of all, the book trade in Canada has suffered chaos ever since.

Reisman agreed to a code of conduct that was supposed to clean up the landfill site left behind by Chapters. She agreed to a standard returns policy, including a set description of the condition of returns, particular payment terms, terms for discounts, and particular placements for Canadian books. But will her good intentions last? Will Indigo last? In August 2001, Indigo released financial information indicating that for the fiscal year ending in January 2001, it had lost $31.7 million on revenues of $94.8 million, losses some $8 million higher than the year before (*Publisher's Weekly*, July 23, 2001, 11). These may appear to be small numbers, especially when compared to companies who work in the billions of dollars, but they are substantial enough to reverberate throughout the Canadian publishing industry, an industry always contingent and tentative, always on edge.

The results reach into the present and the future, with horrific collateral damage. Snug book buyers may not have noticed, but the biggest fallout has been for the specialized literary presses and those people who speak through literary presses, literary writers. Wonderful Canadian poets who don't exactly publish mainstream books opened last year's royalty statements to discover not the modest cheques they might have expected, but statements in the minus thousands. Most writers who publish with small presses report that in 2001 their royalty income was virtually cut in half, and many did not see a penny of actual money. Without the saving grace of the annual Public Lending Right Payment, a reliable if tiny cheque which appears in the lean month of February, many writers would be considering a job at McDonald's.

The bottom line is that publishers and publishing are facing considerable changes, and not all of them related to the 2001 shockwaves. "There is so much blood everywhere, this industry looks like an abattoir" (*Maclean's*, March 26, 2001), said Allan MacDougall of Raincoast Books, a distribution company slightly protected because, on the strength of being the Canadian distributor for the Harry Potter books, they could dictate more favourable terms than other Canadian distributors, and they put the fire to Chapters' shoes. Publishers now are struggling with unpredictable cash flows, and print runs on 2001 fall books were seriously reduced. Print runs on 2002 books were cautiously optimistic, but no publisher risked any excess. Caution plays the note that publishers sound for the future.

In October 2001, I interviewed two important representatives of the publishing industry, Cynthia Good of Penguin Books and Douglas Gibson of McClelland and Stewart, asking them specifically what they saw as the future of publishing in Canada. Both agreed that the industry was changing and that it was difficult to predict what the ultimate result of these sea changes would be, but their attitudes were markedly different. Cynthia Good, of Penguin, perhaps backed by the confidence of the Putnam conglomerate, was optimistic, sure that when the dust settles, the industry will have to occupy a better frame of mind, better able to contend with its challenges. Book publishing in the future, she asserted, would be different, but would prevail as an important reflection of Canadian culture. McClelland and Stewart's publisher Douglas Gibson, on the other hand, despite the support of Random House and the University of Toronto, was greyness and gloom. He foresaw long-range and dire consequences for book publishing in Canada.

Most publishers in the last few years have fought back, determined to ride out this crazy revenge tragedy. All claimed that they would maintain or increase the number of books in their publishing program in 2001 and 2002, and would ignore this bump in the night. In 2001, McClelland and Stewart went ahead with its usual seventy to seventy-five titles; Stoddart, which usually releases around a hundred Canadian titles, was set to release 125. ECW Press, a small literary and critical press, went from twenty titles last year to twenty-seven. But small presses, many of whom publish only a dozen books, were hit very hard by Chapters' ruthlessness, and had to hunker down, many reducing their titles by 20 per cent, translating to one-fifth fewer books chronicling this country's life and culture. The situation was so dire that the Canada Council and the Canadian Heritage department advanced $1.3 million in emergency funding on predictive grants to twenty-two small and struggling publishers just to tide them over (*Globe and Mail,* March 20, 2001). But that relief was merely temporary, and at present some of those small presses that came into being when Canada believed in a national literature and book business are locked in a struggle for survival. Experts predict that it will take years for publishing in this small but culturally vibrant country to recover.

At Book Expo, the industry showcase held in Toronto in June 2001, it seemed as if a tentative peace had been made between Chapters and Indigo. If the future of books depends on bookstores, then the bookstore wars had abated. Chapters, long a non-participant in the event, sent managers and employees to mingle, and John Ralston Saul argued that trying to support or create another bookstore chain out of the remains of Chapters would only lead to the death of independent booksellers, now cast in the impossible role of saviours of the publishing industry (*Globe and Mail,* June 23, 2001). By the summer of 2001, everyone was feeling better. Under Reisman, Chapters was less of a bear, and advance orders for books were good. Publishers even started to bid on manuscripts again. Reisman, who enjoys a friendlier relationship to the book publishing industry than Chapters ever did (perhaps she simply relates to the press better), claimed that she wants to create a chain of "cultural department stores," to fulfill Canadians' interest in their own books and music. Her most philanthropic statement is that she wants to "try and stabilize the industry." Everyone in the food chain of books, writers, agents, publishers, printers, distributors and marketing agents prays she will help to bring about stability.

A slight lull, and then September 11, 2001 stopped all book-buying for a week. Sales froze, and everyone in the business held his/her breath. Would this be the final blow? Books themselves at ground zero? One fascinating example is that of Canadian writer Yann Martell's Booker Prize winning novel, *Life of Pi*. Due to be launched in Canada and the United States on September 12, 2001, it was published but almost completely ignored. Only Martell's winning of the Booker Prize in the UK in 2002 has brought the book the attention it missed. But by the end of October 2001, perhaps as a reaction to that completely unprecedented event, bookstores reported an increase in sales. By Christmas of 2001, it began to look as if the human reaction to September 11 was to curl up at home with a good book. In the final count a good year – for the independents at least – booksellers and publishers relaxed and writers optimistically sat down at their keyboards to put in the long hours that eventually produce manuscripts.

And then the situation worsened again. On April 30, 2002, Jack Stoddart won a thirty-day stay under the Companies' Creditors Arrangement Act. Mr. Stoddart sought bankruptcy court protection from his creditors, creditors who asserted claims of some $45.7 million. Stoddart (one of those publishers early willing to adhere to Chapters' demands) owned General Distribution Services Ltd. (GDS), General Publishing Co. Ltd., Stoddart Publishing Co. Ltd., The Boston Mills Press Ltd., and House of Anansi Press Ltd. This list might seem a small one, but the hardest truth was that General Distribution Services was the largest book distributor in Canada, selling the lists of about two hundred national and international publishers, including about sixty Canadian publishers, all of whom run their programs on very small margins. Bankruptcy protection meant that small Canadian publishers to whom GDS owed money were effectively prevented from suing GDS, and thus prevented from collecting their money from the very book distribution company that was in the business of ensuring that their books were spread across this impossibly huge country.

What a mess. Stoddart owed money to various publishers, including Key Porter Books, Goose Lane Edition, Douglas and McIntyre, Coach House Books, the Porcupine's Quill, Sono Nis Press. The government of Canada, a second-tier creditor because of a loan guarantee of $4.5 million, refused to bail Stoddart out. Knowing that trouble was in the wind, a few client publishers had pulled their books from GDS's warehouses; but the later court order prevented publishers either from getting their books back or demanding payment for their books directly from bookstores. Of course, Stoddart blamed Chapters and their inventory mess, but the newly merged Chapters/Indigo outfit refused to accept blame, claiming that they had followed strict payment rules. The fallout? General Distributing Services and Stoddart Publishing have gone bankrupt. Worse, their demise has had a horrific ripple effect on dozens of small publishers who cannot sustain a high level of loss.

Whatever or wherever the blame, the ultimate result is that a huge number of Canadian publishers, many of them small presses, are now on the edge. What can a small press cut in order to survive? Its staff? Its overhead? Payments to writers or to printers? Ultimately, the one area that can be hacked is in the number of books published. Since publishing is such a gamble anyway – every book that does well in the marketplace is backed by five or six mid-list books – inevitably publishers will refuse to gamble on potentially unprofitable books, which means a certain rise in the number of cookbooks and guidebooks appearing in the future and a certain drop in the number of literary and non-mainstream books about ideas. That is if small presses publishing poetry and other unusual books survive at all. The long-term results? Book prices will go up. New writers will find it increasingly difficult to find a publisher, and they will be the first whose manuscripts are cut, although mid-range writers too will face difficulties. Publishers are making more conservative choices, refusing to take risks, and Canada's literary profile is already more conservative, less diverse. When one small literary publisher goes out of business, its usual eight and ten titles per year vanish from the market. And when five small publishers go bankrupt – a not unlikely number, given General's reach – fifty new books per year will not find a publisher. In Canadian cultural terms, in terms of how Canadians communicate – that is cataclysmic. In ten years, five hundred books that might have met enthusiastic readers will not appear.

And there are other wrinkles in the nation's book publishing industry. Sourcing books has always been difficult in a country as unwieldy for shipping and delivery as Canada is, and predicting sales numbers is guesswork. Small and independent booksellers, who saw their market share drop substantially with Chapters' bulk buying, have reduced their orders, and will in future count on strategy and quick reprint order time rather than on estimating how many books they can sell and ordering larger numbers of copies in advance. A pilot project for Books-on-Demand and Instant Printing was tested by specific bookstores in Toronto in 2002. Certain books would be digitally prepared and participating bookstores could order books from the on-demand site in response to customer orders, bypassing the guessing game of how many books a publisher should print and bind. While printing and binding a book on demand might cost more for each volume, that cost can be offset by publishers avoiding the costs of warehousing, distribution, and long-distance transportation. This practice, too, would permit publishers to reprint books in small runs of something like one hundred copies, again enabling them to control losses and to produce only what the market will buy. On the other hand, Books-on-Demand could also mean that impatient book-buyers who do not want to wait twenty-four hours to get a particular book will more and more resort to buying those books that *are* available, best-sellers printed in the millions and unloaded in dumps, the McDonald's of words. Such commercial approaches are always "dancing on the brink of dissolution" (Bayers 2001). New technologies might seem promising, but the long-term implications for royalties and copyright and intellectual property are unclear, and the additional headache of a smart hacker getting into the system and downloading books without payment is inevitable.

It is an unhappy statistic of the book business that a smaller number of books are taking up a larger and larger share of the market. At one time, publishers were satisfied with 80 per cent of high volume sales subsidizing 20 per cent of risky books, literary books, or unusual and difficult-to-market books. Now that percentage has shifted, and in future, 90 per cent of the books published will have to guarantee their own economic return, leaving only 10 per cent for risky or innovative books. At the Frankfurt Book Fair in 2002, the world's industry marker for books and writing, 6,375 exhibitors from 110 countries enjoyed what evaluators claimed were good to very good levels of business activity. Small and medium-sized publishing companies (those would be Canadian) apparently felt stronger after their attendance at the mammoth fair, but they nevertheless reflected a global sense of caution in an industry that faces the challenge of steering the course of its own economic recovery.

The book market's situation at present means that publishing companies will rely more than ever on predictable bestsellers, restricting their own willingness to experiment and thus limiting the diversity of books on offer. This caution only partly reflects a difficult economic climate. There is a sea change in the production and distribution of books, and the old ways are under threat. While some culture mavens point to e-commerce and electronic publishing companies as potential saviours of the written word, those businesses carry other baggage. Many are run by trend-savvy executives who know little about the complexity of books, one of the most specialized and unpredictable "products" in the world. The difference between books and gadgets is that books are developed and produced by publishers in collaboration with authors and editors, and e-commerce has, virtually or otherwise, no idea of what goes into publishing as a process.

Add to this stew the complex discourse of globalization and the rather unhappy fact that "the world of electronic communication is...American territory" (Gibson 2001, 24). McClelland and Stewart recently conducted an experiment, ordering from Amazon.com a number of Canadian books (authored and published in Canada) also available in an American edition. They were ordered from a Toronto address to be sent to a Toronto address, and in every case, the purchasers were sent American editions (and the GST was magically absent) (Gibson 2001, 25). This is the case for books in American editions by Ondaatje, Atwood, Munro, etc. Books without American publishers enjoy for once a dubious advantage; there being no other edition, Amazon has to send the Canadian edition.

There is no conclusion to be drawn, no prediction to be made, but that Canadian book culture is facing challenges that it has never imagined. Soon we may see no Canadian publishers at all, or only mavericks, fed and hosted by multinationals who enjoy keeping a Canadian cultural lapdog around for amusement. But are there solutions? Stability and reasonable rules of conduct appear to be a desirable goal for every player. The book publishing industry must be recognized as an important cultural medium, needing protection and encouragement and absolutely reliable subsidization. Whatever arguments will continue to be made about culture and free trade, it is still a given fact that Canadian publishing struggles to compete against the thrilling glossy magazines that drift over the border, against Oprah's picks and pans (even after she has discontinued her book club), against the huge jaws of the American publicity machine. Canadians need to recognize that without publishing as an important aspect of how Canadians communicate, the country's distinctive written voice could indeed perish.

But publishing is a complex business, and of even greater concern is the chasm between the writers of books and the big biz who produce and distribute books. Witness poet Fred Wah's comments in the *Newsletter* of the Writers' Union of Canada, written after he attended the twenty-fifth anniversary celebration of Toronto's last independent chain book store, Book City:

> The reception was an early evening post-office-hours affair on a
> high-altitude floor in an upscale Toronto hotel. For myself I expe-
> rienced a slight paranoid edginess about being so high up in a tall
> city building. Perhaps that spiced another paranoia I brought with
> me, the marginalized apprehension of being in a room of about
> three hundred suits dressed up as the "centre" of Canadian pub-
> lishing power. To be fair, there were a few writers, but just a few....
> As a writer I feel more and more alienated from the economics
> that, finally, contain my practice; the frightening implication is
> that my part as a player in cultural politics will become so eroded
> as to be insignificant in the negotiation and formation of the new
> world imaginary (Wah 2001, 1).

The publishing industry flourishes on the dedication and hard work of
mostly economically marginalized people. How long can that disparity last?
As Douglas Gibson declared, "you cannot legislate for genius, but you can
encourage it," (2001, 24) and if diverse writers in Canada are not encouraged, writing will become the enclave of the rich and the leisured few who
can afford to sit at a keyboard idling with their creative thoughts.

So here we are in this large country, with a culture as bright as a
copper penny. Canada bristles with brilliant writers writing brilliant books
and looking for publishers willing to publish them. Publishing houses are
eager to support independent booksellers who won't demand huge discounts. And readers? Despite the CBC and Canada Reads reducing the
whole rainbow of Canadian literature to Michael Ondaatje's *In the Skin of a
Lion,* readers know that there are far more writers than meet the publicizing eye, and are eager to encounter them. Their national enthusiasm must
prevent reading and books from becoming the fetish objects of the rich and
literate, out of the reach of the poor and unlanguaged, literacy itself a privileged site.

Perhaps Canadian publishing must be most unified in its vigilance
with regard to globalization, that blending of cultural diversity into a
common stew of Coca Cola and Stephen King. Hearteningly, it appears
that reading is entering a new age. Booksellers report increasingly healthy
profits, and independent booksellers seem to be holding their own against
Amazon and the big boxes by giving customers the service and selection
that the impersonals cannot. Perhaps in the future people will grow tired of
the repetitiveness of television, sick of the claims of the computer screen not
only at work but at home, and will fall in love with the page all over again.

If September 11 caused a paradigm shift not only in global awareness but in reading habits, it might be possible to hope that in the coming century people will look to books for intelligent and well-thought-out apprehensions of the variable complexities of this unpredictable world and this large, shy country, Canada.

References

Bayers, Chip. 2001. Reprinted from *Wired*, in *Ottawa Citizen*, May 28.

Gibson, Douglas. 2001. "Global Culture." *Literary Review of Canada* (October).

House of Commons Standing Committee on Canadian Heritage [Lincoln Report]. 2000. The Challenge of Change: A Consideration of the Canadian Book Industry June. Available: http://www.parl.gc.ca/InfoComDoc/36/2/HERI/Studies/Reports/heri01/04-toc-e.html.

King, James. 1999. *Jack : A Life with Writers. The Story of Jack McClelland*. Toronto: Alfred A. Knopf.

Wah, Fred. 2001. "Report from the Chair." *Writers' Union of Canada Newsletter* 29(3) (October/November).

Notes

1   See Statistics Canada, Profile of Book Publishing and Exclusive Agents, available at: http://www.statcan.ca/english/Pgdb/arts02.htm

2   Statistics regarding the number and income of writers in Canada come from Statistics Canada, who derived them from the 1996 Census. They are not available online, but directly from Statistics Canada, who keep a Standard Occupation Classification Book. They are happy to provide this information on the telephone.

3   See Statistics Canada, Profile of Book Publishing and Exclusive Agents, available at: http://www.statcan.ca/english/Pgdb/arts02.htm

4   Trade books are those books sold to the general marketplace and readership, while educational books are published and targeted toward a specific educational sector, whether schools, colleges or universities. The textbook market is considerably different from the general retail market. Textbooks are generally more expensive, but may also be more expensive to produce.

5   See http://www.publishers.ca/members.html for members of the Association of Canadian publishers. See also http://oscar.cprost.sfu.ca/group/citation/index.php3?type=Book%20Publishers&CIT_Session=0acfa8eca159d739528af9fc2d478713 for a total list of book publishers in Canada.

6   *University of Toronto Bulletin,* June 26, 2000. See http://www.newsandevents.utoronto.ca/bin1/000626a.asp

7   See McClelland and Stewart at http://www.tceplus.com for a brief history of the company and its founding and development. See also King (1999).

8   *University of Toronto Bulletin,* June 26, 2000. See http://www.newsandevents.utoronto.ca/bin1/000626a.asp

CANADIAN TELEVISION
Industry, Audience and
Technology

**Rebecca Sullivan and
Bart Beaty**

Canadian television occupies a unique space between the private and public sectors, resulting in an almost schizophrenic sense of itself and its role in national society. On the one hand, we look to a strong and diverse television industry as evidence of our status on the global media stage. On the other, the discourses of television are captured by anxieties over cultural sovereignty and notions of national identity that privilege high-minded, middle-brow dramatic programming as evidence of our cultural sophistication versus crass American mass media. As we shall note later, Canadians are avid television viewers. It is the most prevalent entertainment medium in the home. Despite recent claims that a rise in interactive media will cause television to lose its pre-eminence, there is little real evidence to support this suggestion. In Canada, television may have reached a saturation level, but it is also on the brink of major innovations in technology that will expand programming options and also provide new models for how Canadians use television in the home. At this point, although both digital cable and satellite have failed to ignite the industry, they are making slow inroads and challenging the dominance of the generalist, network-oriented model for television broadcasting. This, in turn, fractures audience and increases the costs of producing original dramatic programming. While pundits hail the expansion of the cable grid, there is no guarantee that it will lead toward greater access or a broader multiplicity of voices in Canadian broadcasting. The television industry – as is the case with all media industries in Canada – is witnessing an era of accelerated consolidation and conglomeration. The turn of the twenty-first century in Canadian television highlighted an important and problematic dialectic for Canadians. Based on the expansion of the cable grid, Canadian television is becoming more diverse and plural. However, this expansion is steered by an increasingly concentrated group of powerful media shareholders that has the potential to limit diversity.

Media industries, policy, content regulations and audience development are no longer peripheral issues in Canada – if they ever were. At stake are concerns over who owns the means to produce and disseminate Canadian stories, images and values, both nationally and abroad. Yet the debate is a murky one as regional differences come into play. Canadian television is simply not set up to handle local differences much past a nightly newscast. At best, the country can be divided up regionally so that the CBC, for example, can plan to simultaneously show a Montreal Canadiens game in the east and the Calgary Flames in the west. However, viewers who want to decide which hockey game to watch for themselves will either have to invest in satellite or digital cable plus subscribe to a sports specialty package, or simply learn to root for the team the CBC wants you to watch. This small example brings to light many issues surrounding media ownership and economic convergence while also drawing attention to the unequal access to technological innovations across the country. The divide between media rich and media poor grows wider. In other words, the media centres of Canada (namely, affluent urban centres) continue to control the agenda while rural peripheries are historically ignored as an economic force. At the same time, regulatory agencies and public television advocates increase their support for a cultural ideal of Canadian-ness as having far more in keeping with the Prairie farmer than the Bay Street broker. The extent to which the ideology and the economics of Canadian television don't add up will be explored here.

In order to understand the state of Canadian television today, this paper will bring three key elements to the fore. We will first present a broad picture of media penetration across the country in order to demonstrate patterns of access to broadcasting technologies. Second, we will examine questions of ownership, particularly in the context of the Canadian Radio-Television and Telecommunications Commission (CRTC), the regulatory body charged with ensuring appropriate levels of Canadian representation while fostering a healthy, competitive industry. Finally, we will turn to the question of audience and programming by asking what kind of content is available to Canadian viewers and what Canadians actually watch on television. Within the discussion of television programming and audience choice, we will also briefly discuss the digital television rollout that took place in September, 2001. The new digital channels shed considerable light on the future of television in Canada, in particular because they foreground the triangulation of cable industry, television audience and technological capability and access. It goes some way to express the anxiety felt by the industry with respect to capturing new growth markets, as the penetration of cable across the country appears to have peaked. The annual television season begins in September, with the summer usually left open for tinkering with the schedules, dumping programs that didn't make it during the regular season, and planning new programming for the fall. For the purposes of this chapter, we have chosen to examine closely the period from September 2000 until August 2001. This flexibility with the time constraints allows us to draw a more comprehensive picture of the challenges facing television today.

The Status of the Canadian Television Industry

The picture presented by the Canadian Cable Television Association, based on data provided by the 1999 Statistics Canada census, suggests that television is by far the most prevalent medium in the home. While pundits extol the rapid rise to technological prominence of the Internet, only 33.2 per cent of Canadian homes were actually connected. In comparison, 99 per cent of Canadian homes have at least one colour television and almost 90 per cent have a VCR. That means more people are likely watching television than listening to music (70.3 per cent own a CD player), playing computer games (49.8 per cent own a personal computer) or even talking on the telephone (98.4 per cent). However, the picture isn't entirely rosy for television as a medium. Typical Canadian television viewing hours have been slowly declining over the last decade and reached an all-time low in 1999 with a national average of 21.6 hours per week, or slightly more than three hours per day. This is a decrease of almost two hours per week from the 1988 high of 23.5, and it represents an across-the-board reduction for all demographic groups. Interestingly, in the wake of expanded home cinema technology, increasing DVD sales and the growth of specialty movie channels, television is struggling to compete with its old nemesis, film, as well as the upstart Internet. Movie attendance continues to rise and reached a thirty-eight-year high of 112.8 million, while Internet use also rose (Statistics Canada 2001a). So while television still dominates the media market in Canada, the gap may be starting to close. Furthermore, Canadians may start using their television sets for other things, such as movie rentals or even Web surfing. Since the industry depends on viewers watching their programming, and more importantly, their commercials, the ownership of a television is not the best marker for its popularity as an information and entertainment medium. Thus, the pressure is on the television industry to find new markets and introduce new technologies that will lead to expansion.

If there is one thing that seems certain, the era of the rabbit ears is finally at a close. For decades since the arrival of television in Canada, the image of the rural, northern family struggling with antennas in the vain hope of getting a decent picture for *Hockey Night in Canada* has stood as a symbol of Canada's lack of a viable media market. Today, Canada is a leader in new television broadcasting technology. According to the Canadian Cable Television Association (CCTA), over eleven million Canadian homes have at least one television. Of those, 10.5 million (92 per cent of the total) are cable-ready, and more than nine million (74 per cent), are cable subscribers. This means that cable companies have an untapped market of less than 20 per cent, or just under three million Canadian homes (CCTA 2001). These figures do not take into account those who have abandoned cable as a delivery technology and have switched to satellite television. The market for satellite television remains small in comparison to cable, but already 10 per cent of Canadian homes have at least one satellite hookup, either in conjunction with or in place of cable. The most successful regions for satellite market penetration are remote, rural or northern communities. Currently, cable companies recognize "underserved" areas as only 9 per cent of their total market. The costs associated with introducing a cable grid to areas with scattered population may mitigate the industry's growth in that area (CCTA 2001) so there is no real expectation for that number to drop. The Satellite Communications Association of Canada argues that the primary target market for consumer growth lies in rural regions that are not adequately served by cable nor are likely to be in the future.[2] For now, cable still holds the majority of the television broadcasting market, and the industry is launching a major challenge to satellite companies with the promotion of new digital television channels. Nearly every Canadian home with cable also has access to digital cable, with a difference of less than 100,000 homes between the two totals. However, only 6.5 per cent of cable subscribers have purchased the additional equipment and subscribed to the expanded grid. The other major driver of cable industry growth is high-speed Internet access through cable modems. There, too, the numbers are still quite small. Only 930,000, or 12.5 per cent of potential customers, have signed on to high-speed cable access. While this is a major leap from the 479,000 customers in 1999, there are still seven million more homes to attract to this new service, while other high-speed services from private ISPs or telephone companies are also increasing their services.

Figures indicate that cable penetration grew steadily throughout the 1990s but has slowed as we passed into the twenty-first century. It now appears as if the cable market in Canada may be saturated. Between 1996 and 2000, an additional 220,000 Canadian homes were passed by cable, raising the number of potential subscribers from 10.2 million to 10.5 million. However, only 80,000 of these homes took advantage of their new access, leaving 140,000 homes who have either rejected cable television or have found other means such as satellite technology to provide them with the programming they want. According to the CCTA, that net gain of 80,000 homes came on the heels of a significant loss of 106,000 subscribers in the 1999/2000 year. Cable subscriber growth has been minimal for a number of years. In 1998 and 1999, it was less than 1 per cent. In 2000, the cable growth number was negative, a drop of 1.3 per cent. While precise figures are not available, it seems logical to infer that the decline in cable subscriptions is more accurately seen as consumers switching to satellite than to abandoning television altogether. However, there is still cause for anxiety among broadcasters. As options expand, a larger audience is required to maintain healthy ratings. Indeed, the television audience may be tapped out. It is possible that in the current situation it is now simply a matter of dividing a smaller pie among a rapidly increasing group of hungry broadcasters.

The stability of Canadian cable penetration does not necessarily correlate with increased profitability for the television broadcast industry as a whole. For example, the Maritimes boast the highest cable subscriber rates in the country. New Brunswick and Prince Edward Island lead the way with 87 per cent of all homes passed by cable hooked up, 13 per cent higher than the national average. However, their private television broadcasters posted revenue declines of 8.3 per cent in 2000 (Statistics Canada 2001b). Part of the discrepancy between cable access and broadcasting revenue can be explained through an examination of the demographics of television viewers in Canada. Specifically, 43 per cent of households with televisions have annual household incomes of less than $35,000, and only 20 per cent are in the highest income bracket of $75,000 or more. It's not surprising that lower income households tend to rely on television for their entertainment needs, since television is relatively low-cost compared to live performances and the cinema. However, as the television industry seeks to increase their offerings and new technological innovations are introduced into the market, the cost of keeping up continues to rise. Comprehensive satellite and digital cable subscriptions cost approximately $100 a month, not including any start-up costs for equipment or hook-up fees. Additionally, advertisers keep a close eye on who is watching television to ensure that they are reaching desirable consumers. In the 2000/2001 season, less than half the households with televisions in Canada had viewers with a university education, and slightly less than a third were listed as professionals. That could raise concerns about the levels of disposable income available in most television households. On the plus side, out of a total of approximately thirty million potential viewers, about half were in the advertiser-friendly 18 to 49 demographic, the age group most coveted by advertisers.

As we have already noted, another major problem facing the Canadian broadcast industry is a fracturing of the audience. Lower audience shares affect advertising revenue. As the cable grid extends beyond a hundred channels, viewer choice takes on a kind of elephantine quality that the cable companies are having difficulty controlling. Cable television subscriptions are divided between basic channels and extended options that are sold in packages. Basic cable usually is confined to major Canadian and American network affiliates, mandatory carriage services required by CRTC regulations (such as NewsWorld, APTN and cable community access channels), as well as a smattering of specialty channels such as YTV, Vision or MuchMusic that have broad-based appeal. The basic cable offerings in Canada are usually kept minimal so that cable companies can offer specialty channels to consumers at a higher rate. While there are dozens of specialty channels, many of them duplicating their services in both official languages, the ones that offer news or family-oriented programming tend to have the highest rates of subscription. In other words, the cable companies have given priority to those specialty channels that attract the most general audience. The channels with the most narrow appeal tend to be clustered in smaller, more expensive packages. In English Canada, The Weather Channel is the most widely offered specialty channel, with more than 9.8 million homes receiving the service. After that, NewsWorld follows closely behind at 8.9 million homes,

Rebecca Sullivan and Bart Beaty

Table 1 Canadian Specialty Channels: Monthly Customers 2000
(English Language)

Weather Channel	9.8m
NewsWorld	8.9m
YTV	8.3m
TSN	8.1m
CMT	7.6m
Vision	7.2m
CTV NewsNet	7.1m
CTV SportsNet	7.1m
CPAC	7.0m
MuchMusic	6.9m

Source: Canadian Cable Television Association. 2001. *Annual Report 2000/2001.*

Table 2 Canadian Specialty Channels: Monthly Customers 2000
(French Language)

MéteoMédia*	9.8m
RDI	8.0m
TV5	6.7m
CanalFamille	2.3m
RDS	2.1m
MusiquePlus	2.1m

*jointly reported with the Weather Channel

Source: Canadian Cable Television Association. 2001. *Annual Report 2000/2001.*

Table 3 Top Ten Canadian Specialty Cable Channels 2000–01:
Real vs. Potential Viewers

Channel	Base	Reach (%)	Share (%)
Weather Channel	9.8m	27* (10)***	0.8** (17)***
NewsWorld	8.9m	32 (6)	1.4 (7)
YTV	8.3m	38 (2)	2.8 (2)
TSN	8.1m	42 (1)	3.1 (1)
CMT	7.6m	22 (20)	0.8 (16)
Vision	7.2m	14 (24)	0.4 (24)
CTV NewsNet	7.1m	22 (19)	0.6 (20)
CTV SportsNet	7.1m	31 (5)	1.2 (11)
CPAC	7.0m	---****	---
MuchMusic	6.9m	34 (3)	1.1 (12)

* percentage of cable customers who tune in once per week
** percentage of time spent by cable customers watching this channel
*** ranking compared to all specialty cable channels
****CPAC falls out of the top 25 and therefore was not listed in our data

Source: Canadian Cable Television Association. 2001. *Annual Report 2000/2001.*

with other news, information and family viewing channels rounding out the top ten (see Table 1).

French-language specialty channels show similar composition, with news, information and family viewing holding the highest numbers (see Table 2). It is worth pointing out that the numbers are significantly smaller. MusiquePlus has only 2.1 million customers, five million fewer than their English counterpart, and Canal Famille has six million fewer customers than YTV.

There is, however, a significant difference between customers and viewers. Cable companies refer to audience ratings for specialty channels as "reach." They base reach on the percentage of viewers who are subscribed to a channel and who actually watch something on it at least once per week. The more significant number, however, is "share." That is the percentage of time spent by cable customers watching that particular channel. Table 3 shows the difference between subscriber base, reach and share. It is important to note that since cable companies prefer to offer pre-set packages, the subscriber rate for certain specialty channels in no way actually reflects viewership, ratings or popularity. TSN enjoys the highest rate of viewership, or reach, of the specialty channels, with 42 per cent of cable customers tuning in that channel at least once per week. YTV follows closely behind with 38 per cent reach. The channel with the greatest subscription base in Canada, The Weather Network, has a smaller reach of only 27 per cent. CMT and Vision fare the worst of the major specialty channels with only 22 per cent and 14 per cent reach, respectively. For French-language specialty channels, out of the top five for cable penetration, only two stay at that level in terms of reach. RDS has the highest reach at 43 per cent, with RDI following closely with 42 per cent (see Table 3).

In recent years, specialty and pay-TV services have taken on increasing prominence in the Canadian television viewing spectrum. According to Statistics Canada, specialty and pay-TV channels captured nearly 30 per cent of total viewing hours during the 2000/2001 season. That leaves conventional Canadian and foreign stations that rely on advertisers for the majority of their revenue battling for only 65 per cent of the overall audience share. At the time of the launch of Canadian pay-TV in the early 1980s, conventional television's audience share was at 99 per cent, but in the intervening two decades specialty channels have significantly eroded that figure (Statistics Canada 2001c). This is bad news for network television that relies on generalized programming to reach a wide audience but could be good news for cable companies who hope to attract more customers with specialized pack-

Rebecca Sullivan and Bart Beaty

ages. While it may resolve some of the immediate issues about a flatlined industry, without high audience numbers broadcasting profits may face a decline, sending the industry as a whole into a downward spiral. Already, optional tier penetration is quite high, with 90 per cent of Canadian homes having access to these specialty channels. Further, 87 per cent of cable customers with access to optional tiers subscribe to at least one, again suggesting that we are on the cusp of market saturation. This means that, if a home decides to subscribe to cable, they're highly likely to expend on increased options to maximize their television viewing options. Out of the 7.7 million Canadian homes that have subscribed to cable, 6.7 million have subscribed to an optional tier. Further, the CCTA notes that an additional two million cable subscribers have also added pay-TV to their total television package. Revenue for specialty channels has risen accordingly. According to the CCTA, at the start of the 2000/2001 season, specialty channel revenues, including advertising and subscriptions, were slightly over $1 billion, while pay-TV subscriptions accounted for an additional $213 million in annual revenues. Pay-TV's lower revenues reflect the absence of advertising on their channels, which accounts for about 40 per cent of specialty service revenue, but it also incorporates money from satellite services who pick up their signal (ccta.ca). Movie channels such as MoviePix and The Movie Network enjoy the highest penetration of all the pay-TV channels, with 760,100 and 679,300 monthly subscribers, respectively. The only French-language pay-TV channel in the top five is also a movies channel, Super Écran, with 325,300 monthly subscribers. Interestingly, specialty channel viewing (including pay-TV) is cutting mostly into U.S. broadcasting audiences. In 1989, specialty services had only a 13.8 per cent audience share compared to 31.3 per cent for U.S. broadcasters. In 2001, according to the Canadian Cable Television Association, specialty services had risen by more than 300 per cent to a 48.4 per cent audience share while U.S. broadcasters plummeted to almost half their previous share, 16.1 per cent. That said, Canadian network broadcasters are not safe from the influx of specialty services. Their audience share dropped from 54.8 per cent to 35.5 per cent for English-language channels. For French-language specialty services, audience share has more than doubled, from 14.3 per cent to 31.7 per cent. While that is bad news for Canadian broadcasters on basic cable such as the CBC, CTV and Global, it could potentially be good for cable companies as they expand their grids to attract more and more subscribers.

Table 4 The Canadian Cable Market 2000

Rogers Cable	Central Canada	157 systems	29% of total cable subscribers
Shaw Cable	Western Canada	128 systems	28% of total cable subscribers
Vidéotron	Quebec	53 systems	18% of total cable subscribers
COGECO	Ontario	144 systems	11% of total cable subscribers
EastLink	Eastern Canada	70 systems	2% of total cable subscribers

Source: Canadian Cable Television Association. 2001. *Annual Report 2000/2001.*

Despite the widespread growth of viewing options in Canada, it cannot necessarily be said that competition is growing within the industry. Consolidation in the Canadian television industry has led to serious questions about how we define choice or diversity in the Canadian media environment. The largest cable systems – Class 1 systems that have 6,000 or more subscribers – dominate the Canadian market. There are 140 Class 1 cable systems in Canada, and they control 86.2 per cent of the cable market. In contrast, there are over 1,700 smaller Class 3 systems – those with fewer than 2,000 subscribers – but they only have 8.9 per cent of the total cable market. Five companies control over 88 per cent of the total Canadian cable market (see Table 4).

What becomes apparent is the regional domination within the industry as each cable company has carved out a territory and laid claim to it. This trend has quickened its pace with the swap of cable assets between Rogers Communications Inc. and Shaw Communications Inc. in March 2000. Under the agreement, each relinquished control over systems in the other company's major region so that Rogers would be the most dominant provider in the east and Shaw would control the west. Vidéotron continues to hold strong in Quebec, relying on its French-language selection, while Eastlink remains viable in the Maritimes. Thus, viewer choice occurs only at the micro level. While the cable companies may work to provide more channel selection, there is nothing in the way of direct competition for pricing or access. Increasingly, the only option for dedicated television viewers who are unsatisfied with their cable service is satellite. Currently, Bell ExpressVu and StarChoice dominate the satellite market. The former, especially, has made aggressive moves against smaller satellite providers in the quest for control of the potentially lucrative satellite television market by trying to oust small providers that use grey-market feeds from the U.S.[3] Still, with only 10 per cent of the television households subscribing to satellite services, the era of true consumer choice in the way that Canadians access television programming is still very much a non-reality. As the cable and satellite industry battle for a limited number of subscribers (there are, after all, only thirty

Rebecca Sullivan and Bart Beaty

million people in Canada – about the same as the number of Americans that watch ER in a regular week), the broadcasters suffer the most with an increasingly fractured audience. There is, therefore, a vested interest in actually consolidating ownership between content and service providers, not so much to offer expanded programming, but to expand the venues to air the same programming repeatedly. The question of audience, therefore, is rarely bound to the needs and desires of viewers, but rather to their value to advertisers as consumers. It is perhaps for that reason that Canadian television advocates continue to appeal to a nebulous sense of national identity founded on fur, farms, and fish while marginalizing those very viewers who still make their living in this way.

Governmental Intervention in the Television Industry

Other than satellite or just throwing your TV out the window, *à la* SCTV, the only recourse open to cable television subscribers is the Canadian Radio-Television and Telecommunications Commission (CRTC). This government agency oversees all aspects of television, from programming content to broadcast licences and carriage services. In the 2000/2001 season, the CRTC was kept busy responding to massive changes in the television landscape as companies switched properties, swallowed up competitors, and joined forces with other media outlets to transform the industry. The cable systems swap between Rogers and Shaw was merely the tip of the iceberg. In September 2000, Rogers expanded its entertainment orientation by acquiring a controlling interest in the Toronto Blue Jays baseball team. At the same time, they also purchased CTV SportsNet, ensuring a media outlet for their sports franchise. In November, they launched a television-based Internet service, anticipating a future for interactive television. Consolidation of the eastern cable systems continued, with Rogers' purchase of Newfoundland's Cable Atlantic. Not to be outdone, Shaw purchased the Manitoba-based Moffat Communication in March 2001 and ordered an additional 250,000 cable modems to strengthen the cable industry's lead position in high-speed Internet connections. Not all of the mergers and acquisitions reaffirmed television's position on top of the Canadian media industries. Quebecor, the printing and publishing giant, purchased le Groupe Vidéotron ltée in October 2000, thus adding to its stockpile a majority ownership of cable and broadcasting services in Quebec. Meanwhile BCE purchased CTV. That means that in addition to owning Bell ExpressVu, it also owns the largest privately owned national network in Canada, along with specialty services such as ROB-TV (purchased earlier in the year from CanWest), TSN, the Comedy Network, the History Channel and Outdoor Life Network. BCE is also the owner of the *Globe & Mail*, Canada's major national newspaper, and Sympatico Internet service. Rogers, meanwhile, is continuing to expand both its cable services and its programming content. In addition to its majority (80 per cent) ownership of SportsNet, it has also invested in Biography Channel, Outdoor Life Network, MSNBC and Viewer's Choice, to name a few. Shaw owns Corus Entertainment, which in turn owns a number of popular specialty channels, including YTV, WTN, the Food Network and Teletoon. It is clear, therefore, that 2000/2001 saw enormous steps forward in terms of the conglomeration of the Canadian television industry and its merger with other industries into massive media monopolies. The increasing consolidation of this industry poses a number of possible problems for Canadian television viewers, who are largely absent from discussions about the changing television landscape.

As the line between content providers and broadcast distributors becomes increasingly more fluid, television audiences could be the major losers. No example drives this point home better than the acquisition of Salter Street Films Limited by Alliance Atlantis in February 2001. Prior to the acquisition, the two companies had been bitter rivals in efforts to secure a licence for a new digital television channel that would focus on independent film. Alliance was considered the favourite as it was much larger, was centrally located in Toronto, and had developed a reputation for edgy cinematic programming with its existing Showcase cable channel. Salter Street, by contrast, was based in Halifax and was best known as the originator of the popular CBC television show *This Hour Has 22 Minutes*. It was a shock, then, that the CRTC ultimately awarded the licence to Salter Street. Nonplussed, Alliance simply acquired Salter Street and the broadcasting licence. Alliance was quite blunt in stating that gaining control of the Independent Film Channel was their real intention. "We believe that the specialty channel business, particularly the 'Category 1' *Independent Film Channel Canada*, is an excellent fit with Alliance Atlantis' growth strategy for our Broadcast Group and presents tremendous opportunities to further exploit our extensive motion picture library," stated Michael MacMillan, Chairman and Chief Executive Officer of the company (Alliance Atlantis, 2001). So, months after deciding that Alliance-Atlantis should not own the Independent Film Channel, the CRTC quickly ruled in favour of its acquisition, thus ensuring further consolidation of the television industry in the wake of major channel expansion. While the CRTC could have theoretically blocked the acquisition or withdrawn the licence for the digital channel, that would have been a radical break from the Commission's laissez-faire, pro-business attitude.

There are some outlets beyond the CRTC for consumers frustrated with growing regional monopolies and industry consolidation. The Canadian Cable Television Association maintains the Cable Television Standards Foundation, which hears complaints from the public about television service. According to their 2000/2001 annual report (CCTA 2001), the two primary complaints related to the French specialty service rollout in Quebec and the mandatory inclusion of APTN, the Aboriginal Peoples Television Network, on basic cable at a cost to the consumer. The most prevalent complaints tend to be about quality of service or billing practices. However, a number of complaints concerning programming and digital TV services suggest that cable television consumers are continuing to demand increased choice, selection and flexibility in determining their channel grid. This is not really good news for the industry, as it makes it difficult to sell a faceless "mass" audience to advertisers. This is likely to be the most significant challenge facing television broadcasters as consumers become more technologically adept and other media make inroads into home leisure time. As the industry struggles to convince viewers to upgrade their technology for bigger, better (and pricier) programming choices, they are contributing to lower ratings across the grid for individual channels. This makes programming consistency more difficult, which in turn leads to viewer disgruntlement and a slow but steady decline in actual viewing hours. Change to this business model for television will come slowly, as all channels must submit to periodic review by the CRTC and apply to have their programming policy changed in any significant way.

The CRTC passed approximately a thousand decisions during the 2000/2001 television season, and none of these was particularly earth-shattering. CRTC rulings tend to be primarily concerned with licences and Canadian content regulations. While the former is more often than not a "rubber stamp" exercise, the latter speaks to a constant push-and-pull game between the industry's desire to increase profitability and nationalist concerns over cultural sovereignty that could potentially cut into revenues. This past year, the two largest national private networks, CTV and Global, were both up for licence renewal. Although CTV was in the process of being purchased by BCE, the renewal was approved despite the fact that the company was in the midst of a major reorganization of holdings and subsidiary ownership. Other licence renewals were approved by the CRTC this year also without incident, including RDS, TSN, TLA, Vision, CMT, Showcase, Life and TVA. A number of new channels received their first broadcast licences, although few received the coveted Category 1 classification that guarantees their presence on basic cable grids. The last channel to gain that clearance was APTN in 2000, and that decision led to a small controversy over its mandatory inclusion because a cable channel dedicated to aboriginal issues and native-language programming was seen to have limited appeal. When APTN was first launched, it had the unusually high Canadian content requirement of 90 per cent. However, after its first year of operation the channel applied for and received a reduction in its Canadian content to 70 per cent and is now allowed to run infomercials in overnight time slots.

APTN was the only broadcaster lucky in its attempts to reduce Canadian content. Life, WTN and Bravo all applied to have their commitments to Canadian content reduced, and none met with much success. The case of Bravo illustrates the degree to which Canadian content is a highly contentious issue, subject to microcosmic finagling between private companies and public watchdogs. At the time of its application, Bravo's requirement was to air 60 per cent Canadian content between 6:00 a.m. and 6:00 p.m., 50 per cent Canadian content between 6:00 p.m. and midnight, and no required Canadian content from midnight until 6:00 a.m. Bravo's owner, CHUM, proposed expanding the broadcast day to twenty-four hours with a round-the-clock requirement of 50 per cent. They argued that it would in fact increase total hours of Canadian programming from 10.8 hours per day to twelve hours. Critics of the plan included the Canadian Film and Television Production Association, the Directors' Guild of Canada and national newscaster Don Cameron. They noted that the slight increase in Canadian programming would come during the overnight hours at the expense of daytime programming. Since very few people stay up all night to watch Bravo, the actual reach for this programming would likely be reduced. The Director's Guild further proposed that Bravo's Canadian content requirement actually be increased to 60 per cent for the entire broadcast day, eliminating the prime time reduction. In light of this opposition, CHUM agreed to maintain the requirements as they stood and their motion was denied by the CRTC. This appears on the surface to be a victory for Canadian television producers, but it also speaks to the continuing need for content regulations at this time. While some may have hoped that a time would come in Canadian television where national programming would find an audience without relying on governmental intervention, evidence suggests that the gap between Canadian television producers and audiences continues to widen.

Patterns of Television Viewing in Canada

The most obvious competitors vying for Canadian television audiences are American broadcasters and television producers. This point was driven home in the 2000/2001 season when the announcement of the Canadian television schedule was delayed. According to a report in the *Toronto Star*, both CTV and Global were waiting for the American schedule to be finalized before scheduling their own programs. The U.S. schedule was hamstrung by political wrangling over the dates for presidential debates between Al Gore and George W. Bush. Since both Canadian networks rely overwhelmingly on the simultaneous substitution of American shows, they could not proceed until the American schedules were announced (September 19, 2000). Only five new Canadian dramatic programs debuted on the three major Canadian networks for the 2000/2001 season, and only one of those was from a privately owned network. Global debuted *Blackfly*, a "Canadian history with a twist" sitcom set in the eighteenth century, involving the antics between various backwoodsmen and representatives of the English monarchy at the fur-trading post of Fort Simpson-Eaton. CBC came through with four new programs. They included the more serious take on Canada's origins, *Canada: A People's History*; *Our Hero*, a youth-oriented sitcom about a teenage girl who uses her 'zine to help her sort out life's problems; *PR*, the satire on the public relations business featuring former *Kids in the Hall* writer Diane Flacks; and *These Arms of Mine*, a one-hour drama about the interconnected lives of Vancouver-based professionals. These five shows joined a growing yet uneven existing roster of Canadian-based dramatic programming on network television.

The Canadian television production industry seems split between the development of shows with strong national appeal and those developed for the international syndicated market. The growing acrimony between Hollywood and the Canadian film and television industry is predicated on independent companies relying on Canadian tax breaks, favourable currency conversion and relaxed union relations for their less prestigious productions. While some may argue against any suggestion that Canadian television is not always of the highest quality, a glance at the 2001 Gemini Award nominations reveals some strange discrepancies. While critically acclaimed programs such as *DaVinci's Inquest, Traders* and *Drop the Beat* were well represented, so too were such low-budget genre fare as the science-fiction programs *The Outer Limits* and *StarGate SG-1*. Canadian-based representation prevailed with the winners for best comedy series, *Made in Canada*, and best dramatic series, *DaVinci's Inquest*; however, the award for best mini-series went to a program that few would have recognized as Canadian. *Nuremberg*, starring Alec Baldwin and Jill Hennessey, was a co-production with the Ted Turner-owned specialty channel TNT.

The Gemini awards for 2001 highlight the growing divide between the economics and the ideology facing Canadian television. Nationalist rhetoric falters in the face of increasing globalization. Production companies rely on Canadian content regulations and government incentive programs to maintain their viability in a competitive market. Unfortunately, that too often leads to conceptual leaps about what Canadians actually watch and how television helps to shape cultural identities. A glance at the Nielsen national ratings tells a different story than what Canadian cultural nationalists may want to hear.

Trying to gain a reasonably comprehensive understanding of Canadian television ratings is a rather daunting proposition. National numbers are broken down between English- and French-language television. English-language television viewing is not measured in Quebec. Additionally, Global television is not recognized as a national network so, going by Nielsen reports, CBC and CTV dominate the English market and Global programs remain unmeasured. Unfortunately, there's no way to really overcome these omissions without establishing a rival ratings bureau. Looking at the ratings for regular programming during the 2000/2001 season, the most interesting thing about the top twenty shows on CTV and CBC is that only two are Canadian, and neither are indigenous, dramatic programs. *Hockey Night in Canada* at number 11, and *The CTV Sunday Movie* (which actually shows American films almost exclusively) at number 13, are the only Canadian-produced entries. The rest are U.S.-based network and syndicated programs. In the top ten are *ER, Ally McBeal, Third Watch, The West Wing, The Mole, Law and Order: SVU, CSI, Law and Order, Who Wants to be a Millionaire* and *The Sopranos*. There are a few points worth mentioning about this list. Numbers 2 and 3 are far from the top rankings on U.S. television. *Ally McBeal* enjoyed critical and commercial success in its first two seasons, but the show has declined significantly and routinely fails to crack the top twenty. *Third Watch* has struggled since its debut for

Table 5 Top Ten Shows in Canada: National vs. Regional Differences

National		Vancouver		Toronto	
CTV	ER	CKVU	Survivor:Aus/Outback	GLBL	Survivor:Aus/Outback
CTV	Ally McBeal	CHAN	ER	CTV	ER
CTV	Third Watch	CHAN	The West Wing	CTV	Law and Order
CTV	The West Wing	CIVT	Law and Order	CITY	Temptation Island
CTV	The Mole	CHAN	Nash Bridges	GLBL	Lone Gunmen
CTV	Law and Order: SVU	CHAN	Dark Angel	CTV	The West Wing
CTV	CSI	CBUT	Canada: Peoples Hist	GLBL	X Files
CTV	Law and Order	CHAN	Third Watch	GLBL	Practice
CTV	Who ... Millionaire	CKVU	NYPD Blue	GLBL	Boston Public
CTV	The Sopranos	CHAN	Ally McBeal	CBC	Canada: Peoples Hist

Source: Nielsen Media Research *TV Insights 2001.*

audiences, and ABC's *The Mole* was generally considered a ratings failure in the U.S. Noticeably absent are such standard top ten shows from the U.S. such as *Friends, Frasier, Everybody Loves Raymond* and *Survivor*. These shows are broadcast on Global Television and are therefore not measured nationally in Canada, which tends to skew shows on CBC and CTV higher in the rankings than they should actually be. What's left is an incomplete and rather dubious picture of what Canadians watch. The only way to factor in these shows is to examine regional urban numbers (see Table 5). According to Nielsen data for the Toronto and Vancouver markets, the most watched show last year was *Survivor: Australian Outback*, followed by *ER*. Interestingly, CBC's *Canada: A People's History* ranked in the top ten most watched shows in Vancouver and Toronto but was not as successful on a national scale. This challenges the romantic notion of our national culture that we have noted as speaking to everyday Canadians. Instead, these efforts to bond across the country merely cluster in the densely populated urban centres where cultural politics are the stuff of cocktail banter. In Maritime fishing towns or Prairie farms, the interest in such debates falters in the face of American popular programming.

There are some issues regarding the top ten Canadian programs that should be noted. *The Sopranos*, a critically acclaimed series that began on the American cable network HBO in 1998, debuted on Canadian network television. It drew a great deal of attention, and not all of it was positive. The Canadian Broadcast Standards Council received complaints from viewers offended by the show's sexual and violent content, unprecedented for network television on both sides of the border. As well, the National Congress of Italian Canadians protested what they perceived as the portrayal of negative ethnic stereotypes. In the midst of the controversy, CTV aired the first episode on September 17, 2000, and took sixth place overall in the September ratings. The rest of the episodes ranked from ninth to seventeenth, except for episode 11 (not the season finale) at number 3. The only other shows to even appear on the top twenty rankings for the month of September were *Who Wants to be a Millionaire*, *ER* and the *Emmy Awards*. In 2001, the CBSC ruled in favour of CTV that they had provided adequate warnings of explicit content and did not offend community standards or ethnic values. Ironically, this success was presented as evidence of Canadian audience sophistication. *TV Guide* noted with pride that even FOX had turned down *The Sopranos* when it was originally pitched to the network but Canadian audiences could handle the challenging content. In Canada, the largest number of complaints were that CTV was delaying broadcast of seasons two and three (May 26–28, 2001). Of course, it can only be assumed that part of the reason why CTV was airing the first season was to lure viewers into purchasing The Movie Network, owned by Viewer's Choice, a subsidiary of CTV and the original home to the show in Canada. Therefore they were likely in no great hurry to give away for free one of their more lucrative shows for the specialty channel. This is another example of the industry trying to gain a kind of two-for-one rating from the limited Canadian audience in order to defy the realities of a flatlined industry. If CTV can lure viewers away from their network programming to their specialty cable offerings, then it appears as if they have expanded their audience share. In reality, they've only shifted the audience around in order to spur growth on one end of the business at the expense of the other.

Where Canadian programming does begin to show signs of success is with sports. It is perhaps here that Canadian culture receives its due from television. That in turn challenges liberal nationalist ideals for a decidedly highbrow, or at least middlebrow, Canadian media. Canadians appear to enjoy sports events more than regular dramatic programming. The top-ranked sports program on English national networks for the 2000/2001 season was the CFL championship Grey Cup game on November 26, 2000. It actually beat the number one dramatic series in Canada, *ER*, with 1.3 million viewers compared to *ER*'s seasonal average of one million. The top four sports programs all had higher average audiences than the second-ranked dramatic series, *Ally McBeal*, which attracted an average of 811,000 viewers. Rounding out the top five are all NHL broadcasts, three of them playoff rounds, and the All-Star game. *Hockey Night in Canada*, the only Canadian program to appear in the top twenty for regular programs, is listed as seventh, four positions higher than it appears in the regular program ratings. Again, there are issues with the collection of data since TSN is not considered a national network but a specialty service. The NFL appears nowhere in the rankings, again because Global Television owns the rights for Canadian broadcasting, although the Superbowl outperformed the Grey Cup in Toronto (but not in Vancouver). The Olympics also ranked high in the ratings, although it was decidedly more popular in Quebec. The opening and closing ceremonies were ranked first and third, respectively, and there were four other Olympic broadcasts in the Quebec top twenty. For English Canada, the opening ceremonies failed to crack the top twenty and the closing ceremonies were only ranked eighth. By contrast, the CFL enjoyed seeing all their playoff rounds in the top twenty for English Canada while not even making the cut in Quebec, whose top twenty is exclusively devoted to hockey and the Olympics.

With regular dramatic programming in an uphill battle for recognition, it is not surprising that Canadian television producers are looking to specialty or niche market programming for the industry's health. In 2001 the big news was the digital channel rollout to commence in the 2001/2002 season. It was touted as the largest expansion of a cable grid anywhere in the world (Canadian Association of Broadcasters 2001). The CRTC vetted 450 proposals for channels ranging from the International Film Channel to the Tamil Channel. In the end, they granted sixteen English-language and five French-language licences for Category 1 services, channels that must be offered by cable systems; and 262 Category 2, or optional-carriage, licences. The most important factor is that the CRTC decided to allow cable companies to actually have a share in the ownership of these new digital channels. That means that both the content provider and the broadcaster can now be the same organization, further concentrating the market into the hands of a select few. The English-language Category 1 channels and their principal owners are:

- Biography (Rogers)
- BookTV (CHUM)
- MTV-Canada (Craig)
- Country Canada (Corus, a subsidiary of Shaw)
- Discovery Health (Alliance-Atlantis)
- The Documentary Channel (Corus)
- Fashion TV (CHUM)
- I-Channel (Stornaway)
- The Independent Film Channel (Alliance-Atlantis)

- Men-TV (CanWest-Global)
- The Mystery Channel (CanWest-Global)
- One: Body, Mind and Spirit (Vision)
- PrideVision (Headline Media)
- Tech-TV (Rogers)
- The Travel Channel (Bell Globemedia)
- Women's Television Sports Network (Bell Globemedia).

French-language channels are Réseau Info Sports (BCE Media, RDS), 13ième Rue (Rogers/Global/TVA), LCN Affaires (TVA, Publications Transcontinental Inc./BCE Media), Télé Ha Ha (TVA, Film Rozon Inc., BCE Media), and Perfecto la Chaîne (MusiquePlus). At a glance, it is noted that cable companies have ownership positions in eleven of the twenty-one new channels. On that point, Rogers-owned channels are all joint ventures with U.S.-based companies, and many of the channels are Canadianized versions of existing American specialty services, like the Biography Channel, and MTV-Canada (which is actually a child-oriented affairs and issues station, not music video). Unlike non-digital specialty services that have very high Canadian content requirements, the standard is set at 15 per cent for all channels in their first year. So even though television-viewing options are expanding, perhaps even exploding, in Canada, Canadian content providers face a difficult battle to have their products broadcast over existing American shows. They also must contend with significantly reduced audience share as the market fractures and ad revenue drops. Recent rulings by the CRTC will only make this harder since cable companies now not only have a stake in certain specialty channels but also partner those channels with American counterparts to repackage programming for a Canadian audience. This sets the stage for a very interesting 2001/2002 television season as the duelling forces of industry consolidation, technological advancement and audience demands reshape the television landscape.

Conclusion

It is quite likely that the turn of this century will be looked back upon as a key transitional phase for Canadian television. The heightened activity to consolidate media empires for a global marketplace began in earnest in 2000. The digital rollout the year after was a huge gamble for the cable industry

Rebecca Sullivan and Bart Beaty

and Canadian content providers alike, binding technological and economic convergence even tighter than before. The consumer response could have major ramifications on how the television industry conducts business for years to come. In the meantime, it is stepping up the rhetoric for the future of television: interactive television, Web-TV, digital recording (such as TiVO) and on-demand broadcasting are just some of the services being promised for the future. However, it is highly unlikely that any of these will be delivered immediately. For now, the health of the industry lies in traditional cable and in the start-up business of digital cable, giving satellite broadcasting its first real competition. And television viewers appear content to remain as viewers, and not to turn their televisions into full-time video game consoles or Web browsers.

Yet, the industry needs to find ways to stop itself from flatlining, as it appears to be doing in terms of cable penetration, broadcasting profits and weekly viewership. So it continues to promise whole new levels of technological capability that will revolutionize the medium. Already the hype has begun for high definition television (HDTV), which is anticipated to take hold in 2004 when broadcasters switch their signals to the expanded broadband. We can only speculate on what this will mean in terms of costs to the consumer as we will be encouraged to reinvest in all-new television technology. The gap between media rich and poor looks likely to widen. The question is how this will play out across the Canadian landscape, both economically and geographically. While technological innovation with home sets or broadcasting signals are treated as the hope for the future, Canadian content providers are seemingly left out in the cold. The low Canadian content regulations for the new digital cable channels may be a portent of relaxing controls as it becomes increasingly harder to fill up the airwaves and as the industry itself becomes more oriented toward globalization. The dream of national television produced by and for Canadians forming the cornerstone of the industry is drifting away. There's a new dream now of unlimited viewer choice, but it cloaks a nightmarish vision of media monopolies and limited opportunities for Canadian voices to find an audience.

Works Cited

Alliance Atlantis. 2001. "Alliance Atlantis Reaches Agreement to Acquire Salter Street Films," Available: http://www.allianceatlantis.com/corporate/press_media/archived_inv_releases/AAC01_09.html

Canadian Association of Broadcasters. 2001. *Canada Makes Television History with Largest Digital Channel Launch*. News release. Toronto: CAB Newsroom, September 7.

Canadian Cable Television Association. 2001. *Annual Report 2000/2001*. Available: http://www.ccta.com/english/publications/annual-reports/.

CRTC Multiple Ownership Charts. Available: http://www.crtc.gc.ca/ownership/eng/title_org.htm.

Nielsen Media Research. 2001. TV Insights 2001 (CD-ROM). Toronto: Nielsen Media Research.

Satellite Communications Association of Canada. 1999. "Ian Angus, a very important letter to various Government Departments" Available: http://www.scacanada.com/angus.html

———. 2001. "Bell Canada is a Bully!!!" Available: http://www.scacanada.com/bellbully.html

Statistics Canada. 2001a. "Television Viewing". *The Daily*, January 25. Available: http://www.statcan.ca/Daily/English/010125/d010125a.htm.

———. 2001b. "Private Television Broadcasters." *The Daily*, July 4. Available: http://www.statcan.ca/Daily/English/010704/d010704c.htm.

———. 2001c. "Television Viewing." *The Daily*, October 23. Available: http://www.statcan.ca/Daily/English/011023/d011023a.htm.

Toronto Star. 2000. "New Shows Finally Falling Into Place", September 19.

TV-Guide Live. 2001. *Uncut Sopranos OK*. Available: http://www.tvguidelive.com/newsgossip-archives/01-may/05–26–01.html.

Notes

1   The authors would like to gratefully acknowledge Paul Robinson of Nielsen Media Research for providing us with proprietary data relating to this research.
2   Satellite Communications Association of Canada (1999). The other primary targets for satellite penetration are listed as high-end technology users and people who are just generally dissatisfied with the service they receive from cable companies.
3   Satellite Communication Association of Canada (2001).

IN FROM THE COLD

Aboriginal Media in Canada

Cora Voyageur

The narratives we express are windows on who we are, what we experience, and how we understand and enact ourselves and others. – Gail Guthrie Valaskakis (2000, 76).

Nobody looked like me! As an Indian child growing up in Canada in the 1960s, I saw no reflections or affirmations of myself in the media. Nobody I saw on the television, in the newspapers, or in magazines shared my cultural background as a Canadian Indian. The only Indians on television were "Injun Joe" (who spoke to bears) on the after-school program *The Forest Rangers*; Tonto (which means stupid in Spanish), the Lone Ranger's faithful sidekick; and Chingachcook – the Indian chief who caused pioneers no end of trouble and worry in the television version of James Fenimore Cooper's *Last of the Mohicans*.

There were no "real"[1] Indians on television. What I saw were the White man's images of Indians. Furthermore, the media depictions of Indians that I grew up with were overwhelmingly negative, mythical, or inaccurate – generally all three. Indians were trivialized, demonized, and fictionalized in movies and television. John Wayne movies had us terrorizing the poor White settlers who were only trying to start a new life in the West. We scalped them and burned their wagons. Why the Indians attacked the lying, cheating, stealing Whites was rarely part of the story.[2] We were savages.

Movies and television had us speaking broken-English and we were essentially inarticulate. We expressed ourselves using words like "Ugh" and "How" and other monosyllabic utterances. The "real" Indians I was familiar with were nothing like these caricatures. The Indians I knew were intelligent, reasoned individuals and coherent speakers. In fact, Indians are known for their speech-making and oratory.

As Indians, we did not fare any better in the print media. We were virtually non-existent! However, when we were mentioned, it was mostly in a negative light. Benjamin Singer's content analysis of Aboriginal people in the media found that stories in Ontario newspapers showed Indians either in negotiation with the government over one issue or another, or in conflict with the government or mainstream society (Singer 1982). Charles Ungerleider found that minorities were portrayed as "villains and victims [rather] than as newsmakers, experts, or citizens reacting to contemporary events" (1991, 159). Marlene Mackie's study found that Indians were stereotyped as a people who were poor, uneducated, lazy, dirty, and drank excessively (1974–75, 43).

The media places minorities in a precarious position. The minority depends on it to relay their issues and concerns to the public, but this same media portrays them as being continually at odds with mainstream society. Most of the media reports about minorities focus on conflict or violence (Voyageur 1993). This negative coverage can foster mistrust and misunderstanding between the majority and the minority. Benjamin Singer states:

> The less personal contact that majority members have with the minority members, the more their knowledge of these groups is perceived in the mass media. The typical newspaper reader will encounter Indians or other minorities more frequently in their newspaper than they will in real life (1982, 350).

The public forms its opinions and makes choices based on both the information provided and the context in which the information is set. By selecting, interpreting, and setting events in context, the media filters our news. They can do this by deciding whether to run a story, by where they place the story in the newspaper, by the length of the article, by the size of the headline and by the tone of the message.

The changing relationship between Aboriginal people and mainstream society, in part due to the growth of Native constitutional rights, will impact the media. Another factor that could alter this relationship would be successful land-claim negotiations with the federal government. Aboriginal people could control up to 30 per cent of Canada's land mass (Sloan and Hill 1995). The balance of power between the local Aboriginal people and the resource companies would drastically change.

Another reason the relationship between Aboriginals and non-Aboriginals is changing is that we now have our own media. Our voices are no longer silenced by the courts, politics, or the media. As Aboriginal media scholar Gail Guthrie Valaskakis states, "We construct who we are in the process of identifying with the images and narratives that dominate our ways of seeing and representing the world around us, media also contribute to the formation of social identity" (2000, 76). As Lenore Keeshig-Tobias further states:

> Stories are not just entertainment but power. They reflect the deepest, the most intimate perceptions, relationships and attitudes of a people. Stories show how a people, a culture thinks.... Yet, Native images, stories, symbols and history are all too often used by Canadians and Americans to sell things – cars, tobacco, movies, books (1992, 98–99).

Media observer David Taras comments: "To a large degree, the mass media constitutes a society's meeting ground, its central public square" (2001, 4). Lorimer and McNulty say that mass communications have a social dimension because they serve as an information base around which a community can unite (1991, 17). Aboriginal peoples' role in articulating their stories, issues and concerns in the media allow them to come together and to present their voices to the Canadian public square.

The magnitude and diversity of Aboriginal media has increased in recent years. The year 2000 found a strong Aboriginal presence in print, on television, on the Internet, and on the radio. CFWE Radio, which is broadcast nationwide from Edmonton, Alberta; *The Windspeaker,* a national Aboriginal newspaper also published in Edmonton; the *Aboriginal Times,* a Calgary-based Aboriginal business/trade magazine; and the Aboriginal Peoples Television Network (APTN), a national Aboriginal television network based in Winnipeg, have all been key in the creation of a strong Aboriginal voice. Interviews with media representatives and an analysis of news content and advertising will illustrate the power and depth of the changing image of Aboriginal people, particularly in the print media.

Aboriginal Print Media

The Aboriginal media relays the Aboriginal story. Aboriginal journalist Bud White Eye states that, as an Aboriginal writer, he writes from an Aboriginal perspective and with an Aboriginal style. This means his writing is different than mainstream writing. He believes that passing the information through non-Aboriginal editors takes out the Aboriginal element out of the piece. He argues that, "If you change it to your way, there's no sense in having me. You might as well go out and do it yourself" (1996, 96). The Aboriginal print media examined here are under the editorial control of Aboriginal journalists and financially independent of government funding. The Aboriginal business/trade magazine, the *Aboriginal Times,* has been particularly influential.

Aboriginal Times

The mission statement of *Aboriginal Times,* launched in September 1996 as a trade magazine, states that it is a non-political forum for the exchange of information to enhance the growing relationship between corporate Canada and the economic union of Aboriginal communities (*Aboriginal Times,* January/February, 2000, 3). Its publisher, Roland Bellerose, is a Metis entrepreneur from northern Alberta and a former student at the University of Calgary. He describes the *Aboriginal Times* as "a national business and news magazine that explores the issues and experiences of Aboriginal people in Canada and designed as an executive-style digest with a quick, to-the-point delivery style. Its target market is business people and policy makers" (personal interview, October 11, 2001). He saw a void in the Aboriginal news media for a business/trade-type publication and believed there was an untapped niche market that was not being served by the existing media at that time. The publication is circulated monthly to government, organizations, corporations, companies, Indian bands, and tribal councils.[3]

The magazine's first mandate is to debunk myths about Aboriginal people. As publisher, Bellerose aims to break down stereotypes and quash the belief that Aboriginal people are ill-equipped to operate in the business world and contemporary society. The fact of negative stereotyping of Aboriginal workers that Bellerose speaks of is supported by Aboriginal employment research that found Aboriginal employees suffer from the belief that they are largely unskilled and unreliable workers (Voyageur 1997). Yet the Royal Commission on Aboriginal Peoples (RCAP), in its comprehensive study of Aboriginal Economic Development, found that Aboriginal peoples have long coped with the social and economic changes in Canada. Into the early twentieth century, Aboriginal people were involved in many different types of employment, including farm labour, house construction, building municipal infrastructures, road construction, and railroad construction. They were also involved in logging, milling, mining, shipping and long-shoring. At the same time as they were adapting to a capitalist economy, most Aboriginal people continued traditional pursuits and independent production year-round. Bellerose believes that these negative myths can be discredited by profiling Aboriginal athletes, educators, politicians, businessmen, etc. (personal interview, October 11, 2001).

The magazine's second mandate is to confront and report important, and sometimes controversial, legal/economic/social issues in the Aboriginal community. *AT* investigates and reports some of the grim realities experienced by Aboriginal people, including poverty, unemployment, corruption, legal struggles, and discrimination (personal interview, October 11, 2001). For example, its May issue deals with the Indian Claims Commission and its ineffective and inefficient process for settling land claims (*Aboriginal Times,* May 2000). This type of coverage helps to educate the non-Aboriginal business community and others about issues that Aboriginals face on a day-to-day basis.

Quality is paramount,[4] and Bellerose states that *AT* is constantly under revision. "Revision is integral to the success of the magazine as it responds to an ever-changing market and an ever-changing Aboriginal community" (personal interview, October 11, 2001). In its present form, *Aboriginal Times* contains editorials and feature articles on topical news stories of concern to the Aboriginal community and mainstream society. These concerns include human interest, economic development, leadership, and education. It also includes regular columns that profile national Aboriginal conferences and meetings.

In March 2000, *AT* greatly increased its readership through insertion into the nationally distributed *Globe and Mail*. This moved the publication's monthly circulation from 15,000 to 250,000. The *Globe and Mail* affiliation has not only improved its readership numbers but also its ability to command premium advertising rates for space in its magazine. The increased circulation has brought Bellerose praise, but unfortunately also hate mail. He was amazed, horrified, and disgusted at the vitriolic messages. One such message said, "you god-damned Indians want everything for nothing" (personal interview, October 11, 2001). Bellerose assumed this anonymous writer was alluding to the grants or other assistance given to some in the Canadian publishing industry. He hastened to mention that his publication is entirely privately owned and does not receive any government grants or subsidies (personal interview, October 11, 2001). Advertising and subscriptions pay the bills at *AT*.

Aboriginal Times Content Analysis

Six issues of the *Aboriginal Times* published during 2000 were selected as part of the content analysis exercise[5] to determine the topics covered in articles and discover any trends that might emerge. I also sought to explore the type of advertising space sold and who was buying space in this publication. I coded the data using a number of variables including: feature topic, accompanying photo, advertisement message, size of advertisement, whether the advertiser was Aboriginal or non-Aboriginal, and who was buying the advertising space.

During the period under review, the *Aboriginal Times* averaged thirty-two pages per issue. The July issue had an extraordinary forty-eight pages because of extensive coverage given the Assembly of First Nations' election of the Grand Chief at the AFN's Annual Assembly in July 2000. The *Aboriginal Times* ran two-page feature articles on the candidates vying for the AFN's top job. The candidates featured in this issue included Marilyn Buffalo, Matthew Coon Come (who went on to win the leadership election), Phil Fontaine (the unseated Assembly of First Nations Grand Chief), and Lawrence Martin. Candidates were asked why they were seeking the position; what they believed was the most pressing issue in the First Nations community; what they thought about Indian Affairs' plan to invest heavily into economic development in the First Nations community; and they were

Table 1 Aboriginal Times Content by Month, Category, Number, and Percentage, 2000

2000 Issue	Content Pages				Advertisement Pages		
	Feature (%)	Adver-tising (%)	Inform-ation (%)	Total (%)	Abo (%)	non-Abo (%)	Total (%)
January	22 (69)	4 (13)	6 (18)	32 (100)	2 (50)	2 (50)	4 (100)
March	15 (47)	11 (34)	6 (19)	32 (100)	5 (45)	6 (55)	11 (100)
May	18 (56)	6 (19)	8 (25)	32 (100)	4 (67)	2 (33)	6 (100)
July	24 (50)	17 (37)	7 (15)	48 (100)	8 (47)	9 (53)	17 (100)
September	17 (53)	7 (22)	8 (25)	32 (100)	5 (71)	2 (29)	7 (100)
November	17 (53)	7 (22)	8 (25)	32 (100)	4 (57)	3 (43)	7 (100)
Column Totals	113 (44)	52 (25)	43 (21)	208 (100)	28 (54)	24 (46)	52(100)

Source: *Windspeaker* January 2000, March 2000, May 2000, July 2000, September 2000, and November 2000.

also asked to comment on a *Time Magazine* article about the growing resentment between Aboriginal and non-Aboriginal Canadians resulting from recent successful Aboriginal court cases.[6]

Aboriginal Times' primary focus is the dissemination of information through Features, Advertising, and Information columns.[7] A breakdown of the magazine's 208 pages show that Features comprised 44 per cent, or 113 pages; Advertising comprised 25 per cent, or fifty-two pages; and Information columns comprised 21 per cent, or forty-three pages. Table 1 shows the contents of 208 pages of this publication for the period under review. The Content Pages heading shows the magazine in its entirety (208 pages) while the Advertising Pages category deals with a subset of fifty-two pages of advertising. Advertising pages were divided into Aboriginal or non-Aboriginal advertisers. Is this Aboriginal publication, which shuns external funding, sustained by Aboriginal or non-Aboriginal advertisers and subscribers?

Analysis of the Content Pages found that Features ran between fifteen and twenty-four pages with an average of eighteen pages, Advertising ran between four and seventeen pages with an average of nine pages, while Information ran six to eight pages with an average of seven pages. There were 167 articles, with ninety-three being Features (Features and Information Columns) and seventy-four being Advertisements.

Most of the space in the publication was devoted to the dissemination of information through feature articles. One hundred and thirteen pages, or 44 per cent of the publication, was devoted to news or feature articles. These included information on contentious issues such as the east coast lobster dispute among First Nations fishermen, fisheries officials, and non-Aboriginal fishermen. The articles quote Statistics Canada data that places the lobster industry in Atlantic Canada as a half-billion-dollar per year venture. The Burnt Church First Nations fishermen, who have a right to fish under treaty, obtain between one and two million dollars of the yearly take. Other feature articles include the rise in Aboriginal tourism; the career of Aboriginal senator Len Marchand; and an interview of Judge John Reilly, who caused a row over questioning governance and accountability of elected officials in the First Nations community. Other issues covered in the features category included poor water quality in many Aboriginal communities, employment equity, the National Aboriginal Achievement Awards, legal studies, corporate mentoring, legal cases, and leadership.

The publication's length is determined by both the amount of advertising space sold in any particular issue and by the number of feature articles. A review of *advertising pages* in Table 1 found that slightly more than half (54 per cent) of the advertising pages sold during the period under review were sold to Aboriginal organizations and businesses rather than non-Aboriginal companies and organizations. The latter purchased 46 per cent of the advertising pages. A review of the *actual number* of ads placed in *Aboriginal Times* found seventy-four advertisements, with forty-one (55 per cent) being placed by Aboriginal companies and organizations and thirty-three (45 per cent) by non-Aboriginals. An analysis of advertisement size found that Aboriginals also placed larger ads than non-Aboriginal advertisers.[8] It appears that *Aboriginal Times* is financially supported more by the Aboriginal community than the non-Aboriginal. This could be interpreted as Aboriginal business seeking non-Aboriginal clients. This is particularly true of the *Globe and Mail* readership, which is mostly non-Aboriginal. *Aboriginal Times* would still inform the Aboriginal readership it had acquired prior to the *Globe and Mail* expansion.

Most of the advertising was placed by business or industry to attract potential customers. The largest single group placing ads were Aboriginal companies or organizations providing goods or services. Education institutions from across Canada seeking would-be students were also popular in this publication. This makes sense since an increasing number of post-secondary institutions are initiating Aboriginal programs in the hope that these will attract Aboriginal students.

Perhaps one of the most interesting advertising trends was the large number of financial institutions placing ads. Recently, they have begun to

Table 2 *Aboriginal Times* by Category, Number and Percentage, 2000

Topic	Number (%)	Features (%)	Total Content Advertisements (%)
Culture	5 (3)	3 (2)	2 (3)
Business/Industry	43 (27)	18 (19)	25 (34)
Leadership	15 (9)	15 (16)	*
Indian Affairs/Gov	5 (3)	2 (2)	3 (4)
Legal	10 (6)	10 (12)	*
History	1 (*)	1 (1)	*
Human Resources	6 (4)	4 (4)	2 (3)
Education	15 (9)	7 (8)	8 (11)
Community	2 (1)	2 (2)	*
Medicine	2 (1)	1 (1)	1 (1)
Editorials	8 (5)	8 (9)	*
Natural Resources	1 (*)	1 (1)	*
Information Columns	21 (13)	21 (23)	*
Entertainment	2 (1)	*	2 (3)
AT Advertising	17 (10)	*	17 (23)
Finance	7 (4)	*	7 (9)
Conferences	7 (4)	*	7 (9)
Total Pages	167 (100)	93 (100)	74 (100)
			* denotes percentage less than .05.

Source: *Aboriginal Times*, January, March, May, July, September, and November, 2000.

increase services to Aboriginals. Banks have been setting up on reserves, providing Aboriginal banking services, and advertising in Aboriginal publications. Not long ago, First Nations individuals had problems obtaining bank loans because of the *Indian Act*; now banks are competing for Aboriginal customers (Calliou and Voyageur 1998).

The Aboriginal advertisers included the Aboriginal Peoples Television Network, the National Aboriginal Achievement Foundation, Cree-Ative Media, native businesses, and Aboriginal organizations holding conferences and events. Non-Aboriginal advertisers included the Government of Canada, financial institutions, and car dealerships.

Table 2 shows the further categorization of Features[9] into: culture, business, leadership, Indian Affairs, legal, history, human resources, education, community, medicine, natural resources, information, and others. The data show that Information Columns had the largest number of articles. Information Columns included the Table of Contents,[10] information on Conferences in Canada, a Calendar of Events across Canada, and a clipping service that highlighted newspaper articles featuring Aboriginal topics carried in Canadian newspapers in the preceding month.

The articles covered a range of topics but focused primarily on business-related themes. For example, many articles talk about the success of Aboriginal businesses and of the Aboriginals' willingness to enter into business partnerships. As mentioned by the publisher, the *Aboriginal Times'* mandate is to promote and make non-Aboriginal business people understand and appreciate that investment and development in the Aboriginal community are both viable and desirable. *Aboriginal Times* is "casting Aboriginal people as partners in development" (Calliou and Voyageur 1998, 133).

Leadership was the third most popular topic covered in the *Aboriginal Times*. Various Aboriginal politicians were featured, including Dwight Dorey (Congress of Aboriginal Peoples), Jose Kusagak (Inuit Taperisat of Canada), Matthew Coon Come (Assembly of First Nations), and Gerald Morin (Metis National Council). The concerns of these leaders are highlighted as a means of informing mainstream society. These features help to educate and inform non-Aboriginals, since many studies have documented non-Aboriginals' ignorance of both Aboriginal people and their issues (Ponting 1987). Legal issues included information about various lawsuits either in process or recently completed. These included information about the Samson Cree Nations' $1.4-billion lawsuit against the federal government for breach of trust for misconduct and mismanagement of its share of oil and gas royalties. The Burnt Church fishing conflict coverage featured questions by the Grand Chief about the disparity between the Aboriginal and non-Aboriginal share of Canada's natural resources. The University of Saskatchewan's Program for Legal Studies for Aboriginal Students, which began in 1973, was also featured. The article highlighted the matters before the courts to inform its readers about legal issues affecting Aboriginals, business, and industry.

Windspeaker

A second key Aboriginal newspaper is *Windspeaker*. Again, the analysis below uses the same format as that for *Aboriginal Times*. Six issues are analyzed for topic and advertising trends.

The mission statement of *Windspeaker*'s publisher, the Aboriginal Multi-Media Society of Alberta (AAMSA), is:

> Aboriginal Multi-Media Society of Alberta an independent Aboriginal communications organization committed to facilitating the exchange of information reflecting Aboriginal culture to

a growing and diverse audience. AMMSA is dedicated to providing objective, mature and balanced coverage of news, information and entertainment relevant to Aboriginal issues and peoples while maintaining profound respect for the values, principles, and traditions of Aboriginal peoples (Crowfoot interview, October 15, 2001).

Windspeaker, first published monthly in 1983, intends to serve the Aboriginal people of northern Alberta (http://www.ammsa.co/ammsahistory.htm). *Windspeaker* was so successful in expanding its circulation base that, by its tenth anniversary, it could refocus its editorial policy. It would be Canada's first and only provider of national Aboriginal news, information and opinion (Crowfoot interview, October 15, 2001). With a hundred per cent cut in federal funding in 1990, nine of the eleven Aboriginal publications across Canada closed their doors, as did the Native Communications Program. *Windspeaker* was the only publication west of Ontario to survive the federal cuts and was challenged to fill the void (Crowfoot interview, October 15, 2001). In 1993 *Windspeaker* transformed itself into a national forum that would be supported by readers through subscriptions and advertising. The elimination of government funding meant it could be both financially and politically independent.

Since *Windspeaker*'s national launch, AMMSA has developed three additional publications to serve the needs of Aboriginal people throughout western Canada. *Alberta Sweetgrass* in December 1993; *Saskatchewan Sage* in October 1996, and, most recently, British Columbia and Yukon's *Raven's Eye,* in May 1997 (http://www.ammsa.co/ammsahistory.htm).

As *Windspeaker* prepares to celebrate its nineteenth year of publishing, it is firm in its commitment to maintain a current, relevant, objective and independent viewpoint while reporting news and providing information, current affairs, and entertainment features with the utmost accuracy. *Windspeaker,* published twelve times each year, has a national circulation of more than 18,000 with a readership in excess of 120,000 (Crowfoot interview, October 15, 2001). Given that upwards of 75 per cent of *Windspeaker*'s circulation is paid subscriptions, *Windspeaker,* like the *Aboriginal Times,* is committed to its community. It demonstrates this through its editorials, feature stories, letters to the editor, book reviews, and sections on entertainment, sports, health, education, business and careers.

Windspeaker Content Analysis

To conduct this portion of the research, I selected six issues of *Windspeaker* published during 2000.[11] As with the *Aboriginal Times,* I wanted to determine the nature of the feature articles and any emerging trends in advertising. What type of advertising space sold and to whom? I coded the data using the same variables as in the previous analysis.[12]

Windspeaker issues varied greatly in size, ranging from thirty-two and forty-four pages.[13] Table 3 shows a breakdown of the newspaper's 232 pages for the period under review by month, number, and percentage. The data show that the Features category comprised 41 per cent, or ninety-five pages; Advertising comprised 54 per cent, or 125 pages; and Information Columns comprised 5 per cent, or twelve pages.

The Content Pages heading analyzes the newspaper pages in their entirety (232 pages), while the Features, Advertising, and Information categories are subsets of the Content Pages. The Features column deals with the ninety-five pages of feature stories covered by the newspaper, the Advertising column reports on the 125 pages of advertising, and the Information column shows the number and percentage of pages dedicated to information columns such as Tables of Contents, indexes, and community events. The Advertising category reports the 125 pages of advertising in the publication. The Aboriginal and non-Aboriginal columns show whether the advertisement was placed by an Aboriginal or non-Aboriginal person, company or organization.

Analysis of the Content Pages found that Features ran between ten and twenty pages, with an average of fifteen pages; Advertising ran much higher at between sixteen and twenty-four pages, with an average of approximately twenty-one pages; while Information Columns averaged two pages. There were 955 articles, with 362 being Features (Features and Information Columns) and 593 being Advertisements. Over the months, there was consistently more space dedicated to advertising than features. This can be explained by the fact that this publication is supported solely by advertising revenues.

Feature articles included information on contentious issues such as the Burnt Church fishing dispute and the Supreme Court of Canada's Corbiere decision, which dealt with the issue of voting rights for non-resident Indians.[14] Other topics covered in the Features category included the National Aboriginal Achievement Award, conferences, and community issues such as housing, economic development, and water quality.

Table 3 *Windspeaker* by Month, Category, Number, and Percentage, 2000

Issue	Content Pages				Advertisement Pages		
	Feature	Advert	Info	Total	Abo	Non-Abo	Total
2000	(%)	(%)	(%)	(%)	(%)	(%)	(%)
January	18 (45)	21 (52)	1 (3)	40 (100)	9 (43)	12 (57)	21 (100)
March	10 (28)	24 (67)	2 (5)	36 (100)	12 (50)	12 (50)	24 (100)
May	16 (45)	18 (50)	2 (5)	36 (100)	10 (57)	8 (43)	18 (100)
July	14 (44)	16 (50)	2 (6)	32 (100)	10 (62)	6 (38)	16 (100)
Sept	20 (46)	22 (50)	2 (2)	44 (100)	11 (50)	11 (50)	22 (100)
Nov	17 (38)	24 (55)	3 (7)	44 (100)	8 (33)	16 (67)	24 (100)
Column Totals	95 (41)	125 (54)	12 (5)	232 (100)	60 (48)	65 (52)	125 (100)

Source: *Windspeaker,* January, March, May, July, September, and November 2000.

An analysis of advertising information in Table 3 found that the slight majority (52 per cent) of the advertising pages (sixty-five pages) were sold to non-Aboriginal organizations and businesses. Aboriginal companies and organizations purchased 48 per cent of the advertising pages. A review of the actual number of advertisements placed in *Windspeaker* found 593 advertisements, with 291 (49 per cent) being placed by Aboriginal companies and organizations and 302 (51 per cent) by non-Aboriginals. This means that Aboriginal companies placed fewer but slightly larger ads than non-Aboriginal advertisers. It appears that *Windspeaker* is financially supported slightly more by the non-Aboriginal than the Aboriginal community. This was the opposite of the *Aboriginal Times,* which had more advertising support from the Aboriginal community than the non-Aboriginal. Aboriginal advertisers in *Windspeaker* included companies, organizations, musicians, health providers, educators, the Aboriginal Peoples Television Network, the National Aboriginal Achievement Foundation, Indian bands, and tribal councils. The non-Aboriginal advertisers included the Government of Canada, financial institutions, and mainstream educational institutions.

To determine the types of stories and advertisements placed in *Windspeaker,* Table 4 further breaks down Features[15] and Advertising. The data show that Business and Industry had the largest number of articles. Most of those, 141 of 178, or 79 per cent, were advertising rather than news features. The advertisements were offers of goods or services to the readership. Human Resources followed as the second most popular category. Again, advertising was the majority, with 99 of 124, or 80 per cent. Advertising in this category was primarily employment opportunity notices. The advertisement of education conferences dominated the Education category. These were from all across Canada and were placed mostly by non-Aboriginals.

Table 4 *Windspeaker* by Content, Number, and Percentage, 2000

		Total Content	
Topic	Number (%)	Feature (%)	Advertising (%)
Culture	40 (4)	40 (11)	*
Business/Industry	178 (19)	37 (1)	141 (24)
Leadership	31 (3)	31 (9)	*
Indian Affairs/Gov	37 (4)	24 (7)	13 (2)
Legal	29 (3)	22 (6)	7 (1)
History	3 (*)	3 (1)	*
Human Resources	124 (13)	25 (7)	99 (17)
Education	116 (12)	11 (3)	105 (18)
Conferences	59 (6)	11 (3)	48 (8)
Community/Greetings	39 (4)	25 (7)	14 (2)
Medicine/Health	69 (7)	40 (11)	29 (5)
Editorials	6 (*)	6 (3)	*
Environment	16 (2)	16 (4)	*
Information Columns	18 (2)	18 (5)	*
Letters to Editor	22 (2)	22 (6)	*
Entertainment	70 (7)	13 (4)	57 (10)
Sports	18 (2)	18 (5)	*
AMMSA Advertising	66 (7)	*	66 (11)
Finance	14 (2)	*	14 (2)
Total Articles	955 (100)	362 (100)	593 (100)

Source: *Windspeaker* January, March, May, July, September, and November 2000.

* denotes percentage less than .05.

The articles in the *Windspeaker* covered a much broader range of topics than the *Aboriginal Times*, which was dominated by Information Columns, Business/Industry and Leadership topics. The *Windspeaker*, although concerned with these issues as well, contained more community-based human interest and education stories.

A couple of explanations can be offered. *Aboriginal Times* appears to be more aimed at mainstream society. It is able to target them through insertion into the *Globe and Mail*. It is also due to the size of the publication. Since the *Aboriginal Times* is in digest fomat, and *Windspeaker* is in tabloid format, *Windspeaker* simply has more space to cover more issues.

Windspeaker appears to be the more comprehensive of the two publications since it provides information to the entire Aboriginal community, not just those interested in business and industry. The majority of non-Aboriginal advertisers appear to want to get their information out to the Aboriginal community. *Windspeaker* fulfills its commitment to facilitate the exchange of information from an Aboriginal cultural perspective to a growing and diverse audience by providing a wide range of information to the Aboriginal and non-Aboriginal communities alike.

Cora Voyageur

In closing, when speaking with the publishers of the two print medium examples, *Aboriginal Times* and *Windspeaker*, I asked them what they wanted people who read this article to know about them. They both said they wanted the public to know that these enterprises did not receive government money and that they are supported solely by advertising and subscriptions.

Electronic Media

The electronic media provide the Aboriginal community with both visual and aural means of transmitting and receiving information. Those in the Aboriginal community who might have the ability to read the English language with enough proficiency to understand the print medium's message often still prefer to obtain information electronically. They can watch television or listen to the radio to obtain important information about the community as well as simply watch or listen for pleasure.

CFWE-FM: The Native Perspective

Aboriginal languages have an oral tradition with the exception of written dialogue in a variety of forms, including Wintercounts, Petroglyphs and Pictographs. For this reason, the radio, and especially the service provided by CFWE-FM, The Native Perspective, is the most consistent with our oral tradition.

The written forms of Indian languages came to the prairies with the missionaries (Faries and Watkins 1986, ii). For example, Cree, the most widely spoken of the Algonquin languages, was written into what was called Cree Syllabus by Wesleyan Methodist Minister Rev. James Evans as early as 1840 in Manitoba (Ellis 1983, 636).

In 1986, the Aboriginal Multi-Media Society of Alberta (AMMSA) established CFWE-FM, a radio station located in Edmonton for broadcast through a satellite network to forty-eight communities and settlements throughout northern Alberta (and across North America via satellite). CFWE's programming is diverse, providing music, arts, ethnic programs, public affairs and news, with much of it broadcast in the Cree language.[16]

On August 31, 1987, CFWE-FM made its initial broadcast as a community radio station in the town of Lac La Biche and broadcast for a total of twelve hours per day. This eventually grew to twenty-four hours per day by June, 1989. In June, 1993, CFWE moved its studios and staff to AMMSA's administrative offices in Edmonton. Of all the media assessed in this paper, CFWE is the most easily accessible and readily available to the public. It can be heard across Canada in vehicles, homes, businesses, and in community centres, wherever a radio signal can be transmitted.

The radio station is very popular in communities, and phone-in request shows are always a hit. For example, listeners wait excitedly to hear their names, or the names of community members, usually announced for birthdays or anniversaries. CFWE's radio signal unites Aboriginal peoples as well as their sometimes isolated communities. The phone-in programs and request lines constitute the public square.

Aboriginal Peoples Television Network (APTN)

Aboriginal Peoples Television Network (APTN) was launched on September 1, 1999. For the first time in broadcast history, First Nations, Inuit, and Metis people had an opportunity to share their stories on a national television network dedicated to Aboriginal programming. Through documentaries, news magazines, dramas, entertainment specials, children's series, cooking shows and education programs, APTN offers all Canadians a window into the remarkably diverse worlds of indigenous peoples.

Aboriginal Peoples Television Network's Mission Statement is: "Sharing our peoples' journey, celebrating our cultures, inspiring our children and honouring the wisdom of our Elders." Its motto is "Original People, Original Television." More than 70 per cent of APTN's programming originates in Canada, with 60 per cent of the programs broadcast in English, 15 per cent in French, and 25 per cent in a variety of Aboriginal languages.

APTN got its start back in 1978, when the federal government initiated the Anik B experiments to test communications satellites in applications such as TV broadcasting, community communications, tele-education and tele-health in Northern Canada.

Aboriginal broadcasting was given a boost in 1983, when the Government of Canada announced the Northern Broadcasting Policy and the Northern Native Broadcast Access Program. Public funds were allocated for the production of radio and television programs by thirteen native communications societies across the north. In 1985, the CRTC's Northern Native Broadcasting policy statement recognized the need for a dedicated northern transponder to distribute television programming across the north. For the next several years, the federal government and northern broadcasters established the groundwork for a northern satellite distribution system.

In February, 1998, the CRTC released Public Notice 1998-8, which stated that Television Northern Canada (TVNC) was "a unique and significant undertaking" and that a national Aboriginal channel should be "widely available throughout Canada in order to serve the diverse needs of the various Aboriginal communities, as well as other Canadians."

Television informs individuals on important issues through news broadcasts and current events. It unites the Aboriginal community much as CFWE, the radio channel does. It also gives individuals living in urban areas an opportunity to remain grounded in their Aboriginal traditions and culture. APTN has a significant impact on the Aboriginal community because it gives Aboriginal people the opportunity to see people just like themselves on the television. This is something I did not have when I grew up. It helps to transmit traditions though culturally based programming. It gives people an opportunity to hear their mother tongue. For those born and raised in an urban environment, it might be one of the few opportunities they have for hearing their language.

Conclusion

The year 2000 saw Aboriginal media thriving in Canada. They play a crucial role in informing and entertaining the Aboriginal community and mainstream society. Although Aboriginal people benefit from the existence of their own media sources, mainstream society also reaps the benefits. The media discussed above are dedicated to telling the Aboriginal story. They are also dedicated to maintaining a high degree of quality and integrity. The Aboriginal media in Canada find themselves evolving and adapting to an ever-changing market and increased competition.

These forums get the Aboriginal perspective on various issues out to the world. This helps to break down myths and stereotypes and counter the sometimes negative coverage of Aboriginal issues in mainstream media. They also help to educate and inform the larger society to enable them to gain an understanding of Aboriginal people's concerns. If Canadians want to better understand the basis of Aboriginal people's culture, traditions, beliefs, grievances or claims, they have the opportunity to learn more from the

Aboriginal media. They present Aboriginal views in a way that mainstream media cannot. As mentioned by Singer, the less mainstream society interacts with Aboriginal people, the more they rely on the media for insights about the other. Non-Aboriginals have the opportunity of a voyeuristic view into the Aboriginal community from the comfort and safety of their own home.[17] These media give Aboriginals a voice to get their message across in their own words and own perspective. If Indians wrote the Lone Ranger's script, we would have shown a little more respect to the Indian man who got the Lone Ranger out of predicaments. We would not have called the Lone Ranger's faithful Indian guide "Tonto."

Bibliography

Aboriginal Multi-Media Society of Alberta. 2000. *Windspeaker* 17(9). January. Edmonton.
Aboriginal Multi-Media Society of Alberta. 2000. *Windspeaker* 17(11). March. Edmonton.
Aboriginal Multi-Media Society of Alberta. 2000. *Windspeaker* 18(1). May. Edmonton.
Aboriginal Multi-Media Society of Alberta. 2000. *Windspeaker* 18(3). July. Edmonton.
Aboriginal Multi-Media Society of Alberta. 2000. *Windspeaker* 18(5). September. Edmonton.
Aboriginal Multi-Media Society of Alberta. 2000. *Windspeaker* 18(7). November. Edmonton.
Alia, Valerie. 1999. *Un/Covering the North: News, Media and Aboriginal People.* Vancouver: University of British Columbia Press.
Browne, Donald R. 1996. *Electronic Media and Indigenous Peoples: A Voice of Our Own.* Ames: Iowa State University Press.
Calliou, Brian, and Cora J. Voyageur. 1998. "Aboriginal Economic Development and the Struggle for Self-Government." In *Power and Resistance: Critical Thinking about Canadian Social Issues,* ed. Wayne Antony and Les Samuelson, 115–34. Halifax: Fernwood Press.
Cooke, Katie. 1984. *Images of Indians held by non-Indians: A Review of Current Research.* Ottawa: Indian Affairs and Northern Development.
Cree-Ative Media. 2000. *Windspeaker* 4(5). January/February. Calgary.
Cree-Ative Media. 2000. *Windspeaker* 4(6). March. Calgary.
Cree-Ative Media. 2000. *Windspeaker* 5(8). May. Calgary.
Cree-Ative Media. 2000. *Windspeaker* 5(10). July. Calgary.
Cree-Ative Media. 2000. *Windspeaker* 5(1). September. Calgary.
Cree-Ative Media. 2000. *Windspeaker* 5(3). November. Calgary.
Ellis, C. Douglas. 1983. *Spoken Cree.* Edmonton: Pica Pica Press.
Faries, Ven. R., and Rev. E. A. Watkins. 1986. *A Dictionary of the Cree Language.* Toronto: Anglican Book Centre.
Keeshig-Tobias, Lenore. 1992. "Not Just Entertainment." In *Through Indian Eyes: The Native Experience in Books for Children,* ed. Beverly Slapin and Doris Seale, 98–101. Philadelphia: New Society Publishers.
Mackie, Marlene. 1974–75. "Ethnic Stereotypes and Prejudice – Alberta Indians, Hutterites, and Ukrainians." *Canadian Ethnic Studies* 6–7: 39–52.
Lorimer, Rowland, and Jean McNulty. 1991. *Mass Communications in Canada.* Toronto: McClelland and Stewart.
Ponting, J. Rick. 1987. *Profiles of Public Opinions on Canadian Natives and Native Issues.* Calgary: Research Unit for Public Policy Studies.
Schell, Olie. 1992. Royal Commission on Aboriginal Peoples Hearings. Fort McMurray, June 16.
Sloan, P., and Roger Hill. 1995. *Corporate Aboriginal Relations: Best Practice Case Studies.* Toronto: Sloan Hill Associates.

Singer, Benjamin. 1982. "Minorities and the Media: a Content Analysis of Native Canadians in the Daily Press." *Canadian Review of Sociology and Anthropology* 19(2): 348–59.

Statistics Canada. 1998. "1996 Census: Aboriginal Data." *The Daily*, January 13.

Taras, David. 2001. *Power and Betrayal in the Canadian Media*. Peterborough, ON: Broadview Press.

Ungerleider, Charles. 1991. "Media, Minorities, and Misconceptions: The Portrayal by and Representation of Minorities in Canadian News Media." *Canadian Ethnic Studies* 23(3): 158–65.

Valaskakis, Gail Guthrie. 2000. "Telling our own Stories: the Role, Development, and Future of Aboriginal Communications." In *Aboriginal Education: Fulfilling the Promise*, ed. Marlene Brant Castellano, Lynne Davis and Louise Lahache, 76–96. Vancouver: University of British Columbia Press.

Voyageur, Cora J. 1993. Portrayal of Indians in the Media. Unpublished paper. Edmonton: University of Alberta.

———. 1997. *Employment Equity and Aboriginal People in Canada*. Ph.D. dissertation. Edmonton: University of Alberta.

White Eye, Bud. 1992. Royal Commission on Aboriginal Peoples Hearings. Toronto, November 3.

Interviews:

Roland Bellerose. Personal interview. Calgary. October 11, 2001.

Bert Crowfoot. Telephone Interview. Edmonton. October 15, 2001.

Debra Lockyer Telephone Interview. Edmonton. October 15, 2001.

Internet Sources

Aboriginal Multi-Media Society of Alberta: http://www.ammsa.com

Aboriginal Peoples Television Network. 2001: http://www.aptn.ca

CFWE-FM, The Native Perspective. 2001: http://www.ammsa.com/cfwe

Aboriginal Times. 2001: http://www.aboriginaltimes.com

Notes

1   When I say "real" Indian, I mean any Indian that I could identify with as part of my culture and my lived experience.
2   There is rarely, if ever, any mention of Indians fighting to keep their land from being taken away. People fight over land all through history – the fights are called wars.
3   The *Aboriginal Times* is published eleven times per year.
4   Bellerose is actively involved in all aspects of the magazine's production, and he maintains strict guidelines for the quality of the magazine in both aesthetics and content.
5   I selected the January. March, May, July, September, and November issues of the *Aboriginal Times* published in 2000 for analysis.
6   The article alludes to the recent *Marshall* Case in which the Supreme Court of Canada held that First Nations citizens have the right to earn a "modest" living under the treaty signed with the Micmac in 1760.

7   Feature articles included all articles that were not advertising or regular information columns. This includes the main cover article and others dealing with economic development, natural resources, human resources, youth and education, technology and communications. Advertising included all space used to promote a specific company or product for which a fee was paid to the publisher. Information columns included editorials, table of contents, Across Canada, Across the Nation and Media Snapshots.

8   The only exception to this assertion is a two-page ad placed by the Canadian Armed Forces which was viewed as a non-Aboriginal advertiser.

9   In this table, the Features and Info categories are combined in the Features column.

10   This publication measured five inches by eight inches. Information Columns included the Table of Contents which took up an entire page in this publication.

11   A selection of the January, March, May, July, September, and November issues of the *Aboriginal Times* and *Windspeaker* published in 2000 for analysis.

12   Variables included: length of article, accompanying photo, headlines, feature topic, advertisement message, size of advertisement, whether the advertiser was Aboriginal or non-Aboriginal, and who was buying the advertising space.

13   The increase between thirty-two to forty-four pages constitutes a 38 per cent increase.

14   The *Corbiere* decision stated that off-reserve Indians did have the right to vote in band elections. That right had been denied to some off-reserve Indians because many bands have a residency clause that stated that only those living on reserve could vote.

15   In this table, the Features and Info categories in the previous table are combined in the Features column. This category includes articles dealing with Culture, business/ industry, leadership, Indian Affairs, legal, history, human resources, education, community, medicine, editorials, environment, natural resources, information, and others.

16   Cree is the most widely spoken Aboriginal language in Canada. Cree, along with Inuktitut and Ojibway, is not in danger of extinction according to Statistics Canada (1998, 3).

17   I use the term safety here to counter the uncertainty that some mainstream citizens might experience from entering an unfamiliar environment.

FILM AND FILM CULTURE IN CANADA
Which Way Forward?

Malek Khouri

Introduction

For most Canadians, the 2001 crop of Hollywood-made movies was once again the dominant component of what they went to watch on their theatre screens. As resentful as some of us might feel toward this reoccurring annual reality in our movie-going habits, our fascination with American cinema (one which is by no means unique to Canadians) has consistently reflected broad and deeply rooted social and economic dynamics that have linked us with our southern neighbour. While cultural critics have traditionally created a national pastime out of resenting the domination of American popular culture, and in the process attempted to contemplate various versions of a "unique" or "sovereign" Canadian national cinematic culture, the realities of Canada's cultural landscape today continue to make it almost impossible to take seriously arguments that simply dismiss our attraction to American cinema as an allure to a mythology that is not "ours."

Clearly, Canadians' collective espousal of Hollywood as part of their own cultural myth has its roots in economic interdependence, which is partly entrenched within historical and geographical proximity that links us with our "American cousin." Today's even stronger popular affiliation with aspects of American popular culture – including Hollywood cinema – is consistent with deeper transformations that underlie the increasingly globalized nature of capitalist economy. In fact, no area of Canadian culture reflects the ubiquity of capitalist market dynamics today more than that of film production and reception.

While the American film industry had already consolidated its dominance and its multifaceted popular appeal in Canada as far back as the late 1920s, today's Canadian film culture reflects relatively more recent structural transformations inside and outside this industry. Those transformations are integral to the process of capitalist globalization and the triumph of finance capital over industrial capital as it began to be entrenched toward the end of World War II.[1] While early and mid-twentieth-century film industry seemed more or less autonomous (i.e., as part of an exclusive geographically American and vocationally film-centred industry) today's "Hollywood" has become an integral component of business conglomerates with diverse industrial and commercial interests and a variety of commodities, most of which are multinational in their capital and in their market investment base.

As part of the above-mentioned transformations, national cultures today, including ours, are themselves being transformed and reconstituted within frameworks that largely exist outside the boundaries of the nation-state. Such development will no doubt have diverse and contradictory impacts on the Canadian social and cultural landscape (one which, in the last century, was based largely on a fictional construction of a sovereignty that never really existed).

However, the acceleration of a multi-faceted structural integration of the Canadian economy with that of a vastly global and regionally American-led economy has also been opening new venues for the local film industry. In an ironic twist in the course of its development, this industry now seems to be benefiting, perhaps for the first time in its history, from the American dominance in the area of filmmaking, which itself is increasingly relying on the relatively "cheaper" Canadian work force, the excellent value in currency exchange, and finally the largely beneficial Canadian tax incentives and loopholes. In this context, a more fitting question becomes: Can an integrated cinematic culture, functioning within the global ubiquity of market economy, allow for the survival and possible development of more heterogeneous social, political and artistic forms of film practice? This article will attempt to address this critical question.

Taking the year 2001 as a case study, I will examine several aspects of the spectatorship habits of Canadian moviegoers and then point out several expressions of the increasing solidification of economic interdependency between the Canadian and American film industries. I will then reflect on how this economic interdependency is affecting government film policy and how it is helping to solidify a major shift away from the federal government's traditional emphasis on supporting a largely nationalist interpretation of the notion of "Canadian culture." In the context of accounting for these critical elements in our developing film practice, I will argue that there is an urgent need for us to break with what I conceive as highbrow nationalist and/or artistic emphasis on celebrating the kind of cinema which is given pre-eminence because it somehow reflects a "uniqueness" in, and an "artistic" superiority of, the Canadian cultural experience. In response to this approach I will put forward proposals that incorporate an inclusive understanding of the nature and role of popular and mass cultures as integral to the development of film and film practice in today's society.

Presenting the Obvious: Canadian/North American Movie-going

In view of the earth-shaking events of September 11, it is difficult to predict what themes and stories will dominate our screens in the short and long terms. But if the post-September 2001 film releases were any indication (aside from the postponement of the release dates of several plot-sensitive films), no major change in the annual Hollywood film "masala" is expected to happen in the foreseeable future. The complex set of economic, institutional, social and cultural dynamics that have traditionally contributed to the universal prominence and appeal of American cinema will continue to impel a cinematic outlook which is largely and deeply rooted in the classical Hollywood fictive representation of our world and its realities. In this context, explicit political and ideological messages will mostly remain marginal to how Hollywood will be telling its stories, and ideology will remain a function of a vigorous incorporation of popular "common-sensical ideas and philosophies."[2]

By looking at the data published in *Variety* magazine in the year 2001, for example, one easily recognizes that Canadian moviegoers once again

Table 1 Highest-Grossing Films in Canada in the Year 2001 *

Harry Potter	$21,843,585	Driven	2,931,255
Lord of the Rings: Fellowship of the Ring	20,769,531	Chocolat	2,582,706
Shrek	18,103,401	The Musketeer	2,442,092
Cast Away	14,789,192	Captain Corelli's Mandolin	2,031,404
Pearl Harbor	13,809,900	Heartbreakers	1,817,568
The Mummy Returns	12,549,902	Training Day	1,684,649
American Pie 2	12,157,281	Zoolander	1,622,675
Rush Hour 2	12,141,082	Angel Eyes	1,574,404
Planet of the Apes	11,692,508	The Animal	1,558,140
Lara Croft	10,762,099	Down To Earth	1,527,941
Ocean's Eleven	10,400,239	Jeepers Creepers	1,469,580
The Fast and the Furious	10,142,460	Sweet November	1,426,110
Jurassic Park 3	10,107,877	Kiss of the Dragon	1,422,407
Traffic	9,660,522	Crocodile Dundee in L.A.	1,411,829
Crouching Tiger, Hidden Dragon	9,654,244	The Glass House	1,323,213
Hannibal	7,372,353	Jay and Silent Bob Strike Again	1,319,903
Bridget Jones's Diary	6,918,127	Summer Catch	1,317,675
America's Sweethearts	6,648,652	Hardball	1,288,506
Monsters Inc.	6,416,196	Rock Star	1,179,725
Vanilla Sky	6,258,630	Someone Like You	1,164,343
Moulin Rouge	6,183,419	Serendipity	1,163,078
Swordfish	5,942,046	Tomcats	1,099,460
The Others	5,868,019	Valentine	1,092,562
The Princess Diaries	5,137,279	Hearts of Atlantis	1,081,846
A Knight's Tale	4,938,993	The Tailor of Panama	1,068,922
Spy Kids	4,892,142	The Original Sin	1,064,652
Along Came A Spider	4,734,799	Don't Say a Word	1,038,187
The Score	4,659,233	Joy Ride	949,278
Blow	4,552,922	Memento	896,032
Save the Last Dance	4,179,386	Recess: School's Out	849,113
Scary Movie 2	4,127,947	Le Fabuleux Destin d'Amelie	812,439
Cats and Dogs	4,053,020	What's the Worst that Can Happen	785,869
Dr. Doolittle	3,957,023	Crazy and Beautiful	720,817
Ali	3,944,639	3000 Miles to Graceland	677,957
A.I.	3,801,303	Saving Silverman	663,457
Rat Race	3,774,555	Pokemon 3	602,358
Legally Blonde	3,739,460	American Outlaws	588,379
A Beautiful Mind	3,511,304	John Carpenter's Ghosts of Mars	505,183
Atlantis: The Lost Empire	3,507,266	One Night at McCool's	442,798
The Wedding Planner	3,462,110	Nuit de noces	411,252
Enemy at the Gate	3,426,438	The Forsaken	337,733
Snatch	3,069,133	Max Keebles Big Move	296,717
		Two Can Play That Game	190,241
		MVP2	118,345

* Figures are compiled from *Variety* magazine based on charts of local box office cumulatives originally and intermittently published to indicate ten highest-grossing films in Canada. The data are collected from charts published between January 2001 and January 2002, all of which incorporate numbers only relating to the year 2001. All gross figures are approximate and are by no means final.

expressed their overwhelming fascination with Hollywood films simply by flocking to watch the crop of blockbuster American hits (see Table 1).

Only very minor discrepancies can be detected in comparing the list of Canadian box office movie hits with that of the United States. Major blockbusters such as *Shrek, Castaway, Pearl Harbour,* and *The Mummy Returns* were top choices in Canadian theatres and have generated hundreds of millions of dollars in revenues in the Canadian market. Other less major hits included *American Pie 2, Rush Hour 2, Planet of the Apes, Lara Croft, Traffic, Jurassic Park 3,* and *Crouching Tiger, Hidden Dragon,* among others. The aggregate weekend box office for all No. 1 films also hit a record high in 2001, $514 million as of August 12, compared with $467 million in 2000, and $502 million in 1999 (see Table 1).

Toward the end of the same year, with the release of *Harry Potter and the Philosopher's Stone* and *The Lord of the Rings: The Fellowship of the Ring,* two long-anticipated films quickly turned into major popular culture phenomena. By late December, 2001, the expectation was that the films would each break new box office sales records; Hollywood studios were already preparing to build on this success by producing parts two and three of *The Lord of the Rings* and by turning *Harry Potter* into an annual cinematic franchise ritual featuring further volumes from the J. K. Rowling series.

By late 2001, Hollywood had generated record revenue and a booming economic upturn for major film companies. North American ticket sales for 2001 were estimated at US$8.5 billion, up from another record that was set last year at $7.7 billion (the Canadian share can be estimated within the range of half a billion dollars).[3] After factoring an estimated 4 per cent increase in average prices of tickets, the overall sales were up about 5 per cent. According to Paul Dergarabedian, Exhibitor Relations president, a record five films topped the $200-million mark: *Harry Potter, Shrek, Monsters, Inc., Rush Hour 2,* and *The Mummy Returns.* In fact, *The Lord of the Rings* later became the sixth film release in 2001 to hit that level.[4]

A significant number of Hollywood films in the year 2001 were sequels and remakes, including *The Mummy Returns, Hannibal, Scary Movie 2, Dr. Dolittle 2, Jurassic Park III, Planet of the Apes, Rush Hour 2,* and *American Pie 2.* Many of these blockbusters came out on successive Fridays, in what the industry refers to as "power openings." In this regard, one can argue that the "first" weekend box office had never seen so many power openers. It remains to be seen whether this trend will continue to grow over the next few years. Indications are, however, that slick and expensive marketing methods, and the vigorous utilization of various media for publicizing films (based on accelerating capital integrations between various film and media companies) will continue to provide an ever-stronger base for sending off new releases into today's market.

When it comes to audience age bracket, aside from *Shrek* and *Moulin Rouge*, the major studios appeared to largely target younger audiences. Unlike in 2000, this year we didn't have anything similar to *The Sixth Sense*, a film that appeared to attract crowds from a variety of age categories. In 2001, the studios largely bent toward producing films with largely teenage and pre-teenage appeal, such as *Cats&Dogs* and *Dr. Dolittle 2*, *Spy Kids*, *The Princess Diaries*, and *Monsters Inc.* Highlights included mature teenage films such as *American Pie 2*, *Legally Blonde*, and action films (*The Mummy Returns*, *Rush Hour 2*, *Planet of Apes*, *Jurassic Park 3*), and of course the later releases of *Harry Potter* and *The Lord of the Rings*. If this is any indication, the studios are trying to cash in on an almost guaranteed formula that appeals to audiences between six and eighteen years old. But is the trend to produce more teenage- and pre-teenage-oriented films indicative of a situation where we are forced to choose only from light, unsophisticated, or flat mediocre films? Not necessarily.

On the one hand, and despite their initial success, the grossing numbers of almost all of the number one box office hits in 2001 plunged steeply on their second weekend by 50 to 60 per cent. *Planet of the Apes*, for example, earned 68.5 million during its first weekend and just 27.4 million in its second, a drop of almost 60 per cent. Only two summer movies that opened on top, *The Mummy Returns* and *Pearl Harbor*, managed to stay there for a second week (by contrast, *E.T.* was number one for ten weeks, *Ghostbusters* for eight). An almost identical trend can be detected by assessing the Canadian weekly box office charts. On the other hand, the success of films such as *Shrek* and *Spy Kids* reflected an increased interest in films that, while fitting perfectly into the criteria of younger crowd films, do nevertheless incorporate thematically and stylistically innovative film narratives. Furthermore, films that are traditionally associated with non-mainstream moviegoers also seemed to have scored relatively well in the box office, in some cases even making some profit.

Aside from blockbuster films, many less ostentatious films have also done well at the theatres; a strong compilation of adult art-house films was able to assert its presence in a large number of movie theatres in the U.S. and Canada. Lower-budget winners included films about Hollywood insiders at a get-together that goes all wrong (*The Anniversary Party*); cynical teens (*Ghost World*); a murder mystery (*The Deep End*); an East German transsexual

(*Hedwig and the Angry Inch*); merciless mobsters (*Sexy Beast*); and wretched thugs (*Made*). While all these films did not make enough money to allow them to be within the group of top-grossing films screened in Canada in the year 2001, the fact that in many cases they were produced and/or distributed with the help of major studios testifies to these studios' own increased attention to the growing market demand for alternative films.

One particularly successful independent film in 2001 was *Memento*. The film opened in the spring and played well into the summer, cracking into the top ten highest-grossing movies ($24 million) while playing in only about five hundred theatres (big studio movies often debut in three thousand or more theatres). In Canada, this film eventually came close to garnishing $1 million in box office revenues.

Part of the Hollywood audience (including its Canadian portion) appears to be demanding better quality films. The fact that several movies nose-dive on their second week is not simply an indication that the audiences are fickle and have short attention spans. By turning away from major box office hits after they are seduced to their first glance of the films by snazzy marketing, audiences are perhaps demonstrating that they are increasingly becoming more interested in less homogeneous films. Studio executives may become more sensitive to the market value of such audiences and hence try to increase their share of the profit potential of such a market by moving away from formula films.

Our audiences, however, seemed less keen on watching Canadian films. Based on box office figures, it is clear that none of the wide variety of films produced here came even close to resonating with our audiences to the level of becoming a box office hit. While measuring success exclusively on the basis of revenues is highly problematic, it nevertheless always indicates general trends in film audience reception orientations and habits as well as possible structural problems in the mechanisms of marketing and distribution of Canadian films. But the overall picture of the state of Canadian films was not as dark as it might appear.

Statistics released in January 2002 by the respected Montreal-based box office monitor Alex Films indicated that hockey comedy *Les Boys III* was the highest-grossing Canadian film for 2001 ($3.5 million). This was achieved despite the fact that the film was not released anywhere west of Ottawa. Remarkably, *Les Boys* also accounted for 30 per cent of the total box office generated by Canadian movies and was the sixth biggest box office hit in Quebec, ending just behind *American Pie 2*.

But while most Canadian films did not make it to the 2001 list of the highest-grossing films in Canada, several of these films became very popular among audiences in alternative film-going settings such as film festivals and other tours. The comedy *Nuit de noces* (*Wedding Night*), for example, which also won the Golden Reel Award for the biggest Canadian box office hit (the period which determines the qualification of films for this award is between October 21 and October 20), became also popular with audiences in film festivals outside Quebec. By the end of its run, the film grossed over $400,000.

Other domestic films struck a chord with audiences in a variety of screening venues across the country. Gary Burns's *Waydowntown*, for example, attracted large audiences and positive feedback wherever it was screened. The film was due to open in the United States in January, 2001, after being postponed three months due to the September 11 events. (The reason given for the postponement was the film's depiction of office workers jumping from windows!) Another film with some Canadian connection to it is *Kandahar.* Directed by Iranian filmmaker Mohsen Makhamalbaf, the film casts Afghan-Canadian filmmaker Nelofer Pazira and chronicles a women's quest to get a friend out of the darkness which has engulfed her country of origin for several years.

Canadian films that also attracted attention in the year 2001 were Denis Villeneuve's *Maelstrom,* Robert Lepage's first English-language film *Possible Worlds,* Denys Arcand's *Stardom,* Clement Virgo's *Love Come Down,* and Lea Pool's *Lost and Delirious.* But the overwhelming affection and respect was saved during that year for a film that was first launched at the Cannes Film Festival. This success eventually allowed *Atanarjuat* the opportunity to become a major hit with several film festival audiences in Canada and abroad. *Atanarjuat* (*The Fast Runner*), by Zacharias Kunuk, is a Native-Canadian film based on Inuit oral tradition. It was shot entirely in Nunavut and represented the first screenplay ever written in Inuktitut. The film was the first Canadian feature film to be written, produced, directed, and acted by Inuit. *Atanarjuat* won the best Canadian feature at the 2001 Toronto International Film Festival and was a co-winner of the Guardian Award for best new director at the 2001 Edinburgh International Film Festival. It also won the Camera d'or for best first feature film at Cannes and eventually became a big winner at the Canadian Genies in February, 2002.

No survey of the current film culture is complete without discussing the events of September 11, 2001. No one can tell how the tragic events in New York and the much-celebrated and fetishized "War on Terrorism" will affect our dreams – cinematic nightmarish dreams, that is. However, one thing seems certain at this point. Every generation has its warning tale about the terrors and traumas variously experienced during teenager years, and each generation has sought out the catharsis scary films can deliver. I'm convinced that, in our attempt to deal with the aftermath of September 11, we will also digress into a process of contemplating our own inner fears and that watching movies will be one way of dealing with such fears. This could partially explain the success of several horror films in the period immediately following the terrorist attacks in New York. In post–September, 2001, the relative popularity of films such as *Jeepers Creepers* (the threat comes from nowhere and escapes punishment), *Joy Ride* (two brothers invite evil to "play" with them and pay for their deed), and *The Glass House* (fear of losing one's parents without warning) seems to also point toward a future trend in the horror film genre. But in the context of the cynical attitude toward politics in general, my estimate is that our audiences will continue to watch more escapist kinds of films. Occasionally we will also flock to see films that glorify war and American patriotism. The Iraqi crisis of 2003 may hasten this trend.

Days after the events of September 11, a group of prominent Hollywood producers initiated a meeting with White House officials to discuss ways of supporting Washington's declared "war against terrorism." Director and screenwriter Lionel Chetwynd (a native of Montreal who wrote the screenplay for *The Apprenticeship of Duddy Kravitz* and an organizer of the Wednesday Morning Club, a group of Hollywood Republican Party supporters) led a contingent from Hollywood in a White House meeting, after which he pledged to put more pro-American messages into films (Saunders 2001a). Of course, there is nothing new about the political role played by Hollywood during politically charged situations. At the height of the Cold War, Walt Disney personally submitted each of his films to FBI chief J. Edgar Hoover for editing, and many American filmmakers, scriptwriters, and actors were blacklisted for having dissenting views on various aspects of American government policy. What is relatively new in this instance is how the political and cultural rhetoric of many Canadians in the film industry (both in the U.S. and in Canada) might be shifting in concert with recent events. In this context, Chetwynd's approach might not be isolated for much longer among top executives and producers in the Canadian film industry.

Canada's Film Culture and Globalization

Manifestations of the economic shifts affecting Canadian film policy may also be detected in the new approach taken on various government levels. Since the 1920s, Canadians have struggled to evict Hollywood and the mega-production/distribution complexes that controlled theatres in Canada. In 1987, Federal Communications Minister Flora MacDonald wanted to boost the number of Canadian films on Canadian screens to 15 per cent. Her bill was derailed after furious lobbying by Jack Valenti, Chairman of the Motion Picture Association of America. Marcel Masse, Communications Minister during the Mulroney years, shared MacDonald's goal. He later wrote an article in *Saturday Night* describing the selling out of the Canadian film industry to U.S. interests. The current Liberal government promised, in the Red Book during the 1993 election campaign, to tackle the film distribution issue. No moves in this direction seem to have taken place. If anything, government policy today seems to point in the opposite direction.

Today, Canadian film policy is shifting further toward emphasizing the benefits of increased co-operation between the Canadian and American film industries. This does not come as a surprise. In hindsight, this shift reflects the challenges faced by various sections of the Canadian economy. As it maintains its policy of increasingly restricting funding to public cultural agencies and projects, the Canadian government has also been toning down its official rhetoric about defending Canada's "cultural sovereignty." As government officials intermittently continue to refer to the value of "national" culture, they also seem to voice a favourable appreciation of the idea of creating cultural products that can have a locally as well as internationally more marketable value. They also seem to stress an approach that recognizes the need for an economically more integrated North American film industry.

In November, 2001, Prime Minister Jean Chrétien visited the United States to talk with Hollywood studio representatives from Miramax, Showtime, and other studios and TV networks about the subsidies available for them if they shoot their film and TV programs in Canada. In 2000, American film production in Canada amounted to more than $1.8-billion (about one-third of Canada's film and TV revenues) (Saunders 2001b). For her part, Heritage Minister Sheila Copps stressed that American film production in Canada helps the Canadian movie industry. "I think we've always looked upon [the issue] as, if you invest in Hollywood productions, somehow you're costing jobs for Canadian stories. We now know that's not true [and the two industries] actively promote and protect each other" (Saunders 2001b). What Copps is implicitly admitting is that the rhetoric about an independent Canadian film industry and culture is, at best, wishful thinking. Under the conditions of a globalized market economy, and in the context of increased "free" market competition, this project is destined to become yet another example of imagined hopes and real disappointments. The contradictory attempt by Copps in late 2000 to resurrect talk about supporting the Canadian film industry by injecting a $100 million a year into a fund, $73 million of which would be invested in helping raise the average overall production budget of made-in-Canada films (Adams 2002), will hardly change anything. In the ruthless reality of the capitalist market economy, we simply can't have it both ways. In other words, we can't expect to have our cake and eat it too.

Canada's geographic and economic conditions are critical in determining Hollywood's near full control over the landscape of Canadian film distribution structure. Major U.S. studios such as Universal, Warner Bros., and Disney have well-established distribution offices in Canada. The major U.S. production/distribution houses control 80 to 94 per cent of the theatrical film market in Canada. Any success in the effort to increase the share of Canadian film distribution companies in the local market will eventually have to come at the expense of producing and distributing Canadian films.

Alliance Atlantis's motion picture group, the largest independent distributor of films in Canada with approximately a hundred motion pictures released in 2000, has been showing increased signs of success in its bid to distribute major Hollywood films. Alliance is also Canada's largest producer of feature-length films. The company has been focusing its support on low to mid-size budget art-house productions. Among its relatively recent successes were Isztvan Szabo's *Sunshine*, starring Ralph Fiennes, nominated for three Golden Globe Awards, and Atom Egoyan's Academy Award nominated and Cannes Film Festival Grand Prix winner, *The Sweet Hereafter*. But are the successes of distributors such as Alliance indicative of any possibility for a significant change in what films we see in Canada? The answer is no.

To begin with, the fact that Alliance's recent fortunes have largely been tied to CEO Robert Lantos's successful relationship with Hollywood production/distribution houses, and hence by his ability to secure the Canadian distribution rights for their films, can only indicate that future success will inevitably depend on further reliance on distributing Hollywood films. In the short and the long runs, it is this economic reliance, and not the company's "nationalist" intentions, no matter how genuine they may be, that will determine the kinds of films that it will distribute and support. On the production level, Alliance might continue to back local productions and new emerging artists. But it is the "economic bottom line" that will eventually resolve corporate discussions on the shape of the company's production support policy. In the meantime, Hollywood majors will continue to monopolize film distribution in Canada (and in the process maintain their hegemony over our popular film culture) by:

1. Dominating screen time by buying English-language films from Hollywood, independent, and other international distributors.

2. Attaining North American rights to feature films produced in the United States by independents. This practice has been traditionally based on making deals with major Hollywood studios and then including Canada as part of the American domestic market, thereby preventing Canadian companies from acquiring their own rights to the films.

3. Acquiring entire libraries from international distributors (i.e., from distributors outside Canada). This eradicates even further any possible creation of alternative supplies for Canadian-owned distributors.

If the above gloomy picture of how and why Canadians end up watching films is an indication of anything, it is that our mass cinematic cultural practice is largely determined by the economic interests of the North American film industry, an industry which is privately controlled and owned. Any serious attempt to "democratize" the production and the distribution of and the access to cinema has to revisit the question of implementing public and collective control of the film industry. While such reconsideration is clearly not on the present agenda of our politicians, posing this fundamentally different approach as a politically, economically, and culturally strategic alternative to the private and profit-driven and operated film industry, remains, nevertheless, integral to any meaningful discussion about developing a genuinely democratic and heterogeneous film culture in Canada.

To be sure, reaching a stage at which such fundamental change becomes possible depends on complex dynamics, most of which exist beyond the area of cultural production and reception. Such fundamental change can only occur as part of the materialization of a shift in wider socio-economic and political power relations. This, however, does not mean that Canadian film audiences, as well as artists and workers in the area of film, cannot do anything to lessen some of the negative effects of globalized systems in film production and distribution.

Today, culture has become a domain of political struggle that, although dominated by the interests and perspectives of specific power structures and relations, remains, nevertheless, subject to vigorous contestations and resistance from non-dominant and/or marginalized sections of society. As Walter Benjamin (1992) observed in his significantly misused and eclectically misrepresented seminal piece on "art in the age of mechanical reproduction," by breaking away from isolation, and through new forms of distribution and exhibition, art has been able to dramatically increase the level of human participation in its creation and reception. More than ever before in its history – and one would argue this case even further in the context of today's newer advances in the technology of communications – arts and cultural artifacts have assumed a leading function in ideological and political struggle. Benjamin believed that mechanical reproduction freed the work of art from its dependence and reliance on rituality. This has allowed for the reversal of its functional foundation from the ritual to the political (Benjamin 1992).

In the same context, film has become part of a domain that is largely shaped by its passage through the simulacral territory of what we refer to as mass culture. Canadians are challenged to find ways by which we can reaffirm the heterogeneity of our social and cultural reality by struggling to create and assert a spot for ourselves within popular culture itself. In a world where the global flow of cultural products impacts directly on how we identify (or misidentify) ourselves, marginalized sections of society (including those whose marginality relates to their class, gender, race, ethnicity, sexual orientation, etc.) are challenged to jockey for a position which enables them to bring their perspective to wider mass audiences. Ultimately, this can only be achieved by overcoming old prejudices and affirming a new collective awareness of and for themselves in society.

So what do I propose by way of short-term propositions that, on the one hand, can alleviate some of the negative effects of an increasingly globalized system of "cinematic interaction," and, on the other hand, can contribute to the development of a resistant and more heterogeneous Canadian film culture? It is important here to emphasize that the points I will put forward in the following section are meant as alternatives to the nationalist emphasis on the need to protect the Canadian film industry and market and to the self-indulgent view of filmmaking as an elitist "artistic" practice which does not need to appeal to anyone but its own creator.

Propositions

As I mentioned earlier, the nature of today's development of global capitalism is in turn enhancing a globalized form of cultural ubiquity. The reality of loosening the role of the state in cinema and television and within other cultural production and reception domains necessitates, on the level of alternative cultural political thinking, a departure from earlier emphasis on nationalist-based rhetoric, including the perception of ours as a cinematic culture with somewhat unique artistic and/or national character. This means:

a) Widening, diversifying and empowering various forms of alternative theatrical movie-going culture:

From the unjustifiably labelled "Hollywood-oriented" and increasingly gigantic Toronto Film Festival to the screening of independent and alternative films in smaller Canadian cities and towns, film festivals remain crucial tools that can help forge an alternative grassroots-oriented film culture. By their very nature, and to varying degrees of success, most film festivals tend to encourage new approaches to making and viewing films. As such, film festivals allow large audiences to see films that otherwise would not have been shown in their local theatres. They also allow some films to test and in various cases render themselves popular. This usually encourages profit-driven big distributors to take note of these films.

Major film festivals in Montreal, Toronto, Halifax, and Vancouver, along with many others, are now major and quite significant events that each year attract hundreds of thousands of Canadians (Montreal and Toronto each boasts over 500,000 ticket sales while Vancouver attracts over 135,000 viewers) and introduces them to new and different styles, themes, and forms of filmmaking. With the recent success of new festivals such as the Calgary International Film Festival, which grew within two years of its launching in 2000 from an audience of less than 7,000 to over 25,000 in 2002, there are signs of a renewed and growing interest in supporting and developing parallels to traditional venues for seeing films. As Piers Handling, president of the Toronto Film Festival, has commented on the current state of cinema: "So, where has the culture of film gone? Well, it is alive and well, if not a visible element of our multiplex experience. It appears randomly through myriad film festivals that dot the landscape like hardy weeds that refuse to wither and die. Thirty years ago there was not the same pressing need for them. Now, they are indispensable if one wants to see what cinema is doing" (Handling

2001). Because their budgets are small, the chance of specialty films as well as Canadian-made films getting exposure in film festivals around the country can eventually allow them even to turn a profit.

Another example of a very successful and partially publicly funded venture, which each year since 1994 has allowed audiences across the country the opportunity to view a diverse selection of Canadian films, is the program titled *Moving Pictures: Canadian Films on Tour*. The program finances tours of a good number of recently released Canadian films and is co-sponsored by Telefilm Canada, the Department of Canadian Heritage, the Canada Council for the Arts, the Union of British Columbia Performers, and the British Columbia Arts Council.

Along with seventy-six other films, the year 2001's line-up included Shirley Cheechoo's *Backroads*, the first feature drama written and directed by a Canadian First Nations woman, as well as *Stardom* by Denys Arcand, *Maelstrom* by Denis Villeneuve, and Robert Lepage's first English-language feature *Possible Worlds*. The films toured cities and towns such as Whitehorse, Edmonton, Brandon, Regina, Port Moody, Nanaimo, Kingston, Kelowna, Whitehorse, Prince George, and Yellowknife.

Such screening practices are extremely important when we take into consideration that it is virtually impossible in smaller cities and towns to see anything other than the "blockbuster *du jour*" that is being offered on their local theatre screens. Even megaplexes don't offer alternatives because they often double- or triple-book the same few films. Therefore, encouraging public and private support for existing festivals, as well as for the creation of new theatrical venues to watch films, is critical for building grassroots networks for an alternative and possibly more heterogeneous Canadian film culture. Eventually, expanding and building upon such innovative practices could have a tremendous influence on the way Canadians watch cinema.

b) A new appreciation of the significance and the possibilities of a popular cinema:

Within today's social, economic, and cultural polity, film can no longer effectively be seen as an abstract reflection of individual or collective aesthetics. More than ever before, cinema has assumed an active role as a mode of cultural exchange that forms (desired) social subjectivities. As political spaces (and all films in the end function as political spaces) films contest or naturalize the primacy of those subjectivities necessary to the status quo and suppress or privilege oppositional ones. Therefore, seeking ways through which film production in Canada can contribute to the emergence of an alternative mode of counter-hegemonic social and cultural practice has become integral to the survival of Canadian cinema as an agency that informs and is informed by the heterogeneity of this society.

While Canadian cinema has never operated outside the dominance of capitalist production relations, public institutions such as the National Film Board (NFB), Telefilm, and the Canada Council, along with several provincial agencies, have all historically played a pivotal role in providing Canadians with relatively democratic access to film production. Today, these institutions are challenged to live up to their proud traditions by moving in new creative directions.

The NFB, for example, needs to channel a larger portion of its resources toward forging partnerships with diverse independent producers, specialty television channels, and toward strengthening the utilization of its already excellent Internet and new technology connections (the NFB's Cine Route pilot project already provides Internet access to eight hundred NFB films). But other partnerships are as important; and let's not dread here the possibility of more flexible forms of co-operation with domestic and international film industries.

The NFB is also in a unique position to help develop a film culture which is at once socially conscious and oriented, as well as "popular" and widely appealing. One way to achieve such a goal would be to encourage more docudrama productions. Due to major budget cuts, the NFB has not been contributing lately to any dramatic feature films. But some important and largely successful films produced last year testify to new possibilities. Two highly acclaimed docudrama films made this year with the support of the NFB have qualified for the race for Oscar nominations. *Obaachan's Garden*, a recreation of the story of a Japanese Canadian woman who was interned during World War II, and the highly popular *Atanarjuat*, the Inuit-made film which I referred to earlier, both proved, each in its own way, that cinema is always open to reinvention.

Conclusion

New socio-economic conditions are renewing possibilities for new forms of cultural resistance, ones that transcend the notions of Canadian "cultural sovereignty" and Canadian "aesthetic uniqueness." The totalizing account

of the postmodern itself encompasses a space for various forms of oppositional cultures existing within the boundaries of today's cultural hegemony.
But only when we begin to challenge the dynamics of cultural homogene-
ity (i.e., on the premise of struggling to gain access to grassroots popular
and mass appeal) can a new Canadian film culture become a living process
of appropriating and regaining access to a genuine identity. Such cultural
struggle would reflect a cultural identity that cannot be homogeneous.
Together, the struggle for a common sense of purpose, for unity within
diversity, and toward making room for social and stylistic heterogeneity in
filmmaking, will advance a cinematic agenda that is based on politics and
the politics of culture. Only such an agenda would finally forge a Canadian
cinema, which in the context of its history, becomes capable of evolving and
expressing the dynamics of our collective memory and reality as well as our
collective hopes and dreams.

Works Cited

Adams, James. 2002. *The Globe and Mail*, February 2, R4.
Benjamin, Walter. 1992. "The Work of Art in the Age of Mechanical Reproduction." In *Film
    Theory and Criticism*, ed. G. Mast, M. Cohen, and L. Braudy, 682–89. New York: Oxford
    University Press.
Handling, Piers. 2001. *The Globe and Mail*, September 6, R1, R3.
Pendakur, Manjunath. 1990. *Canadian Dreams and American Control: The Political Economy of the
    Canadian Film Industry*. Detroit: Wayne State University Press.
Saunders, Doug. 2001a. *The Globe and Mail*, October 19, A3.
———. 2001b. *The Globe and Mail*, November 30, A12.
Willemen, Paul. 1995. "The National." In *Fields of Vision*, ed. L. Deveraux and R. Hillman, 21–
    34. Los Angeles: University of California Press.

Notes

1   For more information on aspects of the political economy of cultural development see
    Willemen (1995).
2   This term is used here in the context of Gramsci's emphasis on the construction of a
    system of popular beliefs and values as part of a system of hegemonic class domination.
    This domination relies on the consensual appropriation of ideological perspectives.
3   For details of statistics on box office sales, consult the data complied by Exhibitor
    Relations Company Inc. at http://www.exhibitorelations.com/
4   See www.variety.com

NO FUTURE?
The Canadian Music Industries

Will Straw

In his influential book *Noise*, the French econo-
mist Jacques Attali described music as an early-
warning system. In new ways of making and
disseminating music, Attali suggests, we may
catch a glimpse of imminent changes in the organization of labour and creativity in society as a
whole (Attali 1985). Experimentation and innovation occur in all cultural fields, of course, but
music is relatively unique in that it is produced
and performed in very small-scale intimate circumstances (as is poetry, for example), while
constantly finding new uses for the latest of
technological developments (as do film or multimedia). As the makers of music seek new ways
of distributing it, new relations between the local
and the global are invented. Thus, the past two
decades have seen a rise in the growth of home
computer-based music studios and of musical
undergrounds (like that for UK-based jungle
music), which span the world but remain small-
scale, even artisanal, in many of their activities.
The realm of music allows us an early glimpse of
the paradoxical and contradictory ways in which
new technologies, shifting markets, and changing consumption habits are changing the cultural
sector.

Changes in the character of the music industry have been noted widely over the last half-decade. The "record label," a corporate form typically engaged in signing artists and producing master tapes, has given way to a variety of organizational structures. These include: (a) dance-music production teams, producing CD-masters in home-based computer studios, for distribution via compilation albums often manufactured in other countries; (b) "brokers" of independently produced master recordings, who bypass traditional record label structures and license these to nationally based distributors; (c) custom producers of homemade compact disc albums, who market these via the Internet and duplicate them in response to orders; and a myriad of other structures. The rise of computer-based composition, production, and mastering has made many of the activities of traditional record companies obsolete. Uncertainty over the long-term effects of the Internet has led to predictions that the record store, distribution company, or record label itself will disappear as the industry reorganizes itself. Uncertainty over which of these activities will survive as the basis of a distinct industry is a recurrent theme of music industry discourse at present.

A recent report issued by the British government noted that 80 to 90 per cent of firms active in the sound recording industry were "micro-businesses," that is, firms employing nine people or less (http: //www.culture.gov.uk/creative/mapp_music.htm). In Canada, the federal government claims that there are some two hundred record companies active in the sound recording sector run up against anecdotal evidence that the number is much higher. Historically, Canadian record companies have varied widely in terms of the extent of their involvement in talent, production, or distribution activities. The range of such activities has expanded sharply over the last decade, however. At one level, this diversity of organizational forms is a response to changes in the consumption habits of music consumers. As tastes have become increasingly specialized, they have encouraged a wider range of industry structures, from those companies producing instrumental albums for television-based promotion through to the producers of vinyl, 12-inch singles for the disc jockey market. At the same time, organizational diversity has been one effect of technological change. As the range of channels for distribution and the direct sale of musical recordings expands, companies emerge with distinctive organizational forms suited to these new channels.

This article traces some important developments in the Canadian music industries over the first two years of the new century. Its principal concern is with that sector of the music industries devoted to the production, distribution, and sale of musical recordings, typically in the form of compact discs. We must remember, however, that music is central to many industries, from those which manufacture musical instruments or publish sheet music through to the radio broadcasting sector, for which music is a major source of programming. Over the last few years, all of these industries have confronted changes and uncertainties almost as important as those facing the sound recording industry itself. It is in the making and distribution of musical recordings, however, that these changes have been felt most acutely.

The Canadian Music Industries

On several levels, the past two years have been among the worst for the Canadian music industries in a decade or more. The triumphant international success of Canadian musicians, to which we had grown accustomed in the 1990s (as Celine Dion, Alanis Morrissette, Shania Twain, the Barenaked Ladies, and others rolled through global markets), slowed noticeably in the early 2000s. These successes, in any case, had always been poor indexes of the health of our domestic music industries. Nelly Furtado, Diana Krall, Nickelback, and other Canadian artists have found international success over the past two years. Indeed, in early 2002 the London-based International Federation of Phonographic Industries named Celine Dion "Europe's top multi-million selling-artist" for the period 1996–2001 (IFPI 2002). The biggest news in the Canadian music industries, however, was elsewhere. In 2001, several institutional pillars of Canadian music came crashing down in what seemed like an unending series of cataclysmic events.

In March 2001, *The Record*, Canada's last-remaining industry-oriented music trade magazine, went out of business. In May of the same year, The Song Corporation, Allan Gregg's attempt to build a Canadian-owned "Sixth Major" record company in Canada, filed for bankruptcy. Its failure took down the influential Canadian label Attic Records and battered the balance sheets of several independent companies which had affiliated with The Song Corporation for purposes of distribution. As the year moved on, monthly tallies of unit shipments and dollar sales for the industry showed significant declines from the year before. In November, 2001, the bankruptcy of the Sam the Record Man chain made newspaper front pages across the country.

These events unfolded against the backdrop of general stagnation in the international recording industry. Declining sales and revenues, concern over the impact of technology, and increased corporate concentration fuelled widespread uncertainty about the industry's future. In this context, it was difficult to judge whether problems in the Canadian industry were simply local effects of global trends or whether our national music industries were confronting their own structural weaknesses. *The Record* may have died because it flirted with an unworkable business model. The Song Corporation may have over-extended itself with genres and performers in decline, as one industry executive suggested (off the record). And Sam the Record Man may have finally paid the price for sloppy inventory control and poorly conceived moves into electronic commerce. The cumulative effect of these developments, nevertheless, suggested a broader restructuring of the Canadian industry, one which left U.S. or internationally based interests more firmly in control.

Sales in Decline

The current decline in music sales in Canada may be traced to mid-2000, when monthly sales figures began to drop below those of the same months a year earlier. Initially, this downturn seemed limited to Canada; there was no early evidence that the U.S. market for music was entering a slump. Asked to explain this discrepancy, Randy Lennox, president of Universal Canada, told *Billboard*'s Larry Leblanc that the difference had much to do with the failure of Canadian music fans to embrace the "urban" (in particular, rhythm and blues and Latin) styles currently popular in the United States (Leblanc 2000). Indeed, by the mid-1990s, observers of Canadian music regularly bemoaned the failure of our national industry to develop pop stars working in rhythmic, Top-40-oriented musical idioms. Our expertise in alternative rock and country music had come to seem almost a burden, as the alt.rock boom waned and public tastes moved toward crossover, hit-oriented dance pop.

In 1997, the Canadian Radio-Television and Telecommunications Commission had relaxed rules which limited the frequency at which radio stations could repeat individual records within their programming. This move was intended to spark the production of "hits," through repeated radio airplay; it coincided with a general rise in the popularity of teen-oriented pop. Both developments nourished a rebirth of Top 40 radio formats in Canada. Nevertheless, our industry had, to all intents and purposes, ceased producing records in the single format, and consumers seemed reluctant to buy the full-length, single-artist albums on which hit songs appeared. Compilation albums were one way of selling hit singles, and, by 2001, compilations accounted for 16 per cent of music sales within Canada – a much higher percentage than in the United States (Leblanc 2001a).

The recent success of compilation albums in Canada is often taken as a parable for the broader problems facing our music industry. Once embraced as promotional devices, to introduce consumers to new artists (whose new albums fans would then go on to purchase), compilations increasingly seem to cut into sales of the full album-length works from which they are taken. In a period marked by the rapid turnover of hits and artists, the compilation album can stand as that dose of instant consumer gratification and quick retail revenues whose success masks (and even causes) long-term problems for the music industries. The most negative prognoses for the music industries these days suggest that the old artist-and-repertory functions of record companies – seeking out artists, encouraging their development, building an audience, and so on – are no longer viable in today's commercial climate. Fans seek out tracks or songs, this analysis goes, and will happily acquire these through the Internet, on DJ mix packages, or on the compilations that fill the front racks of music stores.

Even more ominously, the success of compilations has been one factor in making the general merchandise or electronics store (like Wal-Mart or the Future Shop) a more efficient outlet for selling music than the specialty music shop (like HMV or Sam's) (e.g., Adams 2002). General merchandise stories may sell the Top 20 CD albums at discounted prices without the obligation to carry deep inventories of other titles. Alongside the best-selling Now! or Muchdance compilations, Wal-Mart will offer budget compilations of mood music or rerecorded old hits, rather than the major-label jazz reissues or full catalog inventories in which chains like HMV feel they must invest.

Canadian music sales statistics for the year 2001 show a downturn similar to that which transpired in the United States during the same period. Statistics compiled by the Canadian Recording Industry Association (and based on reports from their major-label membership) show declines in both unit sales and dollar revenues for Compact Disc albums of 6 per cent over 2000 (see Table 1). (The catastrophic drop in cassette album sales and unexpected 5 per cent bump in CD single sales over the same period stem mostly

Table 1 Recording Industry Preliminary Industry Statistics for 2001

Sales, year-to-date as of November, 2001 (with comparisons to November, 2000). Unit sales (in thousands of units)

Unit sales*	November 2001	November 2000	% change
Total singles	456	420	9%
Cassette albums	1267	2,637	−52%
CD albums	48,063	51,614	−79%
Total albums	49,330	54,251	−98%

Net value of sales (in thousands of $)

Net value of sales**	November 2001	November 2000	% change
Total singles	2,380	2,171	10%
Cassette albums	6,510	16,687	−61%
CD albums	571,803	617,512	−7%
Total albums	578,313	634,199	−9%

* in thousands of units.
** in thousands of dollars.
Source: Canadian Recording Industry Association figures, posted on CRIA website at http://www.cria.ca/indstats.htm.

from industry decisions to reduce or increase the availability of these con-figurations, and say little about consumer demand.) Statistics tabulated by Soundscan, which tallies retail checkout-counter sales of albums, pointed to a 3.4 per cent decrease in unit sales from 2000 to 2001 (from 63.3 million to 61.0 million units) (LeBlanc 2002).

In the United States, during the same year, album sales declined from 717 to 697 million, a drop of approximately 3 per cent. The most startling statistic on the U.S. industry, perhaps, was that no album had sold more than five million copies during 2001, whereas seven titles had reached those sales levels in 2000 (and one, Eminem's "The Marshall Mathers LP," had sold nine million copies) (Hochman and Leeds 2001). One way of interpreting these figures would be to take them as evidence that sales were now divided more evenly across a wider range of titles – a sign, perhaps, of a healthy plu-ralism in the marketplace.

For major music companies, however, these lowered sales thresholds inspired alternate conclusions. If top-sellers are selling fewer copies, they feel, this has much to do with the fact that sales now decline precipitously after two or three weeks, rather than tracing slow curves through the upper reaches of the charts. In many ways, the life cycles of albums now look more and more like those of movies, whose greatest revenues are derived from the first weekend of release (Ordonez 2001). While saturation booking, concentrated promotion and short public attention spans could explain these life cycle patterns for movies, however, the music industry saw them as confirming the prevalence of illegal CD copying. One group of fans will buy a CD in its first week of release, this theory suggests, then copy it for those who otherwise would have bought an album and kept sales figures afloat in subsequent weeks.

The Canadian Recording Industry Association (CRIA), like its counterparts in other countries, lays the blame for declining sales squarely (and almost exclusively) at the feet of those who copy music illegally. Nevertheless, the attention of these trade groups has shifted in recent years, as the downloading of music for personal use now seems to threaten music industry revenues just as ominously as commercial piracy (which continues to flourish in Latin American, African, and Asian countries). Indeed, while Canada's relative prosperity has made piracy (the mass duplication of illegal copies for sale in grey markets) a relatively minor problem, that same prosperity has made us among the most wired countries in the world. "We are in the middle of a firestorm," Broan Robertson, president of CRIA, claimed in 2001. "High-speed Internet penetration in Canada is among the highest in the world" (Leblanc 2001b).

In music industry crises of the last half-century or more, new technologies have regularly borne the blame for stagnating sales. Radio (in the 1940s), videogames (in the 1980s) and DVDs and the Internet (at present) have been singled out as competing sources of music or objects of youthful attention and obsession. During the music industry slump of the late 1970s and early 1980s, home taping stood as the explanation most commonly offered by the music industry itself. As was the case then, at least two other explanations jostle to explain the current downturn in sales. The most convincing, perhaps, simply links music sales to the general health of the economy, noting that the late-1970s slump coincided with a recession, and that the current decline may likewise reflect a general dip in consumer spending overall.

Music critics and journalists have been more likely to see declining sales as signalling problems of supply rather than demand. In the late 1970s, critics typically blamed low sales on the absence of new superstars with broad, durable appeal, and on the industry's ill-fated investments in disco and New Wave music. (Then, as at regular intervals since, industry watchers bemoan the lack of a new Beatles.) Similar claims have been common over the past two or three years. The music industry's exploitation of the teen-pop fad is regularly denounced as a short-sighted focus on quick revenues, signalling a failure to create the long-lasting careers on which industry stability depends. It needs to be remembered, however, that the careers of many teen-pop artists (such as the Spice Girls) have been longer than almost anyone anticipated, and that the most notable commercial disappointments of the past decade have involved the over-investment in artists groomed for growth and durability who failed to fulfil the enormous expectations laid upon them (such as REM, U2, and, notoriously, Mariah Carey).

I have written elsewhere on the music industry in Quebec, where observers have noticed a growing gap between consumer tastes and the products of a local industry whose structure favours very particular kinds of music (Straw 2000, 2002). Throughout the 1990s, critics and industry observers noted the danger of stagnation, as the music industry in Quebec seemed to be built upon an infrastructure of professional songwriters, studio session musicians, and solo singers. In a report to the Société générale des entreprises culturelles du Québec, Marc Ménard invoked an analysis by *La Presse* music critic Alain Brunet, who claimed that the Quebec industry was unable to meet the increasingly diverse tastes of young Quebeckers. As hip-hop, techno, and world music grow in popularity, an industry organized around professionally managed and media-friendly singer-songwriters might find itself ill-equipped to cater to these tastes (Ménard 1998).

The Song Corporation

The biggest news within the Canadian music industry in recent years was also, perhaps, the most scandalously under-covered business news story of the year. In May, 2001, The Song Corporation, formed in 1999 in an effort to create a Canadian version of a multinational "major" music company, declared bankruptcy. A more detailed history of Song is presented in Table 2, but several key moments in its emergence and unravelling are worth noting. The Song Corporation was pieced together out of various other entities, by Allan Gregg (popularly known as a talkshow host, media commentator, and manager of The Tragically Hip). Gregg announced his intention to create what he called a "Sixth Major." Indeed, at the time of its founding, there was reason to believe the number of vertically oriented multinational music majors in the world might be reduced to four, rather than five (had the proposed merger of EMI with Warner Music and, subsequently, the Bertlesmann Music Group, not been blocked by European Union regulators). Gregg bought up Attic Records, one of the most prominent of Canadian-owned record companies, formed in 1974 amid the optimism that followed the introduction of Canadian content regulations. Gregg also bought a music publishing company, The Music Publisher, from Alliance Atlantis and established a distribution company Oasis Entertainment to distribute recordings. The time was right, Gregg believed, for a major company that would handle the distribution of many small, independent labels.

In 1999, there were good reasons to believe that The Song Corporation was a viable project. Consolidation within the global industry (in particular, the takeover of PolyGram by Universal) had led big companies to shed staff and artists, leaving many of these available on the open market. At the same time, several small, independent labels had been dropped by those majors who distributed them in Canada, leading them to seek affiliations with other companies for the purpose of distribution. In a long interview with Diane Francis of the *National Post*, Gregg called for a new relationship between record companies and artists, one which would allow the latter to share more directly in the profits of the former (Francis 1999). Much of the revenue fuelling these profits would come from the copyrights that were an important part of The Song Corporation's holdings. As of January 1, 1998, radio broadcasters in Canada are subject to a Neighbouring Rights Tariff, which compensates artists and their record companies (and not only songwriters and their publishing companies, as had been the case for over a half-century) for public performance of their music. While the United States has not accepted the principle of neighbouring rights, and while their implementation within Canada has been slow, neighbouring rights leave record companies (and performers) better positioned to derive revenues from the multitude of new music delivery systems that will emerge in coming years. The importance paid to copyright holdings in Song's initial structuring testified to Gregg's belief that rights, as much as physical recordings, were the key to future profitability in the music industries.

After false starts, gimmicky new initiatives, suspicious stock market offerings, hasty reorganizations and rumours of panic, The Song Corporation folded in early 2001. As it turned out, the multinational majors operating in Canada hung onto or reclaimed the distribution of profitable small labels. (The loss of distribution rights to Roadrunner Records in late 2000 is seen by many as the most decisive factor in The Song Corporation's

Table 2 The Short History of the Song Corporation: Chronology

1999

June	Attic Records of Toronto ends its long-term agreement with its distributor, Universal Music.
July	Oasis Entertainment formed by Allan Gregg (co-owner of the Management Trust), Jake Gold (Management Trust), Bill Ott (former President of PolyGram Canada, prior to its take-over by Universal) and Alexander Mair (President of The Attic Group). Gregg states he wants Oasis to be the "sixth major" music company in Canada, and hopes to reach 25 per cent% market share.
	Allan Gregg announces the formation of The Song Corporation. Funding comes from a $15 million private placement raised by Gregg.
	The Song Corporation will include the following:
	· Attic Records (purchased from President/founder Al Mair)
	· The Music Publisher/TMP (purchased from Alliance Atlantis)
	· music publishing catalogues of The Management Trust (Gregg and Gold)
	· Oasis Entertainment (to be headed by Bill Ott)
	The Song Corporation absorbs distributor Page Music, which had folded temporarily when EMI withdrew its ownership involvement. Song will also distribute labels formerly distributed by Attic, including leading US indie Roadrunner.
November	The Song Corporation goes public on Alberta-based Canadian Venture Exchange through reverse take-over of tiny Tertiary Mines, Ltd.

2000

March	Song Corp. announces distribution of thirty labels previously distributed by St. Clair Entertainment.
	Song announces deals with U.S. labels Permanent Press and Razor & Tie for distribution of titles in Canada.
May	Company announces signing of reformed, once-popular Canadian band Grapes of Wrath.
Summer	Song. acquires controlling interest in Canadian label Teenage USA recordings.
August	Song announces agreement with RED Distribution, Inc., "the largest independent distributor of recorded music in the United States" for distribution of RED product in Canada and Song product in USA.
October	Song announces release of first-ever "Companion CD" in Canada. "Companion CDs" serve as sampler compilations, offering buyers of well-known product a selection of materials by lesser-known or up-and-coming artists. Song's Companion CD will be paired with a new album by Maestro (formerly Maestro Fresh-Wes) and will be available through arrangement with the HMV Chain.
	Song announces distribution of shares to recording artists connected to the company.
November	Song announces 3rd-quarter revenues for 2000; loss is $0.04 per share.
	Licensing/distribution agreements announced with U.S.-based companies Venture Video and S-Curve Records.
	Song announces choice of Liquid Audio, Inc., to handle its digital music distribution.
December	Roadrunner Records' deal with Song/Attic ends. Roadrunner signs with Universal for Canadian distribution. Bill Ott will later claim that loss of Roadrunner removed 20 per cent% of Song Corp.'s turnover.
	In conjunction with Microsoft and company called Reciprocal, Song announces the first-ever launch of a "Foreplay" disc, which allows consumers to listen to an album four times before making the decision to buy it. After trial period, consumers can unlock the CD for unlimited play for a further fee.

2001

January	In the face of mounting revenue problems, Allan Gregg announces he will forego salary, but remain as Chair and CEO of Song. Management is restructured: Bill Dawson, Executive Vice President, COO and CFO, announces he will leave the company in May; Bill Ott is named President and COO. The Board of Directors is reduced in numbers.
February	Song signs a worldwide deal giving some worldwide rights to publishing assets to U.S.-based Sony/ATV Music Publishing. Resulting cash injection of $2.4 million is used to pay down company debts.
April	Gold, Mair and Ott (and several others) are no longer on Board of Directors, and all three lose high management positions. Company claims that ongoing efforts to find equity partners haves been unsuccessful.
May	Song Corporation files for bankruptcy, with liabilities of $8.2 million
	Song Corp. CEO Allan Gregg, vice chairman Alexander Mair, and president/COO Bill Ott all resign.
	On May 4th, Mintz & Partners Limited announces it will act as Trustee in the bankruptcy, will liquidate the assets of The Song Corporation and its subsidiaries, and that the respective proceeds of liquidation will be applied toward the payment of the corporations' respective creditors.

Sources: Song Corporation press releases; Buow 1999; Leblanc 1999, 2001b; Olijnyk 2001.

failure.) At the same time, as we have seen, the business entered a significant slump. Song's collapse has been blamed, variously, on an over-commitment to rock music (at the expense of other styles), over-extension during uncertain times, and a shortage of viable distribution pacts with smaller labels. The most tragic consequence of its collapse was the disappearance of Attic Records, which, since 1974, had marketed Canadian music within and outside Canada and distributed smaller labels from the United States and elsewhere. Attic itself had fallen on hard times, and its owner had publicly acknowledged his desire to sell out since Attic's Canadian distributor, Universal, had taken over PolyGram and indicated its priorities were shifting (Bouw 1999). With the news of Attic's death buried amid coverage of The Song Corporation's collapse, tributes to the label's twenty-seven-year history of achievement within the Canadian music industry were sadly absent.

The dream of a Canadian "major" record company – one which combines the production and distribution of recordings with involvement in music publishing and artist management – has inspired few experiments in English Canada. In Quebec, in contrast, the Audiogram record company is one centre of a tightly integrated set of corporations which includes the concert promotion and production company Spectra-scène, the Archambault record store chain, the recording facility Le Studio, the Montreal Féstival du jazz, the gala de l'ADISQ (Association québécoise de l'industrie du disque, du spectacle et de la vidéo) a television program, and the record distribution companies Select and MusicCor.

The problem, for English-Canadian music companies, is that successful integration can no longer be accomplished through the joining together of music-related activities exclusively. In the United States, it has required the absorption of music companies within multimedia conglomerates, who may promote their music through films, magazines, and a variety of multimedia products. (EMI's ongoing search for a new corporate home stems from its own weakness, as the last of the multinational majors to be focused exclusively on music.)

Publications

In November, 2000, *RPM*, the radio and recording industry magazine that Walt Grealis began publishing in 1964, ceased publication. *RPM*'s Golden Leaf Awards, launched with the magazine in 1964, were the forerunner of today's Juno Awards, and *RPM* had played an important role in marshalling the support which led to implementation of Canadian content regulations for radio. By 2000, nevertheless, *RPM*'s influence within the music industries had declined. It steadily lost ground to a slicker, more authoritative trade magazine, *The Record*. After twenty years of publication, *The Record* itself died in March, 2001. It had faced declining advertising revenues for several years, then tried, unsuccessfully, to survive as a subscription-based, Web-only news source. The death of both left English Canada with no print publication covering the music industries. Several websites, most notably Canoe's "Jam!" and the print/web combination "Chartattack," offer charts and lists of new releases, but their news is performer-oriented rather than industry-focused. The Web sites of Canada's two national English-language music industry trade associations fill this gap, but only to a limited extent. The Canadian Recording Industry Association's website (www.cria.ca) publishes monthly sales figures and has links to other sources of statistical information, such as the Soundscan charts published on Jam!. The Canadian Independent Record Production Association (CIRPA) has relaunched its website as www.musicbusinesscanada.com, promising to offer a fuller range of news and industry information than in the past, but this process has just begun. For some time now, the most insightful coverage of the Canadian music industries has been Larry LeBlanc's coverage of the national scene in the U.S. trade magazine *Billboard*.

The death of *RPM* and *The Record* aggravated ongoing difficulties in getting information about the Canadian recording industry. Statistics Canada's reporting on the industry, long a valued source for researchers, has not produced data for years later than 1998. Indeed, obsolete statistics from three or four years ago continue to be trotted out, in "background" packages accompanying speeches by Heritage Minister Sheila Copps, or on the websites of industry associations. While accurate, statistical information on Canadian music remains elusive and scattered, the last couple of years have seen the publication of several milestone books of historical documentation. *Making Music: A Galaxy of Canadian Musical Artists*, by Alex and Ted Barris, focused principally on performers, and on well-known success stories over several decades. Mark Miller's *The Miller Companion to Jazz in Canada* builds on the authoritative treatments of Canadian jazz which Miller has published previously, this time in a useful, encyclopedic form. The most awe-inspiring of these achievements was *Have Not Been the Same: The CanRock Renaissance*, a seven-hundred-page history of Canadian independent rock during the years 1985–95, by Michael Barclay, Ian A. D. Jack, and Jason Schneider. The book's dozens and dozens of case studies – of bands, singers, record companies, and local scenes – are compelling stories on their own, but each serve as parables for the fate of music-makers in Canada. While its authors rarely step outside the boundaries of their chosen focus and apparent tastes (the word "rave" is nowhere to be found here), *Have Not Been the Same* is among the four or five most significant books to date on Canadian popular music.

Retail

When the Sam the Record Man chain declared bankruptcy in November, 2001, journalists in a half-dozen cities documented the outpouring of sentimental regret which resulted. To anyone who had looked closely at music stores, however, the closure was hardly surprising. The chain's key stores had expanded in size with the ascension of the superstore model in the early 1990s, adding new rooms or new sections. Nevertheless, the firm had failed to develop the computer-based inventory-control systems which this model required if chaos was to be avoided. Sam's move into Web-based electronic commerce was a well-documented failure and was quietly halted in April, 2001. As musical tastes shifted toward teen-pop and compilation albums, more and more fans bought their CDs at mass merchandisers, such as Zeller's, or electronic superstores, such as Future Shop. These outlets could sell hit product at low prices without that investment in large, slow-moving inventories to which Sam's (to its credit) was still attached. Indeed, by 2001 it seemed clear that, while fans of mainstream pop had little use for traditional record stores, those with more specialized tastes were often shopping at independent outlets that serviced their particular niche tastes (such as techno or punk), or acquiring music over the Internet. Full-service music stores, like those in the HMV chain, were shifting their emphasis to DVDs or other high-margin items which seemed to generate higher levels of excitement for their customers.

Regret at the loss of Sam's was tempered, as well, by the immediate suspicion that this was principally a restructuring, from which the Sneiderman family (the chain's principal creditors) would emerge as the main beneficiaries. The feeding frenzy of its liquidation sales nourished this suspicion, which was confirmed with the announcement that Sam's Toronto and Halifax stores would remain open under the leadership of the family's second generation. In early 2002, the HMV chain announced that it was ending its liberal returns policy (because fans were returning CDs once they'd copied them at home) and frequent-flyer-like membership card program. HMV, a British-based chain which had invested heavily in Canada (with ninety-eight stores here, compared to only twelve in the United States) itself confronted declining sales and the ongoing competition from general merchandisers and electronics superstores who offered hit product at heavily discounted prices (Bouw 2001). In early 2002, Peter Luckhurst, North American manager for the chain, and the man with principal responsibility for the Canadian stores, announced (like many others that year) that he was retiring in order to spend more time with his family (Shalom 2002; Leblanc 2002).

Artists and Directions

A list of the hundred top-selling albums of 2001 is contained in Table 3. Of the two hundred best-selling albums in Canada in 2001, twenty-eight were by Canadian artists. (Several others were compilations that bore the names of their Canadian compilers, such as M. C. Mario or MuchMusic, but the bulk of the material featured on these was not Canadian.) While the Beatles, for the first time in their history, made the top of year-end album charts in the United States – with "1," their collection of number 1 singles – that album sat at number 17 for the year in Canada. The top five albums in Canada were, in descending order, Shaggy's *Hotshot*, Enya's *Day Without Rain*, the various artists compilation *Big Shiny Tunes 6*, Destiny Child's *Survivor*, and the compilation *Muchdance 2002*. Moving down to number 6 gives us the first album by Canadian performers (Nickelback's *Silver Side Up*), and, arguably, rounds out the range of styles which seemed most commercially successful in 2001. Hip-hop, ethereal pop, crossover teen-pop, hard rock, and the sorts of mainstream dance-pop gathered on the two top-charting compilations would dominate the Canadian Top 200 in 2002. The most surprising aspect of these charts, perhaps, is the low standing of country music, which appears on the Top 100 only because it dominates the soundtrack to the film *Coyote Ugly* (which ranked twelfth).

In the U.S. year-end album charts for 2001, the highest standing by a Canadian was by Nelly Furtado, whose album *Whoa, Nelly!* reached number 54. Sum 41's *All Killer, No Filler*, at 75, and Nickelback's *Silver Side Up*, at number 80, were the only other Canadian albums reaching the U.S. Top 100 album charts for the year. A comparison of these charts for both countries reveals important distinctions in taste and buying patterns. The year-end Top 10 for Canada and the United States share two titles: Shaggy's *Hotshot* and Enya's *Day Without Rain*. We must go down to number 19 on the U.S. 2001 charts before encountering a title which appeared nowhere in the Canadian Top 100 albums – R. Kelly's *TP-2, Com*. (Its absence on the Canadian charts is one more indication of the relatively weak position of rhythm-and-blues in this country.) Overall, though, the list of a hundred best-selling albums in the United States in 2001 contains forty-four titles – almost half the list – which are absent from the same listing for Canada. Because the industries in both countries now rely on SoundScan, the electronic retail scanning system, to compile sales figures, the methodologies of sales tabulation are more similar (and the results more directly comparable) than in the past.

The significant international success of Nickelback (highest chart position in the United States: 2) and Sum 41 (highest U.S. position: 13) has been taken as evidence that Canadians are well-poised to profit from an apparent turn back to hard-edged rock music. Indeed, amid claims that the teeny-pop boom of the last few years is waning, Nickelback have come to stand for the payoffs to be reaped from hard work, lengthy tours and the slow cultivation of a loyal fan base (AntiGUY 2001). Most of these qualities mark the career patterns of the Montreal avant-rock group Godspeed You

217

NO FUTURE?

Table 3 100 Best-Selling Albums in Canada, 2001

Pos	Artist	Album	Label
1	Shaggy	Hotshot	MCA
2	Enya	Day Without Rain	WUK
3	Various Artists	Big Shiny Tunes 6	UNI
4	Destiny's Child	Survivor	COL
5	Various Artists	Muchdance 2002	BMGC
6	Nickelback	Silver Side Up	EMI
7	Alicia Keys	Songs in a Minor	JREC
8	Diana Krall	Look of Love	VER
9	Nelly Furtado	Whoa, Nelly	DRE
10	Jennifer Lopez	J. Lo	EPIC
11	Linkin Park	Hybrid Theory	WBR
12	Coyote Ugly	Original Soundtrack	CUR
13	D12	Devil's Night	INT
14	Enrique Iglesias	Escape	INT
15	Save The Last Dance	Original Soundtrack	HOL
16	Dido	No Angel	ARI
17	Beatles	Beatles 1	EMI
18	U2	All That You Can't Leave Be	ISL
19	Blink 182	Take Off Your Pants and Jac	MCA
20	Nsync	Celebrity	ZOMBA
21	Various Artists	Now! 6	EMI
22	Staind	Break the Cycle	ELE
23	Nelly	Country Grammar	UNI
24	Creed	Weathered	EPIC
25	Pink Floyd	Echoes – Best of	EMI
26	Various	Muchdance 2001	UNI
27	Janet Jackson	All For You	VIRGIN
28	Various Artists	Big Shiny Tunes 5	BS5
29	Britney Spears	Britney	ZOMBA
30	Sum 41	All Killer No Filler	AQU
31	O Brother Where Art Thou?	Original Soundtrack	MER
32	Backstreet Boys	Greatest Hits Chapter 1	ZOMBA
33	Limp Bizkit	Chocolate Starfish and the Hotdog Flavored Water	INT
34	Lifehouse	No Name Face	DRE
35	O-Town	O-Town	JREC
36	Moulin Rouge	Original Soundtrack	INT
37	Various Artists	Planet Pop	BMGC
38	Train	Drops of Jupiter	COL
39	Tool	Lateralus	ZOMBA
40	Various Artists	Women & Songs 5	WCD
41	Lenny Kravitz	Greatest Hits	VIR
42	Dave Matthews Band	Everyday	RCA
43	Andrea Bocelli	Cieli di Toscana	PHI
44	Ja Rule	Pain is Love	DEF
45	Usher	8701	ARI
46	Coldplay	Parachutes	EMI
47	Shrek	Original Soundtrack	DRE
48	Various Artists	Le Lait l'Album Blanc	EMI
49	Barenaked Ladies	Disc One: All Their Greatest	REP
50	Mary J. Blige	No More Drama	MCA
51	Weezer	Weezer (2001)	GEF
52	Garou	Seul	COL
53	Various Artists	Romeo & Juliette	MER

54	Backstreet Boys	Black and Blue	ZOMBA
55	Various Artists	Grammy Nominees 2001: Grammy Pop Nominees	EMI
56	Garth Brooks	Scarecrow	EMI
57	Abba	20th-Century Masters	CEN
58	Radiohead	Amnesiac	EMI
59	Various Artists	YTV Big Fun Party Mix 2	UNI
60	Pink	M!SSUNDAZTOOD	ARI
61	Moby	Play	V2
62	Various	Groove Station 7	BMGC
63	Sade	Lovers Rock	EPIC
64	David Craig	Born To Do It	WST
65	Various Artists	Women & Songs 4	WCD
66	Eve	Scorpion	INT
67	2 PAC	Until the End of Time	INT
68	Isabelle Boulay	Mieux qu'ici	Bas Prod
69	Faith Hill	Breathe	WBR
70	Alien Ant Farm	Anthology	DRE
71	DMX	Great Depression	DEF
72	Creed	Human Clay	EPIC
73	Michael Jackson	Invincible	EPIC
74	Fast and the Furious	Original Soundtrack	DEF
75	Sugar Jones	Sugar Jones	UNI
76	Ssytem of a Down	Toxicity	COL
77	Leonard Cohen	Ten New Songs	COL
78	Blue Rodeo	Greatest Hits Vol. 1	WEA
79	Abba	Gold – Greatest Hits	POL
80	Outkast	Stankonia	ARI
81	Matchbox Twenty	Mad Season	LAV
82	Our Lady Peace	Spiritual Machines	COL
83	Madonna	Music	MAV
84	Gorillaz	Gorillaz	EMI
85	Leann Rimes	I Need You	CUR
86	Paul McCartney and Wings	Wingspan (Hits and History)	EMI
87	M. C. Mario	M. C. Mario Mixdown 2002	SNY
88	Crazy Town	Gift of Game	COL
89	Various Artists	Oh What a Feeling!	INDY
90	Bob Marley	One Love: Very Best Of	UNI
91	Madonna	Greatest Hits Volume 2	MAV
92	Jay-Z	Blueprint	DEF
93	Daft Punk	Discovery	VIR
94	Various Artists	Pure Dance 2001	UNI
95	India Arie	Acoustic Soul	MOT
96	112	Part III	ARI
97	Uncle Kracker	Double Wide	LAV
98	St. Germain	Tourist	EMI
99	Slipknot	Iowa	RDL
100	David Gray	White Ladder	RCA

Source: Soundscan Charts, published on-line at http://www.canoe.ca/JamMusicCharts/
200-2_2001.html

Black Emperor, or of a multitude of techno artists spread across the country, but the latter do not usually imagine themselves struggling toward a possible mainstream success. In 2001, as in most recent years, good music of all kinds seemed to be in great abundance, even when its profitability was often in doubt. Those who, by downloading from the Internet, implicitly make the claim that music should be free, seem just as willing to make music with no expectation of remuneration.

Conclusions

It seems clear that every problem confronting the music industries in Europe or the United States these days will be compounded in Canada. If there is to be no future for record stores – if they are to give way to Internet sales portals, for example – then what, besides the irritation of currency differences, will keep those portals from ignoring Canada and operating out of the United States? If there is to be no future for record companies – if, as some scenarios suggest, we will download music directly from performers – then the proximity to Canadian music sustained by our own industries will disappear, as musics from everywhere become available with equivalent ease. The well-known rapidity with which Canadians adopt new communications technologies has made us one of the most Internet-savvy populations in the world, but this is clearly a double-edged sword. As major media conglomerates have acknowledged for some time, the Internet's offer of abundance will favour those companies with large stockpiles of materials (old and new) whose value may be regularly renewed. Our music companies, few of which are more than a quarter-century old, lack the extensive backlogs of "heritage" musics with which to profit from these new channels of dissemination.

The music industry is notoriously immune to accurate predictions concerning its future. As I noted at the beginning, Jacques Attali described the field of music as one in which we catch an early glimpse of changes which will subsequently affect social and cultural life as a whole. No other realm of activity (and, to be sure, no cultural industry) fulfills this function for music.

Acknowledgments

I would like to thank Grant McCracken, Richard Sutherland, and others whose input into my thinking here was much appreciated. They are not responsible for my errors and misconceptions. I have never met Larry

LeBlanc, Canadian correspondent for *Billboard* magazine, but without his astute and well-informed coverage of the Canadian music industries, we would all be fumbling in the dark. Thank you, as well, to the record company executives who offered their views on the current situation under the guarantee of anonymity.

Bibliography

Adams, James. 2002. "Music is sweet again at Sam's: Sons of venerable record retailer relaunch in wake of bankruptcy." *Globe and Mail*, January 12, A2.

AntiGUY. 2001. "Sophmore: The 2nd Time is the Charm: Nickelback." Rocknworld.com. Available: http://www.rocknworld.com/soph/2001/nb/index.shtml.

Attali, Jacques. 1985. *Noise: The Political Economy of Music*. Translated by Brian Massumi. Minneapolis: University of Minnesota Press.

Bouw, Brenda. 1999. "Music industry veterans target independent artists Oasis formed to compete with the giant record labels." *National Post*, online edition, July 1.

———. 2001. "No. 1 With a Bullet: With Sam's bankrupt, HMV president Peter Luckhurst is king of the land." *National Post*, online edition, December 28.

Francis, Diane. 1999. "Allan Gregg takes on hippest business of them all. Song Corp. to rely on Canada's abundance of musical talent." *National Post*, online edition, July 10.

Hochman, Steve, and Jeff Leeds. 2001. "When the Perfect Storm Hit Labels; The Universal Group leads a diminished derby, battered by artist and fan woes." *Los Angeles Times*, home edition, December 30, F-65.

IFPI. 2002. "Platinum Review: Europe 1996–2001." Available: http://www.ifpi.org/index.html.

Leblanc, Larry. 2000. "Pop's Rise Hurts Canadian Sales: Chains Thrive With Teens; Specialist Stores Fault Release Schedule." *Billboard*, online edition, September 23.

———. 2001a. "Do Compilations Diminish Album Sales? Labels Debate The Impact of Canada's Best-Selling Hits Sets." *Billboard*, online edition, February 3.

———. 2001b. "Canadian Labels, Retailers Call Crisis Meeting Music Merchants and Record Companies Gather to Strategize as Sales Slump." *Billboard*, online edition, May 5.

———. 2002. "Peter Luckhurst leaves HMV." *Billboard*, online edtion, January 19.

Ménard, Marc. 1998. L'industrie du spectacle de chanson au Québec—Portrait économique. Study submitted to the Groupe de travail sur la chanson. Montréal: Société de développement des entreprises culturelles.

Ordonez, Jennifer. 2001. "Music Sales Hit a Sour Note; No Hot New Genres Emerge." *Wall Street Journal*, online edition, August 3.

Shalom, François. 2002. "So long, Sam: Landmark music chain shuts its Ste. Catherine St. doors." *Montreal Gazette*, online edition, January 12.

Straw, Will. 2000. "In and Around Canadian Music." *Journal of Canadian Studies* 35(3) (Fall): 173–83.

———. 2002. "L'industrique du disque au Québec." In *Traité de la Culture*, edited by Denise Lemieux. Québec: Presses de l'Université Laval, pp. 831–46.

United Kingdom. 2001. Creative Industries: Mapping Document 2001. Available: http://www.culture.gov.uk/creative/mapp_music.htm.

NEW MEDIA *and*
CANADIAN SOCIETY

"UNHYPING" THE INTERNET
At Home with a New Medium

Maria Bakardjieva

The Internet: Hits, Heads, and Hype

Over the course of the last few years Canadian statistics have demonstrated a growing rate of Internet adoption. Indicators of this sweeping trend include the following facts:

- In 1999, home became the most popular location for Internet use, surpassing work, school, and all other locations (Statistics Canada 2000);
- In 2000, more than half (51 per cent) of all Canadian households (Statistics Canada 2001b) and 53 per cent of all Canadians, or 13 million people aged fifteen and over, used the Internet at home, at work or at some other location (Statistics Canada 2001c).

- The so-called "digital divide," or the gap between Internet "haves" and "have-nots," showed some signs of narrowing, with the highest growth rate of Internet adoption (41 per cent) occurring among households with incomes less than $36,000 and households headed by seniors (41 per cent). Despite that, higher-income households and households whose members were younger and had higher levels of education were still more likely to use the Internet (Statistics Canada 2001b). Compared to 1994, in 2000 the proportion of men using the Internet had doubled to 56 per cent, while the proportion of women had more than tripled to 50 per cent (Statistics Canada 2001c);
- The two most common uses of the Internet registered in 2000 were e-mail (84 per cent of Canadian users) and searching for goods and services (75 per cent of Canadian users) (Statistics Canada 2001c).

While the prevalence of more highly educated and higher-income users persists, these numbers nonetheless demonstrate that Canadians from all walks of life are bringing a new communication medium into their homes in massive numbers. Consequently, major research centres have undertaken efforts to describe the behaviour of this nascent population of Internet users in order to identify the impacts that the new medium is having on society (Nie and Erbring 2000; Pew Research Center 2000; UCLA Center for Communication Policy 1999). In this country, the task has been taken up by Statistics Canada, which launched its first Household Internet Use Survey in 1997 and has conducted it on an annual basis ever since.

Another strand of quantitative Internet user research is emerging from the rapidly proliferating marketing studies on the nature of the Web "audience." Marketing researchers have worked to provide information for the growing e-commerce enterprise (for example, ComQUEST 1999; Nielsen/NetRatings 2000). These studies aim to capture the characteristics and use habits of home Internet users and, on that basis, advise advertisers and e-commerce managers on how to maximize the effectiveness of their appeal.

So far, very little research on the new phenomenon of massive Internet penetration into Canadian homes has gone beyond counting heads and hits to ask what the Internet *means* to domestic users. "What do they make of what they 'absorb,' receive and pay for? What do they do with it?" (Certeau 1984, 31).

There are several reasons why filling this gap is important. In the home, we can observe the user as a socially situated individual and interpret his or her Internet-related behaviour in relation to the larger picture of his or her life. How do individuals make sense of the new medium? What values and functions do they ascribe to it in their everyday lives? Are these values and functions the same or do they differ in the case of users in different social, economic, and personal contexts? How is Internet use connected with the practices that constitute family and community life? Does it help establish and maintain new relationships between the household and the larger social world? Note that the accent in these questions is not on the medium's effects, but rather on the symbolic processes in which the medium is socially constructed. Silverstone and Haddon (1996), among others, have argued that if we are interested in understanding the complete cycle of the social shaping of any technology, we should include user-appropriation as an important aspect of it. This means that the Internet becomes what it is through the daily practices of its users. Its social and cultural role can be grasped and evaluated adequately only after a careful examination of this immediate level of engagement of people with it in the practice of everyday life.

This article represents an attempt at addressing these less-clear-cut, impossible to quantify, but much more exciting questions by drawing on both quantitative and qualitative research on Internet use in the home. The format of this exercise will involve switching between the macro- and the micro-perspectives. Qualitative research will allow a "zoom in" movement revealing how statistically established trends look in micro-settings and from the standpoint of actual users. The goal will be to juxtapose the macro-narratives about "Internet impacts" with a host of stories like those that people tell each other every day; to capture the numerous small ways in which people dealing with the Internet in everyday life define and shape the new medium through the choices they make. The data furnishing this examination come from two sources: Statistics Canada's most recent Household Internet Use Survey (2000) and General Social Survey: Internet Use (2000), on one hand, and the findings of an ethnographic study of domestic Internet use conducted in Vancouver, Canada, in 1998–99, on the other (Bakardjieva 2000). This study involved in-depth interviews, and "tours" of the home and computer space of nineteen lower-middle-class households with Internet connections.

Growing Internet Penetration or Becoming an Internet User

As the statistical data compellingly demonstrate, the Internet connection has become a home fixture for millions of Canadians of different gender, age, and social and economic standing. Contrary to technological determinism, there is nothing natural or inevitable about this triumphant march. In order to understand how it happened and why, we have to look at actual settings where human agents endowed with reason and independent will make decisions concerning technology. The task of analyzing actual adoption contexts, however, is complicated by the fact that the home Internet connection, at least at this early stage in the development of the medium, is not a simple device such as a microwave or dishwasher that the user brings home with a clearly defined straightforward function in mind. It is a "heterogeneous network" (Callon 1987, 93) comprising technical, social, cultural, and cognitive elements that emerges gradually and bears the formative influence of numerous forces. Ruth Schwartz Cowan has argued that, in order to understand the success or failure of such networks holding user and technology together, one should examine them from "the consumption junction, the place and the time at which the consumer makes choices about competing technologies." This, according to Cowan, is "the interface where technological diffusion occurs" and also "the place where technologies begin to reorganize social structures" (Cowan 1987, 263).

Taking the user as one's analytical entry point, the issue of Internet adoption translates into a set of questions concerning the logic of the relationships users establish with the Internet from within the actualities of their everyday lives. In order to capture these relationships, it becomes necessary to identify the various components or "actors" and "actants" making up the sociotechnical network and to explain how and why the connections among them arose. The following analysis tracks the social trajectory of domestic Internet connections, drawing on the narratives of the participants in the Vancouver study.

The home computer

The computer was the first element to make its way into the future Internet user's home. It had usually gotten there along the line of a productive activity such as work or study performed in the outside world. In most cases, the need to use a computer (its relevance) had been externally imposed by a certain organization, or the expense of buying one had been justified by the expectation of increased efficiency in an income-yielding activity. This external imperative was smuggling the machine into people's homes.

> I went into business for myself for a few years. I had already a computer – a 286, it wasn't good enough for auto-CAD at that point. So I bought a 486 – at that time it was the best and today it is already old and out of date. So, I had everything already there, I only needed to add a modem. I got the modem when I got onto CompuServe. (Reiner, 62, retired mechanical-engineering technician)[1]

> [What were you doing with your computer before you got the Internet?] Writing letters, word processing. I did some work in security business for a while; I did the basics – selling security products like cameras. So I did bookkeeping and record keeping. (Jane, a 35-year-old homemaker)

Taking the computer home usually meant taking work home from one's job site or turning the home into the primary site of paid work. As a direct reflection of the sweeping computerization of the institutions of production and education, computer technology had acquired imposed relevance[2] in the everyday lives of people who were not necessarily "knowledge workers" of high education and status.

For another group of people, the perceived relevance of the computer had an ideological component. Sophie, a thirty-five-year-old nutrition consultant, explained: "When we got the computer first, it was basically for the kids and for us to be upgraded, to be technically upgraded." "To be technically upgraded" stood for an effort to keep up with technological development even when no immediately instrumental applications of it could be found in the home. Similarly, Martha, 41, a meat-wrapper for Safeway, felt compelled to "upgrade" herself with computer equipment and skills in light of her job-related injury that made her look for occupational alternatives. Her exposure to computerized equipment for weighing and labelling at work, and the general discourse of the "computer age," had led her to look in that direction. The computer was presenting itself to her as a source of job opportunities, even if still vague: "And I took a basic programming course a year or two before that. I thought in this computer age I better stay in touch" (Martha).

With a third group of users in this study, the computer had been handed down by a friend or relative who had needed to upgrade his or her own equipment at work or at home. The old computer thus could be given out for free.

> Being retired I basically try to minimize my expenditure on and around the computer. I started with an MX which was free. Someone was throwing it out. Then I bought a second-hand 286, three years ago and then quite recently, this year, a friend of mine who is a computer programmer brought a motherboard for a 386 and put that in the computer. So now I have a 386. All I needed to go out and buy was a hard drive – I didn't have enough memory, so I bought a hard drive. (John, a 73-year-old retired mechanical engineer)

This practice points toward an interesting mechanism of social diffusion of computer technology. The machine, although in a more or less outdated version, becomes available to people in the social networks of computer (and computerized) professionals. Non-professionals and "poor cousins" take up the computer waste and put it to uses of their own. Notably, in some of the cases in this last group, the explicit motivation for accepting the free computer has been its communication function.

> My brother is an actuary, so he uses computers all the time.... So, he was upgrading and he offered me this computer. He had offered it to me 3 or 4 times before and finally I said ok because I had heard – I have had arthritis now since 1992 – that there was a site on there on which I could meet people with arthritis. So I said, here is my chance to use the Internet for something that would be useful to me.... I'd seen them, computers, in the library and I was sort of intrigued, but I could never find how they could be of any use to me. I am not into learning something that is not useful. (Garry, 65, retired naval radio operator)

For Ellen, a former editor with a disability preventing her from working, the home computer gained relevance when she became housebound due to her illness:

My friend came and he said "I'm going to set you up on the Internet, and I'm going to show you how to use it" and this specific function was different from when I used to work. The main purpose was in order for me to be able to connect to a support group. (Ellen)

So, Ellen received an old Macintosh from her friend and got an Internet connection through the local Community Net, also for free. Predictably, Ellen's equipment, as well as that of the other users in this group, was far from being top of the line. The recipients of free computers typically had no or limited knowledge of computer technology and little access to education about it. At the same time, their second-hand, outdated hardware could not handle up-to-date, user-friendly software applications that make use smooth and easy. In this way, ironically, the least knowledgeable had to deal with the most awkward and challenging programs and tools.

Hooking up

Let us now look into the different motivations that led the respondents to make the step from an isolated (stand-alone) computer, a machine for word-processing, bookkeeping, game-playing, etc. into the Internet. Why did they want to bring home a new communication medium? How did the Internet as a technology gain relevance for the people interviewed?

Despite the fact that the respondents in this study were not computer or Internet professionals, quite a few of them had experienced an outside institutional pressure to hook up to the Internet from home. This was most notable in the cases of those who were involved in college or university education. There were also others who felt the need to be able to transfer files between their office and their home, or to do work- or study-oriented research on the Internet from home. The Internet connection at home was seen as relevant in the context of the relations between work/education and family life. It was brought in as a mechanism for extending the work/education space or more precisely, in this case, for blending the spaces of work and education with that of the home:

The Internet came next because I was in nursing [college program], ... and they strongly recommended it as a research resource, for looking up all kinds of different things we'd need to do in nursing.... I thought I just could use the one [connection] at school to deal with the addresses that were assigned to us at school.... But he [her husband] said that the reality was that it's easier to use it from home, from the comfort of my own home, and he was right, because as soon as I was done with classes, I wanted to come home. (Sophie, 35, part-time nutrition consultant)

Much as we saw in the case of computers, a second kind of motivation for connecting to the Internet had to do with a more abstract interest in the technical novelty instigated by public discourses. These were the users whose early motivation to hook up to the Internet had not been predominantly instrumental and institutionally imposed as in the cases quoted above. For them, the Internet had acquired a non-utilitarian, culturally imposed relevance.

Why I wanted to have an account? Because the Internet is something of fashion, there is a lot of talk about the Internet and I can see some business possibilities. The excitement to have something new was the primary reason. (Patrick)

I guess initially I was attracted by curiosity only. It was so much in the news, in the media hype and whatever. I guess you want to see what is really going on. I think one of my sons said once: "If you don't have it, you feel like an outcast. You don't know what is really going on. If you don't have e-mail, who are you?" (Reiner)

In contrast, a third type of motivation for connecting to the Internet from home was characterized by the intrinsic desire to attain something concrete, for example to be able to e-mail friends and family:

Then a friend started telling me about the Internet. He had a son in Calgary and another one in Montreal and he told me how every night he got e-mail letters from them and he would e-mail back. And I said: "How do you do that? How much does it cost you?" And he said: "It doesn't cost me anything. Would you like to try it?" So he came and hooked me up with CompuServe. (John)

Users such as Garry and Ellen, who had acquired computers specifically for the purpose of communication, also fell in this category. They were orienting to the Internet as a matter of free volition, hoping to get access to support groups and, eventually, non-conventional solutions to their personal problems and needs.

A common feature of the people participating in the Vancouver study was their relatively modest disposable income and hence their caution not to undertake unnecessary spending on the computer equipment and Internet service. Yet, there were marked differences in how the reasonable level of expenses was perceived, depending on the kinds of motives people had for bringing information technology into their home.

Intrinsic motivation did not lead users in this lower-middle-class social bracket to make substantive investment in up-to-date equipment. Older people who could not expect any tangible profit or potential increase of earning power and status to ensue from the technology had been reluctant to spend on powerful equipment. With younger people, too, the degree to which they had accepted the idea of the Internet as a vehicle of upward mobility seemed to have an express influence when things came down to equipment expenses.

Emerging stratification: Low-tech, high-tech, and HSA Canadians

The tangible outcome of these differently patterned motivations was a marked variation in the levels of power and speed of the equipment installed in the home. Low-tech users put up with a limited access to the Internet in terms of both time and features and navigated much more cumbersome interfaces than those with advanced equipment, software, and service.

Most of the discussions of unequal access to the Internet have worked with a binary model – a person either has access or not.[3] At this stage of the social diffusion of the technology, the question *what kind of access* is available to a user or a category of users needs to be raised more insistently. The answer to this question could orient the practical shaping of the Internet on the part of site and service designers. The inequality in technical equipment opens new gaps among people who *have* access to the Net. A whole new social stratification seems to be emerging among Internet users themselves.

Both high-tech and low-tech users, as well as a myriad of intermediary states between them, find meaningful applications of the medium. However, commercial and political players chart the course of technical and institutional development of the Internet with consideration of the high-tech users only, or predominantly. One Web-audience researcher company, for example, speaks about those who have high-speed access to the Internet (about 15 per cent of all Canadian Internet users) as "HSA Canadians" and declares them a "key prospect" for Internet information providers (ComQUEST 2001). Thus, while low-tech users are and will remain the predominant number of Internet users in Canada for an unforeseeable number of years, low-tech designs and technical solutions – examples include textual browsers and simple e-mail programs – are not pursued and supported. This marginalizes Internet users with older equipment and slow connections and limits the range of meaningful applications to which they can put the new medium. Seen from this angle, the fact that e-mail is the most popular Internet application may mean that this is all that a substantive number of users do with the Internet because they don't have the time and patience to wait for fancy pages to download and possibly crash their old computers. Using the Internet only or predominantly for e-mail is not necessarily a bad thing. The point here is that the statistically established relatively high rate of Internet penetration should not be interpreted as equalizing opportunities. It would be an even bigger mistake for political bodies and civic organizations to assume that, with an increased penetration rate, Web-based resources are available to the majority of the households and people in Canada.

If the Internet is to be developed as an equitable social resource, the actual circumstances and substantive interests of low-tech users have to be taken into account by software and service designers on the one hand, and content providers, on the other. What sense would it make, for example, to develop flashy Web-based job-ad sites if unemployed users cannot afford the type of connection that would allow them to view these pages? How is the Internet serving parking patrollers, auto body technicians and meat wrappers (all represented in the respondent group of the Vancouver study) if the majority of the positions advertised through this medium are intended for computer professionals?

Content presented on the Internet typically caters to users occupying higher educational, professional, income, and technical-equipment brackets. And this problem is being aggravated by the advent of e-commerce. This deficiency in application and content development can infringe on vital democratic processes allegedly supported by the new medium if it is reproduced by public organizations such as government, unions, and civic associations.

Networking knowledge and skills: The warm expert

The acquisition of a minimum of networking knowledge and skills is a crucial condition for the stabilization of the home Internet connection. The respondents in the Vancouver study had traversed a complex path to pick up such knowledge and skills in both formal settings – an Internet course at the college, an instructional session at the library – and within their own homes with the help of more experienced friends and relatives. Notably, even when the introduction to the Internet had been initiated elsewhere, the "domestication" (Silverstone 1994) of the medium, its appropriation unfolding in one's own home, had been intensively assisted by a close friend. The computer/Internet-literate friend or relative was a recurring character in all of the respondents' stories.

This character appeared initially in the role of someone who precipitated the encounter between the user and the technology. This was the person who "started telling me about the Internet" (John), or insisted that "if you don't have it, you don't know what is really going on" (Reiner), or that the respondent should have it in order to be able to maintain e-mail communication with that friend or relative

An even more important role that the friend's character had played in these stories, however, was one that could be dubbed "the warm expert." The warm expert is an Internet/computer technology expert in the professional sense or simply in a relative sense vis-à-vis the less knowledgeable other. The two characteristic features of the warm expert are that he or she possesses knowledge and skills gained in the world of technology and can operate in this world, but at the same time he or she is immediately accessible in the user's lifeworld as a fellow man or woman. The warm expert mediates between the technological universal and the concrete situation, needs, and background of the novice user with whom he or she is in a close personal relationship.

In Martha's story this role was played by a friend from a remote suburb who came to her house when she bought her new 486 and stayed there for a while helping her with her computer. That friend was on CompuServe, so Martha too took a subscription with CompuServe. Subsequently, the correspondence with that same friend would comprise one of the main streams in the flow of her e-mail.

In Theodore's experience, the warm expert was a cousin (a professional "tech support person") living in the United States who visited like a missionary the homes of his dispersed relatives in North America and hooked them up to the Internet. Theodore's modem and his first mailing list subscription came as gifts from that cousin.

Garry took it upon himself to learn how to use his newly installed computer and Internet connection, relying on what he had heard at an introductory session in the library, and by trial and error. However, when his computer crashed shortly after he started his explorations, he had to call upon a computer knowledgeable friend:

> So there was a misconnection in the mouse and the pointer wouldn't come up, so I thought it was something wrong and pressed every button on the key board in sequence trying to find out.... And during that procedure I crashed the machine. That was the first thing I did. Luckily, I have a friend who is just super technical! He lives and breathes technical things. (Garry)

Less than two years after her initial introduction to the Internet, Sandy was often called upon to teach other people who wanted to set up their own Internet connections at home. In her teaching, she drew on what she had learned from her own discoveries:

> Lots of people now get me to hook them up to the Internet because they know that I hang out there. One of the first things that I download is a chat line program and I say: this is where you go for help – and if they have a Macintosh I will set it up so that they just go in there – in the Macintosh room. And if you go in there and ask for help there are hundreds of people that will help you – they'll tell you where to go and what to do. Then you form relationships with other people who have computers.... [ISP] has their own software, but I don't recommend people to use it.... That's how Stanley taught me – "Don't use [ISP] software, Sandy, use your own software because you are in control of it." (Sandy)

The learning experiences of new domestic users of the Internet recounted here thus exhibit a profoundly social character. The obverse of this social learning process was the process of socialization of personal knowledge of the technology and the medium. Friends and relatives, and to some degree online helpers, had taught the users participating in the study not only how to navigate the interface, but also what they themselves had discovered the Internet was about. They were passing along their definitions of the new technology crystallized from their own experience. As the cases of Sandy and Martha illustrate, the same had happened later, when some of the respondents in the study had become capable of playing the role of the warm expert vis-à-vis less-knowledgeable others.

The registration of the central position of the warm expert in the weaving and stabilizing of the home Internet connection suggests several noteworthy inferences. Initiatives aimed at overcoming the "digital divide" would not be successful even if they offer free computers and Internet access to disadvantaged Canadians. The barrier often consists not only in the level of income and education, but also in the absence of potential warm experts from the social networks of these people. What they need access to the most is somebody "like themselves" who would help them discover what the new medium could do *for them*.

The second message to be drawn from the story is addressed to those who tend to believe that Internet technology itself, or the discourses spun by the powerful players promoting particular versions of it, will single-handedly determine what the broad user population will think of the new medium and do with it. The Internet has proven to be a fruitful field for creative appropriation on the part of "ordinary men" (Silverstone 1994) and women who apply it in their own ways. The prominence of the warm expert, and not the Microsoft manual, in the learning process producing Internet users provides an assurance that networked profiteers may not have it exactly their way. With this thought in mind, the next section will look at electronic commerce.

On Window-Shopping

Slowly but surely, Canadians are living up to their government's vision and plan to make Canada the most connected country in the world. And as more Canadians get connected and become familiar with the Internet, "many are graduating to window-shopping online," we are assured by a backgrounder from the Electronic Commerce Branch of Industry Canada (Industry Canada 2001a). The same publication expresses the expectation that, given some time, window-shoppers become online purchasers and ultimately begin paying for their products directly online. Thus Canada appears to move steadily toward the goal of becoming a world leader in the development and use of electronic commerce foreordained for it in the government's

Electronic Commerce Strategy (Industry Canada 1998). The very fact that in 2000, 75 per cent of Canadian users used the Internet to search for goods and services (Statistics Canada 2001c) seems to suggest that the medium has been irreversibly commercialized, not only in the minds and aspirations of governmental and commercial players, but in the daily practice of ordinary users as well.

Thus, the Internet has followed the course charted by earlier communication technologies, such as radio. In its early years, enthusiasm and hopes that the new technical channel would democratize public communication and invigorate civic life abounded. The image of the Internet as a community-building technology, fuelled by the optimistic predictions of early professional users, analysts, and technological utopians, determined its public understanding. The moment the opportunities for commercial gain emerged, however, this image gave way to visions of dot.com enterprise, online marketing and sales. The Internet was construed by the business world as a medium affording further intimacy between businesses and consumers. Seventy years ago, radio excited businessmen by offering them, according to Harry P. Davis of Westinghouse, "a latch key to nearly every home in the United States" (quoted in Czitrom 1982). The Internet promised to entice consumers to "shop for their underwear in their underwear" (Kalakota and Whinston 1997, 220).

Even though underwear still does not figure among the most popular types of products purchased online, the stream of Canadians who order and pay for their books, magazines, and newspapers, computer software, travel arrangements and music, and most recently, clothing, jewellery, and accessories, over the Internet has grown.[4] This is still a very small fraction of annual consumer spending in Canada,[5] and yet it points to a rising trend (see Industry Canada 2001b and Ellison, 2003). But is it correct to measure and interpret this trend only quantitatively? Are established shopping practices simply migrating online, slowly, due to lingering concerns over transaction security, but inevitably promising – or for some, threatening – to overshadow the face-to-face shopping experience at sites of brick and mortar?

If one listens more closely to Internet users' accounts, however, a whole new dimension of electronic commerce opens up. The common phrase "window-shopping," in fact, may be misleading when applied to "searching for information on products and services online" (Statistics Canada 2001c). References to consumer products and services came up in Internet users' own accounts of their practices under the rubric of "research." From their own point of view, the people interviewed were carrying out *research* on a whole gamut of topics. Equipped with their Internet connections, they seemed to approach their everyday life activities with a heightened awareness of the diverse choices and possibilities available. They were taking a questioning and reflexive stance vis-à-vis their environment and seeking to elaborate rational strategies for dealing with it. The interest in "doing research" was most clearly expressed in the field of medicine, health, and pharmacy. People were drawing on both medical school sites and newsgroups discussions in their effort to figure out and manage their health problems. Research was performed on places to travel to, on apple trees to be planted in one's garden, on forage to feed to one's cows, on historical events drawn into current media discourse, on musical releases, on locating long-lost members of one's family, on equipment and other items to be bought. All of these diverse interests and projects can be subsumed under one trend – the effort to make informed and thus rational choices about matters of daily action, including consumption:

> Another aspect I like – when I want to buy something – whatever it is, be it shoes or books, I can actually get more information about products from the Internet than I can receive from sellers, or a clerk in a store. I think I probably get more factual information because it has been presented to you in a written fashion. It is different when someone puts it on paper and when someone gives it to you verbally. You never know whether this person actually knows anything. So, that I find very helpful – knowledge about anything I would like to purchase ... information is very good for me. I can compare different offers on the Internet and I find I am going to the store much better prepared and I know much more even than the clerk. (Reiner, 62, retired mechanical-engineering technician)
>
> For example, last week I needed a fax, I looked here [on the Internet] what faxes there are on the market.... Instead of asking technical information from the store and the salesmen, who know nothing about that, I went directly to the web site, looked up all things that I needed, downloaded them and chose exactly this fax, which helped me a lot because it saved me a lot of time searching the stores. It also saved me some money because I didn't decide to buy a more expensive fax given that this one would serve me just as well to do what I want. (Alex, 36, jewellery designer)

Thus, in contrast with window-shopping, which typically is frivolous and merchant-led, online product research is rational and consumer-led. It strives at achieving reasonably good understanding of the advantages and disadvantages of the product under consideration and striking a balance between detached analysis and first-hand impression. That is why Internet-based product research is often followed by a personal visit to a local store, especially in the case of products whose feel and appearance matter to consumers. If this turns out to be a persisting practice, then business analysts pointing out the good prospects of hybrid-type click-and-mortar enterprises have a strong argument.

Interestingly, respondents' accounts reveal that often online product research involves consultation with other consumers, especially when a product is related to specific activities – professional or hobbyist – and a respective group or community of informed users of this product can be identified online. For example, one of the respondents was soliciting advice from his hobbyist mailing list before making equipment purchases:

> ... if I wanted a new glider, I would put out an inquiry saying that I was looking at a certain type of glider and ask for comments about it and people will come up with comments. (John, 73, retired mechanical engineer)

Not only advice, but also products themselves seemed to change hands among consumers, inviting the question why this movement has not found recognition as a potentially important aspect of e-commerce. "Electronic commerce encompasses three distinct types of transactions: those between businesses, those between businesses and consumers, and government services" elaborates the Canadian Electronic Commerce Strategy (Industry Canada 1998). A fourth type of transaction, distinctly suited to the new interactive electronic environment, the transactions from consumer to consumer, have remained outside the scope of e-commerce promoters.

> My old radio equipment, needed a crystal to change the frequency. I put an inquiry [in his mailing list] that I was looking for these crystals and somebody in Texas came back: "I've got what you want, John. Seven dollars each, if you like it, send the money, if not – send it back." Without e-mail, that facility would have never existed. A total stranger trusted me. (John, 73, retired mechanical engineer)

There is money to be made on the basis of this type of e-commerce, as the success of online auction sites,[6] glowing survivors of the dot.com bust, has shown. There is a lot to be gained by customers as well, if independent channels for mutual information and advice among buyers are created by non-profit organizations, consumer associations, and various sorts of activity-oriented online communities. The online environment opens up opportunities for more critical and deep-cutting consumer involvement in commercial practices. However, such involvement has to find its own forms and spaces free of market manipulation, a task that the government and existing consumer organizations may want to consider putting on their e-commerce agenda. Not simply strategies for protecting the consumer, but also forms of giving more initiative and power to the consumer need to be devised for the online commercial environment.

Children Driving Internet Penetration

The 2000 edition of the Household Internet Use Survey demonstrates convincingly that children and young people are a significant driving force behind Internet penetration. The survey found that single-family households with unmarried children aged eighteen and under had the highest exposure to the Internet (Statistics Canada 2001b). The data regarding Internet use gleaned through the 2000 General Social Survey reveal that over half of Canadian households with children between five and eighteen have purchased a computer specifically for their children (Dryburgh 2001). A total of 85 per cent of young Canadians between fifteen and twenty-four years were found to have used the Internet from some location in the month preceding the survey. More than half (56 per cent) of the fifteen- to twenty-four-year-olds were connected to the Internet from home, and half of these used the medium every day (Rotermann 2001).

Fifty-two per cent of young home users also accessed the Internet from school, along with 29 per cent of fifteen- to twenty-four-year-olds who didn't have home access. Home users, predictably, spent longer hours on the Internet than those young people who accessed it from school, work, library, Internet café, or other locations.[7] When asked about their reasons for starting to use the Internet, 69 per cent of the males and 57 per cent of the females in this age group pointed to personal interest while 40 per cent of the young women and 28 per cent of the men said that their initial reason for going online was school-related. Having in mind the initiation experiences cited earlier, three powerful factors are at work in bringing young Canadians online: the requirements of school, curiosity, and the desire to keep up with technological and communication developments popular with peers and extolled as the key to future success. Recall: "if you don't have e-mail, who are you?" And finally, young Canadians have access to an abundance of "warm experts" to learn from. That is, they are encountering the new medium in a rich social context.

A cursory count of what young people do on the Internet brings to light the wide popularity of e-mail (used by 71 per cent), while online chatting and game-playing emerge as the second favourite uses for the fifteen- to seventeen-year-olds[8] and then gradually give way to searching for information on goods and services and accessing news sites as age increases. Interestingly, 33 per cent of young Canadians using the Internet have met new people online and become friends with some of them. This percentage is even higher in the teenage group (fifteen- to seventeen-year-olds). The data available so far, however, say little about how the Internet meshes with offline activities and how it becomes embedded in them. How do friendships develop on- and offline? Does the new medium help students learn more or better? Does it widen their horizon in terms of political affairs and civic activism? Do teenagers feel more confident participating in academic, economic, and, generally, social life because of the availability of the Internet? Much more in-depth social research is needed, if we would like to address adequately the "so what?" questions logically following the announcement of the quantitative findings regarding penetration and use. The numbers, useful and remarkable as they are, do little to soothe parents' anxiety as to what the Internet is doing to their children and what their own role in the process should be.

All we know about parents' attempts to make sense of their children's relationship with the new medium is more numbers. The 2000 General Social Survey found that in 64 per cent of Canadian Internet households, parents try to monitor children's Internet use by supervising them directly while they are online. "Hard" approaches such as locking the computer and using different monitoring and filtering techniques are taken by less than 10 per cent of the households, while 33 per cent of Canadian parents with home Internet access do nothing to control their children's exploits on the Internet (Dryburgh 2001). Which of these methods is right and which is wrong? Should this seeming lack of adequate parental control over children's Internet use throw us into moral panic?

Maria Bakardjieva

The passionate engagement of young Canadians with the new medium calls for new parenting practices to be invented in a broad, participatory public learning process. This process starts at the point where individual households coin their own sets of rules and roles around the new medium, grounded in what Silverstone, Hirsch, and Morley (1992, 15–31) have called "the moral economy of the household." It is a process of Internet regulation that doesn't take place at the scene of parliament and government, but in the living room, the bedroom, or home office instead. Let us zoom in on a few domestic settings that can provide a first-hand idea of what goes on when a new communication medium comes to disturb the established everyday norms of family living.

Internet parenting

The primary reason why Sophie, 35, a part-time nutrition consultant and her family had wanted to bring a computer and an Internet connection into their home had been in Sophie's words "for us and the kids to be technically upgraded." But with the arrival of the technical novelty, a whole new set of issues had emerged. One important thing Sophie wanted to ensure was that she or her husband were home when their sons went on the Internet. The location of the computer in their living room was central enough to allow the parents to keep an eye on what their boys were doing in cyberspace, even while they were busy with something else around the house. Monitoring children's use of paid Internet time and the printer was part of the incentive for this:

> They'd like to download a lot of pictures and things and get them printed out, but we try do discourage them because it is too expensive. I mean, if they need a picture for a project or something like that, that's fine. But if they just want to hang it on the wall or whatever, they've got to kind'a watch that. (Sophie)

The second and more alarming reason for keeping an eye on the boys' Internet use was pornography. Sophie's anxiety did not stem simply from the knowledge of pornography being available "out there" in cyberspace. She was disturbed by the fact that pornography was actively reaching into her home uninvited and intruding on her and, potentially, her teenage sons' attention. One small-scale technology-out-of-control experience had prompted Sophie and her husband to start looking for preventive measures against the inflow of pornography: "Because you can put in something very innocent and have quite surprising things come up on the Internet."

What had happened to Sophie was that she entered "Toyota Previa" as a search term in a search engine because she and her husband were thinking about buying one. All of a sudden, she was confronted with a number of shocking "previews" of hard-core pornographic sites. The search engine, she thought, "must have misunderstood." Or, because she was in a car-related site, Sophie speculated: "maybe those [cars and pornography] go together, maybe people think they go together, I don't know." In any case, it was not only too easy to get into these hard porn previews, it was confusingly difficult to get out: "cuz when you push 'back' you'd normally get out of the site quite easily, but this one just kept going with this horrid stuff." If the kids had been looking at the computer at that moment, Sophie concluded, she would have been very unhappy. That was why she and her husband bought two different patrol programs and installed them on the computer – only to be disappointed quite soon. The patrols, they found, were useless, "too overbearing, too nit-picky." Next thing Sophie knew, she couldn't get into a herbology site. The CyberPatrol was coming up saying that the site was being protected. In the end, Sophie and her husband decided that they simply had to be present when the boys were online.

Considerations of common access and monitoring children had kept the computer in the living room also in Carol's case: "For the first year and a half I had it right here in my living room, so I could see it, so I could see what was happening." Their Pentium PC computer with Internet connection was used by Carol and her two sons, eleven and fourteen years old. Her husband, who used his own Macintosh mostly for the purposes of his job as a movie producer, hadn't yet figured out how to find his way on the Internet. So, it fell upon Carol to follow their sons' exploits in cyberspace. Having the computer in the living room and going on the Internet herself helped her intercept a disturbing phenomenon:

> Now, after about half a year, I don't know exactly how it happened, but my son somehow got connected to some pornography sites and we started to get a lot of pornographic mail, and we still do to this day. I get 2 sometimes up to 7 pieces of pornographic mail every single day on my AOL account. It's a line that says: "X-rated sites, open us up" and really horrible stuff ... and I have that computer here in the living room and at one point my 11-year-old downloaded pictures, *dis-gusting* [speaks with indignation] pic-

tures, so I disconnected the Internet for about a week. They didn't know how I'd done it, I disconnected the phone lines from the box and I told them that if I ever caught them on…. (Carol)

When she contacted their Internet service provider, America Online, Carol found that most probably her sons were not to blame for what was going on. They had not been necessarily actively searching for pornography. Pornography had intruded on them by way of seemingly "innocent," as Sophie had put it, activities. AOL explained to Carol that "these pornographic people" would go into the chat rooms, and most certainly into the teen chat rooms that her sons frequented at the time, and they would collect up all the addresses of the users they found in there and start sending them stuff. Then, if one of her kids ever went into a pornographic site, his address would be picked up and "be sold over, and over, and over again" to similar content providers.

This put Carol on the alert and looking for measures to closely supervise her sons' use of the Internet. The placement of the computer in the living room contributed to that for some time.

> But finally after that length of time my husband wanted the mess gone. The kids had their games everywhere and they were always downloading stuff and the computer was always sitting here in the living room and my husband wanted to sit here and listen to music and, he is a very quiet man, and that really bothered him. (Carol)

Thus, the computer and Internet activities were relocated from the central, shared, visible, lively space of the living room into a designated separate space with open access for whoever in the family wanted to use the computer. The ensuing competition with her sons and the felt obligation to weed out pornography from their mailbox had shaped Carol's temporal pattern of using the Internet. Carol would go into the "computer room" more often at night "because the kids are in bed and they are not on the computer." Usually, in the morning she would do her "computer work" – writing reports, announcements, etc., related to the voluntary organizations she belonged to – and she might also "sit on the Internet to see whether I've got any messages and to clear off any pornography mail that's coming through the night."

Sharing computer/Internet-related space and time with her sixteen-year-old son was also an issue that Martha, a single mother, had to consider.

In a two-bedroom townhouse, Martha had to be flexible and creative, and so she came up with the hallway. A neutral place, where she did not feel secluded, could be aware of what was going on, and had the rest of the home facilities close at hand, turned out to be a good solution. Martha dealt with the pornographic threat in a more relaxed manner than the previous two mothers, although she too had to do her share of monitoring her son's Internet use:

> He has done the typical teen-age boy thing – gone to porno-graphic sites. He leaves a trail of crumbs behind. I can always tell where he has been. [Laughs.] I can check in the cache and see what graphics are there. So I say: "Oh, okay." But I don't make a big thing out of it because it is there. There is freedom of speech and there is going to be subversive information out there but I think it is like television – you don't have to turn it on, you don't have to go there. I knew that he would go through this stage and he did and it is not a big deal any more. (Martha)

On one occasion, a Yahoo chat partner had led her son to believe that he was communicating with a fourteen-year-old girl, when actually, after real addresses, telephone numbers, and names were exchanged, it turned out that the chat partner was a boy sexually interested in Martha's son. That had come as a shock to Martha's son. She, however, had not disconnected her telephone line, as Carol had once done. Instead, she had taken the opportunity to educate her son about how "it is totally whatever you want to perceive and whatever they want to tell you. You are totally at the mercy of this thing, so you have to be very cautious."

All three stories recounted here involved computer- and Internet-literate mothers vividly aware of the shadowy side of cyberspace and deeply concerned about the threats it posed to the moral and social sanity of their sons. For these mothers, the Internet had added one more line of development to watch for, one more area of their children's upbringing to work on. Canadian sociologist Dorothy Smith (1999) has argued that the "dominant school-mother T-discourse"[9] in this society lays the primary responsibility for the individual child's school achievement, and even further, his or her success as an adult, on the family. The ideological code of the "Standard North American Family" (Smith 1999, 157–61) helps to translate in practical settings "family" into "mother." Thus, mothers are charged with the responsibility for the overall success or failure of the child in terms of academic and moral accomplishment and are expected to do the work required for fulfilling that responsibility. Thus the arrival of the Internet was bringing in more work for mother, as had happened with earlier domestic technologies (Cowan 1987). Understood in this way, the work of mothering that had to be done in these Internet-connected families had become more complex and demanding. It required technical competence and knowledge of the medium on the part of the mother.

Notably, the different reactions the three mothers had displayed with regard to cyber-pornography were not based simply on different moral philosophies or parenting styles. At the core of those reactions was the Internet experience of the mother herself. Sophie and Carol were unconfident novice users. They were coming to know the new medium alongside and maybe even a step behind their sons. For them, cyberspace was still an unpredictable terrain, the technology was hard to harness, and these two circumstances put together represented a major source of anxiety. Martha's reaction, on the other hand, was based on her superior knowledge and understanding of the medium compared to her son. She was moving ahead of him, knew what could be expected, and felt capable of educating him, while the other two women were looking for mechanisms for protection.

Furthermore, Martha was making a conscious effort to disclose to her son the creative and knowledge-yielding powers of the medium. She was in the process of developing a website for his art: "He's an artist – he draws a lot and I want to get his pictures out there. It's a sort of self-esteem thing. He can feel really good about his work."

She had downloaded an English–Spanish translator program to help him with his Spanish classes and kept his bookmarks organized in a separate folder in Netscape. A look into this folder gave her a synopsis of at least some of her son's interests and pursuits at any given moment so that she could better understand those interests and possibly shape them as far as she could: "Art Crime – he is very much into world graffiti and what people are doing out there and what kind of impact and statement they are making."

Thus, in Martha's case, a not-so-easily predictable mother–son bond seemed to be growing out of Internet use. Mother and son were jointly exploring cyberspace and learning more about each other along the way.

Jane, a thirty-five-year-old homemaker, and her twelve-year-old son represented another example of this phenomenon. Jane had two boys and a girl. Her husband, a metal builder, had no interest in the Internet, mostly because he worked long hours, but also because, as he put it himself, he was more "mechanically inclined." Mechanical versus literary, or symbolic,

247

inclination was a line of identity formation in this family. The older boy, 14, according to Jane's characterization, was like his father:

> ... interested in mechanical things, how to repair [machines]. He fixes cars, he can make an oil change.... He likes to work with his hands, to see how things work, and machines. He would use a computer to make a card for someone's birthday, or make a sign, or do his homework. He is not that interested in the Internet at this point. (Jane)

The younger son, 12, for his part, was perceived to be like his mom and like her was a voracious reader. He was attracted to the Internet "for the reading part." Jane and her younger boy would often dial up the Internet together after he came back from school. They tried different search strategies: "He'll show me different things he's done to find something, and I'll show him things that I have done and we sort of exchange information." She encouraged him and helped him correspond with e-mail pals from other parts of the country. This was a collaborative project between the two of them as her son would write to those pen pals about his Lego, Tamagotchi, and boy scout activities, while Jane would add geographical descriptions of their area, their city, and other information that she thought might be educational. Thus, in this family, the Internet was being appropriated by the mother as a tool for building a new kind of special bond between herself and her growing son.[10] For the time being, it was competing successfully with the "male" mechanical stuff involving machines, cars, carpentry, etc.

A complex dialectic of oppression and empowerment with regard to these women can be detected in their everyday stories. On one hand, the technological system was invading their homes through the ideologies of progress, personal success, and motherly responsibilities. It was forcing them to do additional work in order to meet the challenges involved in ensuring adequate technological and moral education of their children in the unsettled context of the new medium. A boy's toy was turning into a mother's toil.

At the same time, the new medium was delivering a new tool into the hands of the mother to teach creativity and implant curiosity and self-respect. Internet mothers worked to make homes where their children could strive to be "subjects, not objects" (hooks 1990, 42) vis-à-vis a powerful technological system driven, among other forces, by the impetus to transform these children into perfect consumers.[11] In order to be able to play that role, mothers had to understand the technology critically and to imagine alternative possibilities for its use that would affirm the subjectivity of their children as learners and creators. The three women whose experiences were discussed here found themselves at different stages in this process. Each of them had needed to make her own journey of critical discovery in order to learn how to interpret the new phenomenon.

Similar to what was argued about consumers in the previous section, it is evident that much more than children's protection is at stake as the Internet makes its way into Canadian homes. Children cannot be effectively sheltered from the possible negative effects of the new medium if they are not proactively taught how to enact and take advantage of its potentialities that their parents perceive as positive. Needless to say, young people themselves will discover possibilities unimaginable to parents and educators. These emergent activities need to be considered with an open mind. All this means that a new branch of education involving parents, children, teachers, and researchers needs to emerge if Canadians are to be able to adequately steer their children's Internet use. The time of hyperbolized promises occasionally challenged by gloomy predictions about the effects of the Internet on the young generation is over. At this point, Canadians should engage in an empirically informed rational-critical discussion of what in fact is going on in individual homes, what problems arise out of the everyday experiences of "wired" families, and what solutions are devised in the context of diverse configurations of family roles and value systems.

Conclusion: "Unhyping" the Internet

This article took seriously the proposition that users represent an active force in shaping technology alongside various groups of experts and political players (Feenberg 1991, 1999; Lie and Sorensen 1996; Silverstone and Haddon 1996). As the Internet penetrates into the everyday life of a vast user population and one of its core sites – the home – heavy involvement of these users in signifying work with regard to the new medium takes place. That is, people need to create meanings and values to correspond to specific tasks and problems they face in their immediate environment. In this process users actively discover the relevance of the Internet to their situations and initiate Internet-based practices that designers and promoters had not been able to imagine. Taking the Internet home, users not only act *with* it, but also *upon* it.

The emergent practices involving Internet use in everyday-life contexts represent a rich resource of ideas that can direct the pursuit of a democratic Internet development. The point is not to concoct utopian schemes for realizing the visions of theorists, technologists and political leaders, but rather the opposite – to elaborate visions to be asserted in a political process with an eye and ear turned to the unglamorous everyday initiatives of ordinary users. Such a project necessitates the complementing of large-scale quantitative studies with qualitative, ethnographically informed approaches that provide a holistic contextualized understanding of the Internet as a technology and a communication medium. The examination of concrete human activities embedded in local situations uncovers important and previously missing aspects of this medium's social shaping.

The standpoint of users proves to be a crucial vantage point with respect to the present and future of the Internet. The images of the medium captured from this perspective represent a healthy mixture of realism and optimism that can inform and direct its development. The Internet can evolve into an inclusive and empowering communication medium if technical and content-related problems are defined, and their solutions sought, with conscious consideration of users' perspectives. The Internet can stabilize as an exploitative, alienating technology and institution if users' perspectives and situated knowledges are systematically ignored or counteracted. The important dilemma still to be tackled is, to paraphrase Lefebvre (1971, 230), whether human beings simply will be made profitable through new high-tech mechanisms, or whether their everyday lives will be changed for the better, leaning on the possibilities brought about by the new powerful technology.

References

Bakardjieva, Maria. 2000. "The Internet in everyday life: Computer networking from the standpoint of the domestic user." Ph.D. diss., Simon Fraser University, Burnaby.

Callon, Michele. 1987. "Society in the making: The study of technology as a tool for sociological analysis." In *The Social Construction of Technological Systems: New Directions in the Sociology and History of Technology*, ed. Wiebe E. Bijker, Thomas P. Hughes, and Trevor J. Pinch, 83–103. Cambridge, MA: MIT Press.

Center for Media Education. 1996. "Web of deception: Threats to children from online marketing" [Online]. Available: http://www.cme.org/children/marketing/deception.pdf [November 20, 2001].

Certeau, Michel de. 1984. *The Practice of Everyday Life*. Berkeley: University of California Press.

ComQUEST. 1999. "Media metrix announces Canadian expansion" [Online]. October 20. Available: http://www.bbm.ca/Press_Releases/Press_Release_Archives/body_press_release_archives.html#october201999 [March 20, 2003].

———. 2001. "High Speed Access: The Canadian Internet Engine." *CyberTrends*, Fall.

Cowan, Ruth Schwartz. 1987. "The consumption junction: A proposal for research strategies in the sociology of technology." In *The Social Construction of Technological Systems: New Directions in the Sociology and History of Technology*, ed. Wiebe E. Bijker, Thomas P. Hughes, and Trevor J. Pinch, 261–80). Cambridge, MA: MIT Press.

Czitrom, Daniel, J. 1982. *Media and the American Mind: From Morse to McLuhan*. Chapel Hill: University of North Carolina Press.

Dryburgh, Heather. 2001. "Changing our ways: Why and how Canadians use the Internet" [Online]. Statistics Canada Catalogue no. 56F006XIE, 2001. Available: http://www.statcan.ca/english/IPS/Data/56F0006XIE.htm [January 22, 2002].

Ellison, Jonathan. 2003. "Electronic commerce: Household shopping on the Internet," *Innovation Analysis Bulletin*, vol.5 no.1, pp.8–9. Available: http://www.statcan.ca:80/english/freepub/88-003-XIE/88-003-XIE03001.pdf [March 20, 2003].

Feenberg, Andrew. 1991. *The Critical Theory of Technology*. New York: Oxford University Press.

———. 1999. Questioning Technology. London: Routledge.

hooks, bell. 1990. *Yearning*. Boston: South End Press.

Industry Canada. 1998. "The Canadian electronic commerce strategy" [Online]. Available: http://e-com.ic.gc.ca/english/strat/doc/ecom_eng.pdf [February 12, 2002].

———. 2001a. "Household internet use survey, Electronic commerce release." Electronic Commerce Branch [Online]. Available: http://e-com.ic.gc.ca/english/research/rep/backgounder_oct23_01.pdf [January 8, 2002].

———. 2001b. "Canadian Internet commerce statistics summary sheet." Task Force on Electronic Commerce [Online]. Available: http://e-com.ic.gc.ca/english/research/rep/e-comstats.pdf [March 20, 2003].

Kalakota, Ravi, and Andrew B. Whinston. 1997. *Electronic Commerce: A Manager's Guide*. Reading, MA: Addison-Wesley.

Lie, Marette, and Sorensen, Knut H. 1996. "Making technology our own? Domesticating technology into everyday life." In *Making Technology Our Own? Domesticating Technology into Everyday Life*, ed. Lie Marette and Knut H. Sorensen, 1–30. Oslo: Scandinavian University Press.

Lefebvre, Henri. 1971. *Everyday Life in the Modern World*. New York: Harper & Row.

Nie, Norman H., and Erbring, Lutz. 2000. "Internet and Society: A preliminary report" [Online]. Available: http://www.stanford.edu/group/siqss/Press_Release/Preliminary_Report.pdf [August 15, 2000].

Nielsen//NetRatings. 2000. "Defining the standard in Internet research" [Online]. Available: http://www.nielsen-netratings.com [October 8, 2000].

Pew Research Center. 2000. Pew Internet & American Life Project [Online]. Available: http://www.pewinternet.org/about/about.asp?page=4 [August 20, 2000].

Reddick, Andrew, Christian Boucher, and Manon Groseilliers. 2000. "The dual digital divide: The information highway in Canada" [Online]. The Public Interest Advocacy Centre. Available: http://olt-bta.hrdc-drhc.gc.ca/resources/oltdualdivide_e.pdf [March 20, 2003].

Rotermann, Michelle. 2001. "Wired young Canadians." *Canadian Social Trends* (Winter). Available: http://www.statcan.ca/english/indepth/11-008/feature/star2001063000s4a01.pdf [January 12, 2002].

Schutz, Alfred. 1970. *On Phenomenology and Social Relations. Selected Writings*, ed. and with an introduction by Helmut R. Wagner. Chicago: University of Chicago Press.

Schutz, Alfred, and Thomas Luckmann. 1973. *The Structures of the Life-World*. Evanston, IL: Northwestern University Press.

Silverstone, Roger. 1994. *Television and Everyday Life*. London: Routledge.

Silverstone, Roger, and Leslie Haddon. 1996. "Design and the domestication of information and communication technologies: Technical change and everyday life." In *Communication by Design: The Politics of Information and Communication Technologies*, ed. Robin Mansell and Roger Silverstone, 44–74. Oxford: Oxford University Press.

Silverstone, Roger, Eric Hirsch, and David Morley. 1992. "Information and communication technologies and the moral economy of the household." In *Consuming Technologies: Media and Information in Domestic Spaces*, ed. Roger Silverstone and Eric Hirsch, 15–31. London: Routledge.

Smith, Dorothy. 1999. *Writing the Social*. Toronto: University of Toronto Press.

———. 1987. *The Everyday World as Problematic: A Feminist Sociology.* Toronto: University of Toronto Press.

Statistics Canada. 2000. "Household Internet Use." *The Daily*, May 19 [Online]. Available: http://www.statcan.ca/Daily/English/000519/d000519b.htm [October 4, 2000].

———. 2001a. "E-commerce: Household shopping on the Internet." *The Daily*, October 23 [Online]. Available: http://www.statcan.ca/Daily/English/011023/d011023b.htm [February 6, 2002].

———. 2001b. "Household Internet Use Survey." *The Daily*, July 26 [Online]. Available: www.statcan.ca/Daily/English/010726/d010726a.htm [December 10, 2001].

———. 2001c. "General social survey: Internet use." *The Daily*, March 26 [Online]. Available: http://www.statcan.ca/Daily/English/010326/d010326a.htm [December 10, 2001].

———. 2001d. "E-commerce: Household shopping on the Internet." The Daily, March 1 [Online]. Available: http://www.statcan.ca/Daily/English/010301/d010301a.htm [February 12, 2002].

UCLA Center for Communication Policy. 1999. "Landmark UCLA study will explore the evolution and impact of personal computers and the Internet" [Online]. Available: http://ccp.ucla.edu/pages/InternetStudy.asp [March 20, 2003].

Notes

1 Pseudonyms are used everywhere in this paper in order to protect respondents' privacy.
2 This analysis employs Alfred Schutz's notion of system of relevance. (Schutz and Luckmann 1973; Schutz 1970). Schutz (1970) distinguishes between "intrinsic relevances" and "imposed relevances." Intrinsic relevances are "the outcome of our chosen interests, established by our spontaneous decision to solve a problem by our thinking, to attain a goal by our action, to bring forth a projected state of affairs" (p. 113). Imposed relevances, on the contrary, are the outcomes of our being not only "centres of spontaneity" but also "passive recipients of events beyond our control" (p. 113) that occur without our interference. Imposed relevances are not connected with interests chosen by us. Having no power to remould them by our spontaneous activities, we have to take them just as they are (see p. 114).
3 For an interesting analysis of the stratification among non-users, see Reddick, Boucher, and Groseilliers (2000).
4 In 2000, 12.3 per cent of Canadians households made purchases over the Internet, up from 6.9 per cent in 1999. This amounted to an increase of the total dollars spent online from 417 million (1999) to 1.1 billion (2000) (Statistics Canada 2001a).
5 Purchases over the Internet made by private households from home represented less than one-tenth of 1 per cent of personal expenditure on products and services in 1999 (Statistics Canada 2001d). The increase registered in 2001 did not mark a quantum leap with regard to the share of online purchases in the total household expenditure in Canada (see Ellison, 2003).
6 A prominent example is eBay.
7 Home users averaged twelve hours per week on the Internet, while those accessing it from other places spent about 3.4 hours weekly online (Rotermann 2001).
8 Named respectively by 71 per cent and 65 per cent of the young people in this age group (Rotermann, Michelle, 2001).
9 In Smith's terminology, this concept refers to discourses mediated by texts representing "skeins of social relations mediated and organized textually" that connect and coordinate the activities of actual individuals whose local historical sites of reading/hearing/viewing may be geographically and temporarily dispersed and institutionally various (Smith 1999, 158).
10 Pornography was not that big an issue in this home because they were using a text browser and still could not access any graphical files on the Internet. Nevertheless, Jane had learned from her experience with newsgroups that "you have to watch them [newsgroup postings] though. Some have really horrible pornographic stuff in the text, even on kids' stuff. People put really weird stuff."
11 A comprehensive discussion of the commercial exploitation of children through the Internet can be found, for example, in Center for Media Education (1996).

TELEHEALTH IN CANADA

M. A. Hebert,
P. A. Jennett,
and
R. E. Scott

1. Introduction

Innovations in health care delivery have become possible through advances in information and communications technologies (ICT). Telehealth applications represent an important opportunity to expand how Canadians communicate in the context of providing and receiving health care in Canada. These innovations are particularly important in countries like Canada that have geographic challenges as well as moral and political imperatives to provide equitable access to health care. The purpose of this paper is to discuss the changes and important factors influencing the field of telehealth in Canada.

This discussion will include: a definition of telehealth; background on the use of telehealth applications; the micro level – factors influencing telehealth communications directly related to health care provision; the macro level – government and policy influences on telehealth development; the context – communications shaping our understanding of telehealth use and adoption.

2. Definition of Telehealth

According to Reid, telehealth applications use advanced information and communications technology (ICT)[1] to deliver health services, expertise and information over distance, geographic, time, social, and cultural barriers (Reid 1996). This well-known definition is particularly useful because it recognizes that distance may not be the only barrier to care. While there are many variations on this definition, they have three elements in common: separation of provider and receiver of care, use of advanced ICT, and delivery of health care services and information. The Health Telematics Unit (University of Calgary) website extends this definition of telehealth to include: "Internet or web-based 'e-health' and video-based applications, [which] can be delivered 'real-time' or through 'store-and-forward' mode."[2]

While this is a common understanding, other distinctions have been made. For example, in determining how telehealth fits within global health strategies, the World Health Organization (1997) distinguishes between health promotion and curative aspects of health care:

> If telehealth is understood to mean the integration of telecommunications systems into the practice of protecting and promoting health, while telemedicine is the incorporation of these systems into curative medicine, then it must be acknowledged that telehealth corresponds more closely to the international activities of WHO in the field of public health.

The term "e-health" has also been recently introduced into this field, and, as for "telehealth," there is no single definition. Although, as the definition from the Health Telematics Unit website suggests, there is some common

M. A. Hebert, P. A. Jennett, and R. E. Scott

Table 1 **Examples of Telehealth Applications**

Clinical Specialty	Process Supported	Location of Service	Type of data
Teleradiology	X-ray consultation	Hospital, physician practice	Images
Teleultrasound	Ultrasonography	Hospital	Images
Telepsychiatry	Consultation	Hospital, clinic	Images, audio
Teleophthalmology	Consultation	Clinic, physician practice	Images
Telepathology	Consultation on laboratory slides for diagnosis	Hospital	Digital images Text (laboratory reports)
Teleconsultation	Post-operative cardiac care	Hospital, clinic, home	Images, audio, sensory; physiological (e.g., blood pressure)
Telehomecare	Care, support	Home, community	Images, audio, physiological (e.g., heart monitor)
Telecare	Telephone advice	Home, community	Audio

understanding that e-health, like other "e" initiatives, reflects use of the Internet:

> "e-Health" was first introduced as a term that distinguished web-based telehealth activities from the use of videoconferencing. It is now gaining in popularity as an over-arching term for the use of information and communications technology in health care.[3]

Maheu, Whitten, and Allen (2001, 4) also note another key difference in that "e-health differs from telehealth and telemedicine by not being *professional centric*." In other words, the "e-health groundswell is being led by people who are not health professionals."

Telehealth communications take place in a variety of ways and in different settings. Therefore, telehealth applications can be characterized by clinical specialty, health care processes or activities that are being supported, or location of the service, as well as by the type of data being transmitted. Examples of these characteristics are outlined in Table 1.

Understanding the important factors shaping telehealth activity in Canada requires some background knowledge of the telehealth field generally. Section 3 reviews why telehealth is important as a medium of communication, how it has added flexibility to the communication paradigm, and its role in society.

3. Background Review

Telehealth presents an important opportunity to expand the way Canadians communicate as health care consumers with health care providers and with the health care system at large. This background review explores aspects of communication in health care and why telehealth is becoming a medium of choice. Sections 4, 5, and 6 then take a retrospective view of specific aspects of telehealth that reveal important micro, macro and contextual aspects of the field in Canada.

3.1. Choosing Telehealth as a Means of Communication

The complexities of communication in the health care arena are related to the many types of data communicated and the players involved. Multiple factors contribute to the success of these communications, such as who is involved and the reason for the communication, as well as the timing and type of information to be communicated. Clinical, educational, research, and administrative activities within the health sector all require communication. These communications involve a variety of participants such as health care professionals, patients, families, and the public, as well as policy and decision-makers at many levels within the health care system.

The communication may be ad hoc, scheduled (e.g., clinics, face-to-face meetings) or event-driven (e.g., emergent and urgent consultations, problem-driven interactions). The timing of communication may also be immediate (e.g., in person or via telephone) or delayed (e.g., EKGs and X-rays are sent via mail or fax to a specialist at a tertiary centre for interpretation). ICT can be used to support each of these processes at many levels.

3.2. Flexibility Introduced Into the Communication Paradigm

For centuries, health care communication has occurred most commonly on an interpersonal level between a health care professional and patient. This communication has been based on a time and space consideration that required, for the most part, in-person communication. But in recent times, this basic paradigm has taken on new dimensions. Interactions have extended to include multidisciplinary health care teams, family members and other caregivers. As well, such communications are no longer bound by a face-to-face requirement.

Indeed, with the rapid and continual advances in ICT, this paradigm is changing in ways not previously imagined. Today, virtual visits between patients and their caregivers can occur across barriers of time and distance. In addition, consumers can access personal health information, as well as detailed health and health care information, without a health care provider intervening as interpreter or guide.

Traditionally, in the communication paradigm of sender-transmitter-receiver within a health care context, there is usually one person talking, one person listening and the interaction occurs in "real-time" (i.e., both people are present at the time and engaged in the communication).

Within telehealth applications, communication may be affected at three places: at the point of data capture, during data transmission, and data receipt. For example, in a consultation conducted via videoconference, both audio and video data are captured (through cameras and microphones), transmitted (over a cable line), and received (on a monitor and speakers). To enable communication, the system's technical capability must be sufficient to support the quality of data types being transmitted (as previously noted in Table 1).

While the use of ICT doesn't change the communication paradigm, the technology introduces flexibility in the variables and their temporal relationships. For example, a "store and forward" facility allows the sender to transmit information when it is convenient, while the receiver can do the same. Event-driven communications, such as consultation with a trauma expert, no longer depend on the expert being present. Instead, the expert can provide advice based on transmitted images and simultaneous discussion with one or more colleagues.

3.3. Societal Role for Telehealth

On a broader, societal level, there are a number of reasons why the use of ICT in health delivery and health care is considered timely. Telehealth provides a partial solution to such Canadian challenges as vast geography, harsh climate, and cultural diversity, as well as health provider mal-distribution, shortage, or isolation. It addresses the need for cost containment while also responding to the five principles of Canada's Health Act, i.e., that health care should be comprehensive, universal, accessible, portable, and publicly administered.

Jennett, Kulas, Mok, and Watanabe (1998) note that telehealth technologies play a role in supporting many changes that have occurred in the health care environment over the past decade. These health reform initiatives and restructuring include regionalization of services and workforce management. As well, in an effort to contain costs, there has been a shift from tertiary care to the community and home care. This shift has been accompanied by a philosophical change from curative to preventive health care, along with evolving health views that draw attention to the determinants of health (e.g., social and economic factors), evidence-based medicine, population health, and self-responsibility for health.

There are three areas where changes are occurring in the field of telehealth: a) at the micro level between patient and provider; b) at the macro level with government and policy influences; and c) the contextual aspect of communications around this innovation. Each of these areas is discussed further.

4. The Micro Level:
Factors Shaping Telehealth Communications between Patient, Provider, and Facility

4.1. Introduction

Telehealth communications that support health care processes are at the heart of this innovation. Issues important in this area include changes in consumers' abilities to interact with the technology and with others using the technology (including how easy it is to use). Equally important are the factors that influence health care professionals to use the technology and how this use changes their roles and responsibilities within the health care system.

4.2. Changing Role of the Consumer

Consumers are taking a more active role in seeking health-related information, which has raised issues of availability of culturally appropriate material and participation in interactive health communication opportunities. These relatively new activities include "the interaction of an individual – consumer, patient, caregiver, professional – with an electronic device or

M. A. Hebert, P. A. Jennett, and R. E. Scott

communication technology to access or transmit health information or to receive guidance on a health-related issue."[4]

As noted in one definition of "e-health," the active use of the Internet to communicate is expanding, as illustrated by the development of websites such as *GrannyBarb and Art's Leukemia Links*.[5] This website highlights the trend for consumers to use the Internet to both seek and share health-related information without intervention by health care professionals. When "Granny Barb" was diagnosed with adult leukemia, she was overwhelmed by the diagnosis as well as by the lack of readily accessible, consumable information. To counter this, she set up a website and began collecting information to share with others. In addition, a listserv was introduced as an option for consumers to actively interact with others facing the same diagnosis. It has drawn active participation from around the world, including many Canadians who were active in promoting the website and listserv in Canada.

Not only are patients initiating these online resources, but health care providers are beginning to see the benefits of an online medium to provide education and support to patients and families. For example, the electronic Child Health Network (eCHN), a non-profit organization operating out of Sick Kids Hospital in Toronto, is dedicated to sharing child health information electronically (Neale 2001, 15). The team has developed interactive online resources for pediatric health care providers, children, and their families. Included in this portfolio is a public website called "Your Child's Health," which covers a variety of children's health and safety issues in formats appropriate to both children and their parents.

As telehealth applications increase access to resources, the resulting developments emphasize another challenge: that of developing culturally appropriate material and making it available. This was exemplified in the case of Nunavut during their development of territorial telehealth opportunities. The telehealth network was seen as a tool to bridge the gap between the residents' needs and their access to services. While the technology was available, there were limited opportunities for interactive communication or for consumers to access relevant material in their own language or in a culturally sensitive context (McKinnon 2001).

The availability and use of telehealth and Internet technologies in these novel ways are certainly changing the ways in which communication occurs. For this reason, these developments have also prompted a call for more understanding around the influence of the Internet on consumers' health-related behaviours, such as seeking information (Brown 2001, 51–52).

4.3. Changing Role of the Healthcare Professional

Use of telehealth technology is also changing the role of health care professionals in their provision of care and their relationships with patients. However, they, unlike consumers, have been hampered in the adoption and implementation of telehealth initiatives by barriers such as sluggish policy reform, the lack of recognized training opportunities, and the absence of standardization.

This is beginning to change, as evidenced by the development of professional training sites. For example, as a counterpart to their consumer information, eCHN has developed a health care professional development and collaboration website for Ontario, called PROFOR (Edmonds 2001, 14–15). It is intended to facilitate communication, collaboration, and knowledge exchange among health care professionals. This innovative website combines material from many health care specialities and illustrates the potential of the technology to support multidisciplinary education.

Another type of initiative that is changing the role of health care professionals is the development and dissemination of health products and services online. Biggs (2001, 97–98) describes such an area where practitioners and service providers offer interactive mental health interventions, or e-therapy. He notes this type of service offers benefits to clients who are unable or unwilling to access face-to-face services; however, there are additional benefits to the practitioner such as convenience of working at home. While the technology supports these changes in service delivery, the training and policy mechanisms have not kept pace.

Policy related to physician reimbursement for telehealth activities is another area that has lagged behind the technology development. In the publicly funded Canadian health care system, physicians provide care and are reimbursed through a traditional "fee-for-service" system. This means that when physicians see patients in person, they bill the government for the services provided. However, decisions around what constitutes an "electronic visit" have not been consistent or rapid, although agreements have been reached in some jurisdictions for specialities such as telepsychiatry, teledermatology, and teleradiology (Hogenbirk, Pong, and Liboiron 2001). The question of which telehealth specialties to reimburse services is confounded by the location of the physician in relation to the patient, i.e., whether they

M. A. Hebert, P. A. Jennett, and R. E. Scott

are located in the same province and if care is deemed to occur where the patient or physician is located.

The overarching need to address medico-legal factors, training, standards development, and "change" issues was identified in a recent study commissioned by the Canadian Council of Health Technology Assessment (Noorani and Picot 2001). Although the study focused on the state of videoconferencing in telehealth in Canada, the findings were broadly applicable and identified continuing human resource issues in the adoption of videoconferencing that require urgent resolution.

4.4. Advances in Technology

Important changes in technology include better images available through videoconferencing technology operating over POTS (plain old telephone system). For telehealth applications this provides two benefits – increased affordability and increased access in many homes that do not have high-speed cable. Both these features support tele-homecare applications, such as the use of videophones to deliver home visits. While the tele-homecare market remains relatively small in Canada, vendors wishing to explore and expand this opportunity are actively seeking partnerships with suppliers and technical support.[6]

On the opposite end of the technical spectrum are advances in the development of broadband capabilities that support transmission of much larger files containing higher resolution images, movies, and multimedia applications. As more of these innovations emerge, whether low tech or high tech, the need for some standardization becomes evident – much like the standards for videotapes.

4.5. Need for Standards

When considering the technology associated with telehealth, there are four aspects to consider: hardware, software, transmission mode, and network. The hardware includes the physical components of the system that are used to send and receive data. Much like computer workstations, telehealth workstations have evolved to cope with the need for a complex array of equipment that must all be compatible, including monitors, speakers, microphones, and computers. With advances in the technology, workstations have become more portable, less expensive, and increasingly user-friendly (because of the tailored human–machine interfaces). If there is a need to capture clinical data during the teleconsultation, peripheral devices, such as a stethoscope or ophthalmoscope, may be included in the workstation.

Software is used to manage the formatting, storage, transmission, and receiving of data. This may include databases (e.g., such as those used to store clinical practice guidelines or drug information) and electronic health records.

Transmitting the data from the sender to the receiver requires a transmission mode, or a means to move the data from one location to another. This may include telephone lines, the Internet, cable, ISDN lines, wireless or satellite (Jennett and Siedlecki 2001). Each of these modes varies in the speed of data transmission and carrying capacity. For example, data containing moving images such as those captured with an ultrasound examination require much higher transmission capability than audio or still images, such as an X-ray.

A technology network is required to support multipoint distribution of data. This technology network accepts one or more of the various transmission modes required to connect users in various locations as well as different types of equipment. Networks can be national, provincial or territorial, regional, or local in scope. Examples include the telephone system or a videoconferencing bridge.

As telehealth technology becomes more integrated into the mainstream of health care delivery, the need for national leadership around technical standards and interoperability becomes critically important (Bergman, Ulmer, and Sargious 2001). Interoperability is being considered at many levels, including the four technical areas mentioned in this section (hardware, software, transmission mode, and network) as well as clinical and operational levels.

4.6. Organizational Issues

A number of issues are important in telehealth success, including the role of telehealth technologies in supporting organizational change through new avenues of informal and formal communication; the implementation of telehealth applications and ensuring sustainability of those services; and the evaluation of effectiveness of telehealth as a service delivery mechanism.

Regionalization of health services in provinces and territories has been a major change over the last decade and one that telehealth supports well. What has been surprising is the number of videoconferences conducted in support of administrative functions relative to the number used for clinical consultations. For example, in a 2001 report by Alberta we//net (Alberta we//net 2001), the number of clinical consultations reported in the province during 2000–2001 was 1,057 with 2,743 participants, while the number of administrative and educational sessions totalled 1,311 with 28,691 participants. This parallels trends reported in other provinces and territories.

One reason suggested for this unanticipated balance of use may be the reduced travel for administrators and participants in education sessions. This represents direct savings to the health care system. In contrast, when patients do not have to travel, personal financial benefits accrue, and these are not reflected in the health care budget.

5. The Macro Level:
Government and Policy Influences on Telehealth Development

5.1. Introduction

On a broader scale, political and social forces shape decisions and expectations for access to services as well as underlying beliefs around provision of public services. Government funding opportunities also influence choices for telehealth-facilitated application development and service delivery. These are important factors in the development of telehealth service mechanisms and may or may not be in alignment with provincial or territorial strategic plans.

5.2. Government Funding Sources and National Policy Influences

It is important to be aware of provincial and federal initiatives because they help determine which projects get funded and where they are located across the country. Policy also influences which projects and activities will be viewed favourably. An example of this is the CHIPP (Canada Health Infostructure Partnerships Program) awards.

The website for Health Canada's Office of Health and Information Highway (OHIH) describes the CHIPP program and telehealth projects funded through this initiative:

The Canada Health Infostructure Partnerships Program (CHIPP) is a two-year, $80 million, shared-cost incentive program, aimed at supporting collaboration, innovation, and renewal in health care delivery through the use of information and communication technologies. CHIPP will invest in model implementation projects in two strategic areas: telehealth and electronic health records model projects. The Program will help improve accessibility and quality of care for all Canadians while enhancing the efficiency and long-term viability of the health system.

Telehealth Projects: Projects funded through CHIPP advance the development of innovative solutions to health care delivery that affect all Canadians. Telehealth projects, for example, will bring the expertise of urban-based specialists to patients living in rural and remote communities, including First Nations. By using technology to shrink Canada's vast geography, telehealth can improve access to health services for all Canadians, no matter where they live.

For example: 1. Remote screening for diabetic complications for First Nations living on reserve in Alberta; 2. Telemedicine services in over 30 disciplines for 47 Northern Ontario communities; 3. Access to psychiatric care using video-conferencing technology for rural and remote communities in Ontario and British Columbia.[7]

Although this funding opportunity was by no means the only one available, ongoing project funding was also provided federally through CANARIE, Industry Canada, and Health Canada, and provincially through various initiatives.

In spite of these funding initiatives, a recent government report titled *The Health of Canadians: The Federal Role* notes that health care continues to operate as a "cottage industry" and is not making use of ICT as much as other information-intensive industries (Kirby and LeBreton 2001). The report suggests greater use of these technologies, as well as better integration of providers and institutions, is a means to improve evidence-based decision-making at all levels. As a result, national policy is directed toward building a Canadian Health Infostructure (CHI),[8] which is a network of networks that builds on initiatives already in place or under development. From this, interprovincial collaborations have arisen (Appendix A). These are important alliances, as national funding opportunities favour multi-province projects, which typically must involve three or more provinces.

The funding opportunities and rapid advancements in technology have prompted attention to be focused on the need for national standards. A National Interoperability Workshop played a lead role in this (see 6.3). However, other national organizations are actively involved in activities related to standards, including the Canadian Council of Health Services Accreditation (CCHSA) and Canadian Institute of Health Information (CIHI).

5.2. Provincial Telehealth Policy Influences

National telehealth policies directly and indirectly influence the activities undertaken within each province and territory. Each province and territory has enunciated its own policy position, which reflects both its individual goals and support of national initiatives. Information on key plans and priorities for health infostructure development, and specific initiatives, can be found at the Health Canada OHIH web site.[9] Taken together, this information provides an overview of current and planned activity toward creating the CHI and highlights the overarching influence that policy has on regional and national telehealth initiatives.

6. The Context:
Communication Shaping Our Understanding of the Telehealth Industry

6.1. Introduction

Within the telehealth industry, a variety of communications advance our ability to understand and share information around issues. These communications include reference databases, conferences, meetings, and reports.

6.2. Reference Databases

The gathering momentum in telehealth use is reflected in the efforts of Health Canada to develop a reference database of telehealth projects and programs. Launched by Health Canada through OHIH, contributors are invited to share information about ICTs in health and to contribute to the development of the *ICTs in Health Initiatives Database*. OHIH has initiated other communication support tools[10] to share information with   and among – those interested in ICT's and health. These include:

1. An ongoing history of the Canadian federal government's involvement in the development of a Canadian Health Infostructure;
2. A searchable database of global ICT and telehealth conferences;
3. A searchable database of current online literature on ICTs in health, with links to online full text documents and periodicals;
4. A listing of online periodicals with links to latest issues;
5. A listing of organizations and initiatives related to ICTs in health;
6. Provincial plans and priorities regarding the use of ICTs in health; and
7. Professional development resources.[11]

This database is one example of many sources of information around telehealth projects, for example: Health Canada, CANARIE, Industry Canada, CIHI, CCHRA, and provincial and territorial websites. However, at this time there is no single source of information on telehealth activities in Canada, which would be an important resource for those interested in research and development, implementation of systems, and evaluation.

6.3. Meetings, Conferences and Reports

Members of various professional societies in Canada meet on an annual basis to exchange information at conferences, or they contribute to special meetings on defined topics. Both modes of communication influence future directions of inquiry into ICT use in health care. Examples of these forums include:

- e-Health: COACH – Canada's National Health Informatics Organization Annual Conference
- Canadian Society of Telehealth 4th Annual Conference
- Telehealth Research Summer Institute

The field is expanding at a rapid rate. In 2001, for instance, key reports influenced thinking in the telehealth field in Canada. Let's look at two examples that illustrate the diversity of topics examined:

M. A. Hebert, P. A. Jennett, and R. E. Scott

- **Canadian Council of Health Technology Assessment**. The importance of the trend toward implementing telehealth applications and understanding the context of their use was highlighted through a study to assess the state of videoconferencing in telehealth in Canada, commissioned by the Canadian Council of Health Technology Assessment (Noorani and Picot 2001). The study concluded that, while the size and population of Canada was appropriate for this use of technology, the number of patients seen by videoconferencing remained small. Sustainable, long-term funding remained a challenge. The authors concluded there remained a need for quality outcome studies regarding clinical effectiveness and cost-effectiveness; guidelines for planning and implementation; and user training and program sustainability over the long term.
- **Interoperability Workshop Report**. In response to the urgent need for standards, the Canadian Society for Telehealth and the Alberta Research Council organized a National Interoperability Workshop in Calgary in February 2001. The resulting report[12] provided key recommendations, including: national leadership was required, given over forty organizations involved in different aspects of telehealth interoperability; resources and a business plan were needed to move this process forward; and synthesis and compilation of the telehealth interoperability elements into a framework was needed to address telehealth interoperability, implementation, and sustainability.

These conferences, meetings, and reports provided key opportunities to share information around the developing fields of telehealth and e-health. They are meant to serve as examples of the many ongoing activities but also to illustrate the wide-ranging efforts in this area. What they also point out is that, while there are many resources, they are not easily located or accessed. Therefore, to advance our understanding of this field, there is a need to coordinate the communication around these activities, both within provinces and territories as well as nationally.

7. Conclusions and Future Directions

7.1. Introduction

We conclude this discussion by asking what will be the important influences for Canadian telehealth initiatives in the near future? The role of telehealth in the delivery of health care is just beginning to be explored, as Mr. Roy Romanow, head of the Commission on the Future of Health Care in Canada noted:

> The task before us is to draw upon the ingenuity of all Canadians to ensure ... that our health system meets the challenges of the 21st century. Join us as we work toward making recommendations to ensure the sustainability of a universally accessible, publicly funded health system, that offers quality services to Canadians and strikes an appropriate balance between investments in prevention and health maintenance and those directed to care and treatment.[13]

Telehealth is a rapidly advancing field, but at least six general themes are likely to be influential:

- Recently funded activities such as the National Telehealth Outcome Indicator Project (Health Canada 2000; Scott 2001) and evaluation framework development (Hebert 2001; 2001a) can be anticipated to lead to advances in evaluation criteria;
- Pursuit of the recommendations from the Interoperability Workshop will influence increased interoperability;
- Creation of Canada Health Infoway Inc., with its $500-million budget and mandate to identify investment opportunities with vendors and systems integrators, will accelerate computerized health information networks;[14]
- Awareness of the contribution of telehealth to global health may also influence Canadian activity;
- Recognition of the urgent need to resolve privacy, confidentiality, and security issues will lead to technical and organizational solutions; and
- Resolution of the need to provide coordinated access to the many telehealth resources, such as current telehealth implementation activities, conferences, research results, funding opportunities, and policy development.

M. A. Hebert, P. A. Jennett, and R. E. Scott

Table 2　Continuing Challenges in Telehealth Adoption in Canada[15]

Challenges Related to Human Factors	
Patients/Public	**Practitioners**
Depersonalization	Change in role
Readiness	Incentives
Training –experience	Scheduling
Cultural–ethical issues	Access to equipment
Dissemination	Workflow
Challenges Related to Technical and Administrative Issues	
Integration	Sustainability/scalability
Interoperability	Funding
Connectivity	Standards
Infrastructure	Consistent performance and functionality
Challenges in Policy Areas	
Licensing/privileging	Multidisciplinary and culturally diverse partners
Reimbursement	Diverse outcomes and goals
Regulation	Intellectual property, copyright
Confidentiality and privacy	Complex, multiple partners
Challenges in the Health System	
Institutional inertia	Quality control, incomplete or inadequate content
Marketing/business case and supporting inventories	Provincial/National/International plans, along with proven governance models needed
Evaluation	Integration into other modes of care
Business models	Acquisition and service agreements

7.2. Identified Challenges

Although studies to date have shown that technology is not only a medium but also a catalyst for human development and change (organizational, cultural, and economic), a number of challenges remain unresolved. These occur in both human and technical areas as well as at individual, organizational, and administrative levels (Table 2).

7.3. The Future of Telehealth in Canada

The integration of telehealth as a successful communication vehicle within the health context requires a comprehensive understanding of how effective communications take place within the current health care system, with and without the use of technologies. While recognized as important, the evidence in this area is not yet well developed. In addition, introducing telehealth applications requires understanding change from the viewpoints of patients, providers, organizations, health systems, and the public. Therefore, successful implementation needs to address both these issues in an ongoing critical assessment of the evidence for using this approach.

The vision for telehealth communication in the future is a seamless, sustainable, low-cost, efficient, technological, clinically necessary solution. The characteristics of a successful technological solution include:

- Simplicity: ease of use
- Interoperability: systems that work with other systems
- Low-cost: affordable
- Ubiquitous: available to multiple users from multiple locations
- Sustainability: able to transition from a pilot project to a program
- Open standards: "plug & play" modules as in computing environments
- Portability: solution has multiple uses
- Reliability: users are assured the system works
- Controlled access: Privacy, confidentiality, security issues addressed
- Scalability: can start small, but expand as needed
- Open architecture: not limited to one vendor
- Internet platform: Web-based technologies and standard protocols
- Standard browser (Jennett, Bates, Bluow, Cairns, Fischer, Gilbert, Healy, Ho, Kazanjian, Lesinger, Richardson, and Woolard 2000).

While all of these characteristics are important, their development will require a complex interplay of human and financial resources. This is a process that will occur over time with incremental success in each of the areas.

7.4. Conclusions and Implications

There is evidence that conceptual shifts around communicating and providing care via telehealth have been occurring in Canada. This retrospective review of important factors illustrates that conferences, reports, government funding opportunities, and policy development are influencing the thinking and knowledge development in this area. In addition, opportunities for change are being presented to both health care consumers and providers. Telehealth is establishing:

- New avenues for communicating about health and health care;
- New ways for maintaining health;
- New forms of health practice;

- New models for continuing learning;
- New approaches to administering health;
- Global communities and networks (Jennett and Siedlicki 2001).

With all of these potential areas for change, there remains much for us to learn about this emerging form of communication for Canadians.

Appendix A:
Interprovincial Collaboration on Telehealth Initiatives

Health Infostructure Atlantic Alliance (HIA)

In the fall of 1999, the four Atlantic premiers requested that their respective departments of health collaborate on health information technology across the Atlantic region. The departments of health of New Brunswick, Newfoundland and Labrador, Nova Scotia, and Prince Edward Island signed a memorandum of understanding in January, 2000, to form an organization known as Health Infostructure Atlantic alliance, or HIA. The purpose of HIA is to share health information/technology initiatives, and to identify projects or strategies for collaborative development and the use of best practices. HIA consists of the Chief Information Officers/Directors of Information Technology and senior staff from the four departments of health.

   The alliance identified six collaborative areas:

1. Picture Archiving Communications System (teleradiology);
2. Hospital Information System Standards;
3. Telehealth (different provinces have different priorities, e.g., teleoncology, rural palliative homecare, etc.);
4. Public Health Surveillance (chronic and communicable diseases);
5. Emergency Department Information System; and
6. Electronic Health Records.

Western Health Infostructure Collaborative (WHIC)

WHIC (www.whic.org) provides a forum for the identification, planning, and coordination of collaborative opportunities with Western Canada for health information systems standards, architecture and product development and implementation. These opportunities may then be implemented by the appropriate bodies. Membership consists of British Columbia, Alberta, Saskatchewan, Manitoba, Northwest Territories, Nunavut, and Yukon. The following key provincial infostructure initiatives, HealthNet BC, Alberta we//net, and the Saskatchewan Health Information Network, are also members.

The work is focused on joint development of seven major projects:

1. Continuing Care Electronic Health Records Initiative (CCEHRI);
2. Provider Registry;
3. Laboratory Test Standards;
4. Pharmacy Information Network (PIN);
5. e-Claims;
6. Telehealth; and
7. Consumer Access to Health Information

Ontario

Ontario works closely with Health Canada and a number of other provinces and territories toward the development of the Canadian Integrated Public Health Surveillance System (CIPHS). In addition, Ontario maintains close relations with the western provinces through WHIC, especially in the areas of continuing care (Alberta) and all provinces and territories for electronic health records).

Quebec

Quebec had no interprovincial collaboration initiatives listed on their website.

Acknowledgments

The authors wish to acknowledge the assistance provided by Susan Brownell, Neera Datta, and Pat Engel in the compilation and clerical aspects of developing this manuscript.

References

Alberta we//net. 2001. "Toward sustainable telehealth in Alberta." Discussion Draft from the Provincial Telehealth Committee. August.

Bergman, D., R. Ulmer, and P. Sargious. 2001. "Telehealth technical interoperability." Presentation at the National Telehealth Interoperability Workshop. Calgary, February 5.

Biggs, S. 2001. "E-therapy: Consumer experience, potentials and pitfalls." E-Health 2001: The Future of Healthcare. *Proceedings of the Annual COACH Conference*. Toronto.

Brown, A. 2001. "Consumers and health care performance information on the Internet." e-Health 2001: The Future of Healthcare. *Proceedings of the Annual COACH Conference*. Toronto.

Edmonds, J. 2001. "PROFOR: A health care professional development and collaboration web site for Ontario." e-Health 2001: The Future of Healthcare. *Proceedings of the Annual COACH Conference*.

e-Health 2001: The Future of Healthcare. *Proceedings of the Annual COACH Conference*. Toronto, May 26–29.

e-Volving Telehealth: The Next Level. Telehealth 2001: *The 4th Annual Meeting of the Canadian Society of Telehealth*. On-site Program and Proceedings Book. Toronto, October 20–23.

Health Canada. *ICTs in Health Infoway: About the Canada Health Infostructure Partnerships Program*. Office of Health and Information Highway [Online]. Available: http://www.hc-sc.gc.ca/ohih-bsi/whatfund/chipp-ppics/chippics-intro_e.html.

——. 2000. "Evaluating Telehealth 'Solutions': A Review and Synthesis of the Telehealth Evaluation Literature – March 2000" [Online]. Available: http://www.hc-sc.gc.ca/ohih-bsi/whatnew/index_e.html.

Hebert, MA. 2001. "New Approaches to Telehealth Evaluation." *Canadian Evaluation Society Conference 2001: The Odyssey Continues*. Banff, Alberta, May 20–23.

Hebert, MA. 2001a. "Telehealth Success: Evaluation Framework Development." *MedInfo 2001: 10th World Congress on Medical Informatics*. London, England, September 2–5.

Hogenbirk, J.C., R.W. Pong, and L.J. Liboiron. 2001. "Fee-for-service Reimbursement of Telemedicine Services in Canada in 1999/2000." Centre for Rural and Northern Health Research, Laurentian University. April. Available: http://www.rohcg.on.ca/tao/docs/reimburse.pdf [January 21, 2002].

Jennett, P., and B. Siedlecki. 2001. "Telehealth: Analysis of present and future Applications." Presentation at E-health and Telehealth Conference. Edmonton, February 20.

Jennett, P., J. Bates, M. Blouw, J. Cairns, R. Fischer, J. Gilbert, T. Healy, K. Ho, A. Kazanjian, M. Lesinger, D. Richardson, and B. Woolard. 2000. "Developing a technological infrastructure for telehealth services for rural and remote areas." Presentation at the Second Annual Meeting of the International Society for Telemedicine and the 5th International Conference on the Medical Aspects of Telemedicine. Montreal, October 2–4.

Jennett, P., D.P. Kulas, D.C. Mok, and M. Watanabe. 1998. "Telehealth: A timely technology to facilitate health decision making and clinical service support." In *Health Decision Support Systems*. Gaithersburg, Maryland: Aspens Publishing.

Jennett, P., D. Urness, and S. Stayberg. 2001. "Making the right choices: Lessons learned and best practices for decision makers." Presentation made at *The Telehealth Connection*. Vancouver, March 29–31.

Kirby, M.J.L. (Chair), and M. LeBreton (Deputy Chair). 2001. "The Health of Canadians: The Federal Role." Interim Report, vol. 4, Issues and Options. Standing Committee on Social Affairs, Science and Technology, September. Available: http://www.parl.gc.ca/37/1/parlbus/commbus/senate/com-e/soci-e/rep-e/repintsep01-e.htm [December 6, 2001].

Maheu, M.M., P. Whitten, and A. Allen. 2001. *E-Health, Telehealth, and Telemedicine: A Guide to Start-Up and Success*. San Francisco: Jossey-Bass.

McKinnon, T. 2001. "Telehealth initiatives in Canada 2001: The IIU Network, Nunavut – Bridging the gap." E-Volving Telehealth: The Next Level. *Canadian Society of Telehealth Annual Conference*. Toronto, October 20–23.

Neale, J. 2001. "Electronic health: Interactive learning for parents and children." e-Health 2001: The Future of Healthcare. *Proceedings of the Annual COACH Conference*. Toronto.

Noorani, H.Z., and J. Picot. 2001. "Assessment of Videoconferencing in Telehealth in Canada." *Canadian Coordinating Office for Health Technology Assessment: Technology Report Number 14*. Ottawa, May 2001.

Reid, M. J., ed. 1996. *Telemedicine: A Guide to Assessing Telecommunications in Health Care*. Institute of Medicine Committee on Evaluating Clinical Applications of Telemedicine. Washington, DC: National Academy Press.

Scott, R. 2001. "Evaluation of Telehealth: Time to Prove Value." In *Business Briefing: Next Generation HealthCare*, 65–67. World Markets Research Centre, October 2001.

World Health Organization. 1997. Telemedicine will henceforth be part of the strategy for health for all. Geneva, December 23. Available: http://www.who.int/archives/inf-pr-1997/en/pr97-98.html [January 28, 2002].

Notes

1   ICT is defined on the HTU website at http://www.fp.ucalgary.ca/telehealth to include: "The application of modern electronic and computing capabilities (technology) to the creation and storage of meaningful and useful facts or data (information), and to its transmission to users by various electronic means (communication). The ultimate goal is for ICT to transform data into information, and information into knowledge."

2   Health Telematics Unit, University of Calgary. Glossary on the website accessed January 29, 2002 at http://www.fp.ucalgary.ca/telehealth.

3   Health Telematics Unit website.

4   Health Telematics Unit website.

5   *GrannyBarb and Art's Leukemia Links*: Where to get leukemia information on the Internet, http://www.acor.org/leukemia

6   See the Healthworks TMS® website for more information at http://www.healthworkstms.com/homecare_solutions.asp [accessed February 12, 2002].

7   Health Canada: Office of Health and Information Highway, *ICTs in Health Infoway: About the Canada Health Infostructure Partnerships Program*, http://www.hc-sc.gc.ca/ohih-bsi/about_apropos/chipp-ppics/chippics-intro_e.html [accessed March 17, 2003].

8   Canadian Health Infostructure Website, http://www.hc-sc.gc.ca/ohih-bsi/chics/index_e.html [accessed March 17, 2003].

9   Health Canada OHIH website, http://www.hc-sc.gc.ca/ohih-bsi/chics/pt/index_e.html [accessed March 17, 2003].

10   Office of Health and the Information Highway website, http://www.hc-sc.gc.ca/ohih-bsi [accessed December 2001].

11   Mr. Bill Pascal, Director General, Office of Health and Information Highway, e-mail communication to e-Health Program Committee, December 7, 2001.

12   See HTU website http://www.fp.ucalgary.ca/telehealth/Interoperability_Report.pdf [accessed March 17, 2003].

13   See http://www.healthcarecommission.ca/ [accessed December 2001].

14   See http://www.infoway-inforoute.ca/preview/aboutinfoway/index.php?lang=en [accessed March 17, 2003].

15   Table adapted from Jennett, Urness, and Stayberg (2001).

M. A. Hebert, P. A. Jennett, and R. E. Scott

FROM THE "ELECTRONIC COTTAGE" TO THE "SILICON SWEATSHOP"
Social Implications of Telemediated Work in Canada

Graham D. Longford and
Barbara A. Crow

The work and workplaces of Canadians have undergone profound change over the last few decades, from the relative decline of jobs in manufacturing and primary industries and subsequent rise in service-sector employment, to the increasing use of contingent (part-time, temporary, and contract) workers and the entry of millions of women into the paid labour force. While such changes originate from a complex blend of global and domestic economic and social forces, the emergence of new information and communications technologies (ICTs) has also played an important part. In this essay we survey and evaluate the extent and effects of telemediated work in Canada, that is, work that depends upon or is carried out through the use of ICTs. Numerous and often conflicting studies on work and technology have appeared in the last decade, some controversial. Works by Rifkin (1995), Noble (1995), and Menzies (1996), for example, invoke near apocalyptic scenarios about the "end of work" and the formation of a mass cyber-tariat. Technology gurus like Don Tapscott, on the other hand, argue that work involving the production or use of ICTs constitutes the fastest growing source of employment in the new economy (Tapscott 1996, 188). Our task is rendered more difficult by the relative lack of empirical data in the area. Compared with recent studies of the impacts of organizational change, there is a lack of adequate study and analysis of the impact of telemediated work on such things as the availability of employment, skills and income, job security, and working conditions for many workers in the "knowledge-based economy." In an age when ICTs have been elevated to the status of a universal panacea, the need for better research and understanding is compelling.

Business and government leaders endorse the rapid proliferation and diffusion of new ICTs throughout the economy and workplace as key to Canada's future economic growth, prosperity, and competitiveness, and have portrayed them as enabling technologies capable of breaking down barriers to economic opportunity based on gender, race, disability, and geography (Boston Consulting Group [Canada] 2000; Information Highway Advisory Council 1997; National Broadband Task Force 2001). In our view, however, evidence for such widespread positive effects of ICTs is inconclusive at best. In fact, there is mounting evidence that the impact of ICTs on the nature, quantity, and quality of work in Canada is one of polarization, by reproducing and intensifying rather than overcoming historically recalcitrant barriers to economic opportunity and self-sufficiency. Without denying the benefits new ICTs have brought to many, their effects have been highly uneven.

For some, albeit a minority, the effect of ICTs on the nature of work and employment in the new economy has had many positive aspects: swelling their bank accounts, providing new opportunities for autonomy and creative collaboration with distant colleagues, and helping to accommodate family commitments, such as childcare or eldercare. At the other end of the spectrum lie hundreds of thousands of relatively unskilled, poorly paid teleservice agents working in conditions best described as "silicon sweatshops," where they are crowded into call centres, seated at workstations that will inevitably injure them, and subjected to continuous electronic monitoring. Somewhere in the middle lies a substantial majority of Canadians who share a simultaneous fascination with new technologies such as cell phones, pagers, and the Internet,[1] and an abiding suspicion that new technology poses a threat to their jobs and intrudes on their privacy and leisure time (Reid 1996, 127–44). Finally, even those who have succeeded in prospering in the new economy have paid a price, in the form of increased hours of work, increased stress, and a blurring of the distinction between work and home life.

Graham D. Longford and Barbara A. Crow

In this essay, we follow the contours of the contemporary landscape of work in Canada, with particular attention paid to how it has been restructured and reshaped in recent years by the growing use of computer and telecommunications technology, and with a view to identifying emerging trends and issues with which employers, workers, policy-makers, and Canadian citizens in general must contend. With so much ink and air time in the popular media devoted to celebrating the benefits of these technologies, we have elected to focus on a number of more troublesome impacts. Among these emerging trends and issues are: increased polarization of the workforce between highly skilled, well-paid knowledge workers and a large pool of semi- and unskilled workers occupying poorly paid and increasingly precarious part-time, temporary, and contract positions; rising numbers of home-based teleworkers for whom coverage by employment standards and occupational health and safety legislation is uncertain; the persistence of a gendered and racialized division of labour in the new economy; geographic "clustering" of economic and employment opportunities in already economically privileged urban regions; declining working conditions and employment standards for all workers in the knowledge-based economy in terms of employment standards, job security, and stress; and the use of technology to electronically monitor the activities, performance, whereabouts, and, increasingly, the private thoughts of growing numbers of workers. Current public policy, with its focus on promoting further technological innovation, has yet to acknowledge, let alone address, many of the issues raised below.

ICTs in the Canadian Workplace

Before examining the effects of ICTs on work and employment, let us first get an appreciation for the extent to which they have been incorporated into and are a part of the daily life of working Canadians. Two recent Statistics Canada surveys provide useful snapshots of the diffusion of ICTs in the paid workplace in Canada. Its 2001 *Electronic Commerce and Technology Use* survey reports that while e-commerce itself constitutes only a small part of economic activity, the use of ICTs such as the Internet, e-mail, electronic data interchange (EDI), and wireless communications in the workplace is significant. In 2000, 63 per cent of businesses used the Internet, 60 per cent used e-mail, 51 per cent used wireless communications, 26 per cent had websites, and 12 per cent used an intranet (Peterson 2001, 11–16). Public sector organizations report even higher use: 99 per cent use the Internet and e-mail; 73 per cent had websites; and 52 per cent used an intranet (Peterson 2001, 13, 16–17).

Another method used by Statistics Canada to measure the phenomenon has been to measure the prevalence of computer use by individual workers. As of 2000, computer use in private and public sector workplaces stood at 81 per cent and 100 per cent, respectively (Peterson 2001, 11). At the level of the individual worker, six out of ten employed Canadians use computers in their work, 80 per cent of these on a daily basis (Marshall 2001, 5–11). The latter figure represents roughly 6.5 million workers. These figures also represent a striking increase over the number using computers only a decade ago – a mere three in ten (Marshall 2001, 5).[2]

Not surprisingly, however, computer use at work varies across industrial sectors, occupational groups, and other demographic categories, including gender and education level. Public sector workers, firstly, were significantly more likely to work with computers (77 per cent) than private sector counterparts (56 per cent). Within the private sector, meanwhile, professional, scientific, and technical services firms report 95 per cent computer use, while only 66 per cent of firms in the accommodation and food services industry use them (Peterson 2001, 12). Incidence of use also varies according to occupation, education, income, and gender. Professionals and managers had among the highest rates of computer use, at 86 per cent and 78 per cent, respectively. In sales and service occupations, meanwhile, the figure stood at 39 per cent. Of workers with high school education or less, only 41 per cent report using computers, as compared to 85 per cent of those with university degrees. Computer use also correlates with income level; with a mere 36 per cent of those with incomes under $20,000 reporting computer use at work, while 80 per cent of those with incomes in excess of $60,000 use them (Marshall 2001, 6–7). Finally, women were more likely to use computers at work than men, by a margin of 60 per cent to 54 per cent. Much of this gap can be accounted for by the prevalence of women in clerical positions, however, who recorded 84 per cent computer use. Based on these figures, it is fair to say that computers and computer use have rapidly, albeit unevenly, become prevalent in the Canadian workplace.

Aside from computers, the proliferation of other new ICTs such as cell phones, pagers, and various other wireless devices has been significant. Cellular phone subscriptions in Canada rocketed from less than 100,000 to 9.9 million between 1987 and 2001 (Statistics Canada 1998b; 2001d). A sub-

Graham D. Longford and Barbara A. Crow

stantial portion of these are used for business purposes. The growing importance of ICTs to the economy overall is also reflected in the magnitude of investment that has been poured into ICTs over the last decade. Private sector capital investment in ICTs grew by approximately 20 per cent per year in Canada throughout much of the 1990s, reaching $13.6 billion (CAN) by 1997 (Ertl 2001, 46; Rubin 2001), and overall expenditures on ICTs as a percentage of sales increased as well (Peterson 2001, 4). Public sector spending increases on ICTs have also risen dramatically in recent years. Federal government annual ICT expenditures, for example, increased from $3 billion to $5 billion between 1993 and 2000 (Longford 2001, 6).

With an appreciation for the rapid diffusion of new ICTs throughout the Canadian economy and paid workplace in recent decades, let us now turn to the question of what effects they have had on work, workers, and Canadian society as a whole.

Impact of ICTs on Work I: Demand, Security, Skills

The End of Work?

Competitive pressures, organizational changes, and human resource strategies – especially downsizing, delayering, outsourcing, and an increased reliance on part-time and temporary employment – have had a major impact on employment in the last two decades. There has been a significant shakeout in industries such as manufacturing and in occupations such as clerical work as a result of the introduction of new technologies over the last few decades. Thanks to robotics and computer-controlled just-in-time delivery, automotive manufacturers are able to produce cars at a much greater rate than even ten years ago, despite employing significantly fewer workers (McNally 2000, 268–70). Successive waves of automation have enabled Canada Post to handle a 45 per cent increase in mail volume since 1982, despite a 32 per cent drop in full-time employment (Bickerton and Louli 1995, 220). Overall employment in clerical positions in Canada decreased by 250,000 positions during the 1990s as a result of new technologies that increased productivity and enabled managers to assume responsibility themselves for clerical functions like word processing (Betcherman and McMullen 1998, 10). Similarly, airline ticket agents have suffered deskilling and job loss over the past decade and find those jobs remaining threatened by self-serve check-in kiosks currently being rolled out across the country (Shalla 1997, 76–96). Finally, in the mid-1990s, Human Resources Development Canada (HRDC) replaced 5,000 frontline staff with several thousand electronic self-serve kiosks, resulting in an annual personnel cost-savings of $200 million (Longford 2001, 12–13).

New ICTs have also facilitated the transfer of work out of Canada and into other countries. Between 1989 and 1992, 338,000 manufacturing jobs disappeared from Canada (Reid 1996). The loss of these jobs coincided with the Canada-U.S. Free Trade Agreement, which enabled employers to relocate operations south of the border. Many of Canada's high-tech corporate darlings of the 1990s, such as Nortel and JDS Uniphase, created more positions outside Canada than inside (Reid 1996, 292). Such transfers of work and the control and coordination of work in production facilities thousands of kilometres distant from head offices was also rendered possible by the introduction of new ICTs, including the fax machine, Electronic Data Interchange (EDI), cellular phones, and corporate intranets.

Still, for all the doomsday talk of the "end of work," it warrants pointing out that the employment rate in Canada has declined only marginally over the last couple of decades and hovers just over the 62 per cent mark (Statistics Canada 2001a).[3] Meanwhile, for all the hype about the knowledge-based economy, demand for many workers in occupations such as truck driving, cleaning, personal services, home care, and retail sales persists (Burke and Shields 2000, 103). Therefore, the fears of doomsayers appear at least somewhat exaggerated (Walters 2001, 78–83).

On the other hand, in spite of considerable hyperbole regarding the positive correlation between ICTs and economic and employment growth,[4] sober analysis has demonstrated that, while it hasn't been a "job killer," information technology has produced no employment bonanza either (Conference Board of Canada 1996). The average annual rate of employment growth ran at 2 per cent through the 1990s, the very same period during which, as we have seen, Canadian firms invested very heavily in ICTs. In fact, the experience of the information technology sector in Canada itself mirrors this phenomenon of near jobless growth in the wider economy. Between 1990 and 1997, the ICT sector's contribution to GDP in Canada grew at an annual rate of 6 per cent, eventually reaching 6.1 per cent of total output. Meanwhile, employment growth in the sector lagged at 2.8 per cent. In some sectors, such as telecommunications services and computer manufacturing, downsizing and restructuring led to net losses in employment (Denton and Pereboom 2000, 4–10). All told, the sector added perhaps 100,000 jobs to the economy of the 1990s, rising from 3.1 per cent to 3.5 per cent of all jobs in Canada (Ertl 2001, 18). While investment in the production and use of digital technologies clearly has the potential both to create as well as destroy jobs, there is little evidence supporting the claim that ICTs create as many, if not more, jobs as they destroy.[5] What is clear is that new ICTs eliminate certain kinds of work and displace workers, mostly of a low to intermediate nature in skill level, and thus create problems of adjustment in the near term at least (Betcherman and McMullen 1998, 12).

Just-in-time Work

One of the most significant changes in the way Canadians work has been in the area of work arrangements, particularly the rise of "non-standard" employment such as part-time, temporary, and contract work, and own-account self-employment. As many as half of all Canadian workers, depending on one's definition of non-standard work, now find themselves working under such arrangements (Lowe 1999, 5). One and a half million, or 13 per cent, of employed Canadians are in temporary jobs (jobs with a specified end date), a 60 per cent increase since 1989 (Canadian Policy Research Networks 2002). Many of the firms taking advantage of new work arrangements are closely connected with either the use or production of new ICTs.[6] Numerous studies reveal a significant correlation between ICTs and the flexibilization of the workforce in terms of employment arrangements, such as increased use of part-time, temporary, outsourced, or contract workers (Benner and Dean 2000, 361–75; Betcherman and McMullen 1998, 1; Lowe, Schellenberg, and Davidman 1999, 43; Vosko 2000). Today, computerized systems offer employers an increasingly fine-grained view of workers' activities, productivity, and workload in real time. Such information can be used to optimize staffing levels according to demand and workload, to the point where employers can rely on "just-in-time" workers. At call centres, for example, phone systems compile data on such factors as average time on hold, number of calls in queue, average call length, and number of hang-ups. As one call centre software developer puts it: "Its whole purpose is to optimize the relationship between the number of people that they have on the phones versus the number of calls coming into their centre so that they can have just the right amount of people"(Guly 2000). The call centre industry in Canada employs half a million people, roughly 60 per cent of these on a part-time basis (Human Resources Development Canada 2002).

Such technology is not confined to call centres by any means. Increasingly, it is being used to "optimize" work and staffing levels throughout all sectors of the private and public sector.

High-tech firms in the ICT sector itself, meanwhile, use such flexible staffing arrangements at an increasing rate, on the grounds that rapid technological change and pressure to reduce time-to-market for new products necessitates doing so. Firms in so-called high-tech "cluster" regions like Ottawa, or Silicon Valley and Seattle in the United States, have made liberal use of innovations like outsourcing, contract employment, and the use of temporary workers (Benner and Dean 2000, 361–66; Chun 2001, 127–54). Such regions serve as laboratories for incubating new employment practices and offer a window into the future landscape of work and employment in the new economy, where even the most skilled workers may find plenty of work in non-standard employment arrangements, but fewer jobs in the traditional sense. Silicon Valley in California has been singled out as the capital of non-standard work in the United States, where as much as 40 per cent of the region's workforce works under non-standard employment contracts (Benner and Dean 2000, 363–64). In Canada's software and computer services industry, meanwhile, fully 65,000 of 190,000 workers were reported to be self-employed in 1998, or almost 35 per cent. (Industry Canada 2000, 3, 8). In addition, Canada's high-tech sector is dependent upon a steady supply of skilled foreign workers coming on temporary work visas (Rao 2001). A project begun in 1997 to fast-track the processing of such visas for IT software development workers helped bring three thousand individuals into Canada by early 2000 (Citizenship and Immigration Canada 2000).

While such flexible work arrangements are clearly desired by many workers, an increasingly significant proportion find themselves in such arrangements involuntarily, indicating a considerable amount of underemployment (Jackson, Robinson, Baldwin, and Wiggins. 2000, 63). Furthermore, surveys consistently report that non-permanent, contingent workers are paid lower wages and salaries and enjoy little protection under labour laws and few if any benefits (United States General Accounting Office 2000, 18–30; Jackson, Robinson, Baldwin, and Wiggins 2000, 58–73; Vosko 2000, 200–29). Thus, even in the heart of the new economy, the bonanza of high paying jobs alleged to accompany the transition to a knowledge-based economy is part illusion.[7] As this population of contingent workers continues to grow, calls to close the gap in wages, security, employment standards, and working conditions between the permanent and "flexible" workforces may grow louder. The struggle to improve working con-

Graham D. Longford and Barbara A. Crow

ditions and extend protection to such workers will be difficult, however, as employers and governments alike have worked to limit and roll back rather than extend protection to such workers.[8]

As more highly skilled and professional groups find themselves among the ranks of the temporary workforce, there are signs of renewed interest in union-organizing to defend and protect their interests. Witness the re-emergence of occupational unionism among temporary workers in Silicon Valley and Seattle under the banners of organizations like WashTech, FACEIntel, and Alliance@IBM (Alliance@IBM; Andresky Fraser 2001, 150–52; Washington Alliance of Technology Workers/CWA 2001). While this remains a largely American phenomenon, it may only be a matter of time before it emerges in Canada as well. What implications this might have for the broader labour movement, and for improvements in working conditions for contingent workers in general, remains to be seen.

Skills in the New Economy: Knowledge Workers or Cybertariat?

By some measures, workers in today's economy are more skilled and better educated than previous generations. Over half of Canada's workers possess a university or college degree, up from one-fifth twenty-five years ago. Jobs themselves have also been said to be more complex on the whole. The rising skill intensity of some forms of work and the increasingly qualified nature of the workforce have been portrayed as symptomatic of the growing importance of ICTs; hence mounting pressure to expose school children to computers as early as possible through programs such as the federal government's SchoolNet, and the mass production of diploma-wielding "IT" graduates from private and public business colleges. Evidence on the effect of ICTs on workplace skills is mixed, however. Betcherman and McMullen have found evidence of a modest up-skilling effect (McMullen 2001). According to their research, over half of job-types created as a result of introducing new computer technologies were of a professional nature, whereas only 11 per cent required intermediate levels of skill. Of the positions eliminated as a result of new computer-based technology, 60 per cent came from the lower skilled job-types, and only 7 per cent from the professional category. As well, workers in occupations with the most intensive use of computers – such as managers, administrators, and clerical workers – also report increases in the skill requirements, problem-solving, and autonomy involved in their jobs (Betcherman and McMullen 1998, 14).

On the other hand, a recent Statistics Canada survey reveals that uses of computers at work vary considerably and that not all involve a high degree of skill. The most common task reportedly performed on computers was word processing (83 per cent), followed by data entry (72 per cent), record keeping (69 per cent), spreadsheets (63 per cent), and Internet use (54 per cent). Other tasks requiring specialized skills and training were performed less frequently, and only 16 per cent engaged in any programming activities (Marshall 2001, 9). The evident increased use of computers in the workplace should not, therefore, automatically be equated with knowledge work. To what extent does it make sense to call a task like word processing a "skill" if already 83 per cent of computer users report proficiency at it? (Barney 2000, 153–55) Of course, many managers and other skilled workers use word processing and Web surfing to support highly cognate tasks such as report writing, but the mere fact that computer equipment is used in a given workplace is not an automatic indication of the deployment of highly skilled labour.

The varying degrees of skill involved in using computers are also indicated by where and how users report getting their training. Most employees report acquiring the ability to use computers in a relatively informal manner, as a result of trial-and-error or learning from family and co-workers (Statistics Canada 2001e). By way of contrast, the kind of "critical skills" deemed necessary for core occupations in knowledge-based industries like the ICT sector itself are obtainable only through pursuit of an advanced engineering or computer science degree at a limited number of elite institutions, followed by three to ten years of experience in a relevant technology area (Denton and Pereboom 2000, 13). Clearly, then, the prevalence of computers at work is not a reliable indicator of the growth of knowledge-intensive work. As we look, therefore, to assess and secure Canada's place in the emerging knowledge-based economy, we must be careful not to make a fetish of computers and other information technologies, the presence of which can be just as indicative of relatively simplified forms of work such as data entry or telemarketing as it is of high value-added knowledge work.

What the Betcherman and McMullen study also fails to shed light on is where and in what kinds of occupations those holding low to intermediate skill jobs that were eliminated wound up. Highly skilled occupations in knowledge-based sectors carry with them high costs of entry, in the form of specialized university education and professional training, which places them beyond the reach of a large portion of the population. With few new avenues of comparable employment open to them, many end up accepting jobs increasingly likely to involve less skill, pay and security than previous positions. Indeed, for all the discussion of Canada's transition to a knowledge-based economy, a list of the top ten jobs for men and women contains few associated with so-called "knowledge work," according to the 1996 Census. The leading job types included truck driver, janitor, retail sales, secretary, and cashier (Statistics Canada 1998a, 3–6). In other words, the up-skilling effect observed by Betcherman and McMullen is also a polarizing one, as it increases the widening skills, pay, and job security gap between skilled and unskilled workers.

The bifurcation of the labour force on the basis of skill also shows up in income distribution, where a growing trend toward an "hour-glass" economy is evident in Canada. Polarization between rich and poor and a general decline of middle- and working-class incomes are readily apparent (Jackson, Robinson, Baldwin, and Wiggins 2000, 113–38). While it is difficult to disentangle the distributional effects of ICTs from other factors, given what is known about its employment and labour market impacts, there can be little doubt that it plays some role in shaping distribution patterns in the Canadian political economy.[9] The two-tier system increasingly characteristic of occupational structures and income distribution in the information economy is reproduced in the quality of working life as well. Elite knowledge workers experience high degrees of autonomy and flexibility in their work, take advantage of high demand and highly portable skills, and operate on the basis of relations of co-operation, creative collaboration and partnering with peers (Symons 1997, 195–215). The information-worker "underclass," meanwhile, often engages in repetitive and stultifying tasks related to data entry, processing, and extraction, under working conditions in which hierarchy, subordination, and electronic surveillance figure prominently (Bryant 1995, 505–21; Symons 1997, 195–215; Whitaker 1999, 115–18).

Impact of ICTs on Work II:
A Gendered and Racialized Division of Labour

The intensifying occupational and distributional hierarchies characteristic of the new economy are cross-cut by distinct gender and racial cleavages as well. New ICTs have been seen as having the potential to overcome systemic barriers to economic and educational opportunity based on gender, race, and disability. New forms of teleworking, for example, have been held out as particularly advantageous to women, racial minorities, and the disabled. For women, telework offers the possibility of combining work with family commitments and may provide an entry point into the workforce for less skilled or new immigrant women. The virtual workplace, others have argued, reduces the chances that a worker might be penalized or discriminated against based on their race, since the visual clues to racial difference are eliminated. Finally, telemediated work has also been portrayed as offering the potential to more fully integrate the disabled into the workforce by enabling such accommodations as telecommuting.[10] Unfortunately, aggregate trends in the place and status of women, racial minorities, and the disabled in the new information economy are not very encouraging.

Feminist analyses of digital technology have revealed the profoundly gendered nature of the division of labour within the new information economy. In addition to its contribution to the "feminization" of work in general, many new telemediated forms of non-standard employment, such as home-based call centre and clerical work, are doubly feminized insofar as women are disproportionately over-represented in them (Menzies 1997). The nature of computer use at work also varies by gender. Overall, while more women than men report using computers (largely a reflection of the prevalence of women in clerical positions), men were more likely to perform a greater variety of tasks than women, particularly those associated with so-called knowledge work. Men were twice as likely to engage in programming tasks, and significantly more likely to use the Internet, produce graphics, or analyze data (Marshall 2001, 8). We are also witnessing a certain "technological masculinism" within high-tech employment itself (Sawchuck and Crow 1995). The effects of the gendered division of labour are manifested in the masculinization of scientific and computer technical expertise and hardware and software development (Brunet and Prioux 1989, 77–84; Stromber and Arnold 1987; Ullman 1995, 131–44).

In Canada, female employment in professional, technical, and managerial positions related to ICTs averages approximately 20 per cent in the private and public sectors (Avon 1996, 13; Treasury Board of Canada Secretariat 2000). Moreover, at the same time as the ICT sector has been experiencing impressive growth, there has been a worldwide decrease in the numbers of women in computer science (Wright 1997). Women tend to be concentrated in positions such as call centre agents, which are relatively low-paying (under $30,000) (Buchanan and Koch-Schulte 2001, 9–14), while being under-represented in the much more highly paid and secure positions in occupations like computer services and software development, where salaries regularly exceed $100,000. Such gender-based occupational and distributional hierarchies in the new economy are to some extent the reflection of gendered conceptions of the skills used by various workers (Buchanan and Koch-Schulte 2001, 9–14; Eyerman 2000; Putman and Fenety 2000; Shalla 1997). "Communication" skills highly regarded in the service industry, for example, and particularly in call centre work, are viewed as a "feminine" skill, as something that comes "naturally" to women, and hence is not highly valued and is not translatable into higher wages. Paradoxically, "communication" skills are highly valued in the managerial classes in telemediated work, but not in call centre work. All this suggests that the bifurcation of the labour force and polarization of incomes increasingly characteristic of the new economy will place a disproportionate share of the burden of poorly paid and insecure work upon the backs of women.

While there is little empirical research on the status of racialized peoples in terms of occupation and income in ICT-related forms of work, there is ample evidence pointing to the fact that they, too, tend to occupy the lower regions of occupational and income hierarchies in Canada. As Galabuzi argues, "adults in racialised groups are less likely than others to be employed in professional or managerial occupations. Instead, many are concentrated in lower-paying, clerical, service and manual jobs" (2001, 111).

Inequality and Social Cohesion in the New Economy

Increasingly, commentators from a variety of perspectives worry about the implications of such polarization and hierarchy for social cohesion. The mainstream consensus on dealing with the problem has focused on investments in "human capital" through education, training, and skills development (Courchene 2000, 6–14). Workers will best protect themselves from skills-obsolescence in the new economy, and the attendant decline in the demand and remuneration for their services, by engaging in continuous skills upgrading and "lifelong learning." There are some grounds for this view. University graduates in Canada, for example, benefited from a 47 per cent increase in employment during the 1990s, while non-graduates saw their total employment increase by a mere 2 per cent (Statistics Canada 2001e, 30). There is less consensus among governments, policy-makers, business, and educators however, regarding how best to support education and training. While governments and employers have paid lip service to their importance to society as a whole, the last decade has seen a contraction in opportunities for the most vulnerable workers and members of society in terms of education and training (Schmidt 2001). Government budget cuts and the deregulation of tuition fees in most provinces have led to shrinking budgets and rising costs to students and parents for education at all levels.[11] Meanwhile, publicly funded training infrastructure in Canada has been cut back and increasingly privatized (McBride 2000, 167–71). Employer-sponsored training and skills development is significant, but is increasingly focused on those who already possess high levels of education and skill, thereby entrenching existing inequalities of access to the kinds of education and training that would enable the less skilled to create opportunity for themselves.[12] Furthermore, the growth of non-standard work will lead to less employer-sponsored training, as part-time and temporary workers are much less likely to receive such training than those in traditional, full-time permanent positions (Statistics Canada 2001e).

Again, the patterns of gender and racial inequality in terms of employment in the new economy show up in terms of access to education and training opportunities as well (Galabuzi 2001, 111). The general thrust of current trends is toward the privatization of education, training, and skills development, and the placing of responsibility on individuals for their own employment outcomes, by inculcating the rhetoric and values of lifelong learning. Such a shifting of responsibility onto individuals, in our view, threatens to harden attitudes toward those deemed a "failure" in the new economy and to undermine societal cohesion as a result. As access to favourable employment opportunities and their associated social outcomes becomes increasingly dependent upon the possession of higher levels of skill and education, a commitment to equity requires a levelling of the playing field and a renewed dedication to creating universally accessible institutions for education and training.

Also cause for concern is a growing body of research suggesting that human-capital investment is only weakly correlated with favourable employment and economic outcomes. As a number of researchers have pointed out, the problem of accessing "good jobs" is more structural than the human-capital approach suggests. No matter how well educated we become, as one commentator notes, "we can't all be web designers," for the simple reason that the economy does not supply enough positions (Stanford 2001, 31). There are, for example, fifteen retail clerk positions in Canada for every

Graham D. Longford and Barbara A. Crow

job as a computer technician, and one-quarter of all university and college graduates are employed in clerical, sales, and menial jobs, suggesting significant levels of underemployment (Stanford 2001, 31).

Impact of ICTs on Work III: Locational Dynamics

The Eclipse of Geography and Distance? New Locational Dynamics of Work in Canada

In addition to their effects on the supply, quality, skill-intensity, and distributional patterns of work, new ICTs have been correlated with changes in the location of work, both within and between regions and countries. By detaching work from locale, a process dubbed "delocalization," ICTs have enabled the ready transfer of many kinds of work across regional and territorial boundaries, as well as the blurring of the boundary between the workplace and the home. The rise of networked computing, the Internet, and the growth of broadband infrastructure have encouraged the relocation of work along a number of vectors, reshaping the nature of work and employment in the process. In this section we examine the emergence and implications of four important shifts in the locational dynamics of work in Canada: the rising incidence of home-based telework; the growth of mobile telework; the increasing concentration of knowledge work in urban centres and surrounding regional high tech "clusters"; and the insertion of Canada into the emerging international division of telemediated labour. Popular views of these changes have been dominated by pastoral images of electronic cottaging offered up by Rheingold, among others, in which telecommuting professionals take advantage of ICTs to enjoy greater autonomy, contact with family, and freedom from the aggravation of daily commuting (Rheingold 1994). While some do enjoy these advantages, the shifting locational dynamics of work raise new concerns such as employment standards enforcement, work/home-life balance, traffic congestion, urban sprawl, and regional economic disparity. In several of these respects, what is perhaps most noteworthy is the *failure* of ICTs to produce positive effects.

Home-based Telework:
Telecommuting or Cyberserfdom?

New ICTs like computers, fax machines, and modems have played a role in the recent resurgence of home-based work in Canada. The number of home-based workers, including employees and the self-employed, rose markedly between 1971 and 1995, from 613,000 to 2.8 million, increasing from 8 per cent to 17 per cent of the workforce (Akyeampong and Nadwodny 2001, 12–13). The percentage of employed Canadians performing some or all work from home increased from 3 per cent to 10 per cent between 1971 and 2000, according to Statistics Canada. Ekos Research, however, reported in 2001 that 11 per cent of employed Canadians work primarily from home, and that when periodic work at home (unpaid overtime, catching up on e-mail and paperwork, etc.) was included, the figure rose to 40 per cent (Ekos Research Associates 2001). By 1997, meanwhile, nearly 2.5 million Canadians were self-employed (twice as many as in the late 1970s), amounting to 16.2 per cent of the total labour force. During the 1990s, self-employment accounted for over three out of four new jobs added to the economy (Lin, Yates, and Picot 1999, 2). Such a dramatic rise was bound to have an impact on the incidence of home work, given that 50 per cent of the self-employed work at or from home. Upper estimates of the total number of such workers who could be classified as "teleworkers," that is, those whose home-based work is enabled by information and communications technologies, range from one million to 1.5 million (InnoVisions Canada/Canadian Telework Association 2001).

Since some of the largest annual increases in the number of self-employed homeworkers took place during the 1990s, a decade marked by significant corporate downsizing in white collar as well as blue collar occupations, many have argued that the rise in home-based self-employment reflects the existence of a large group of former employees unable to find traditional full-time work (Jackson, Robinson, Baldwin, and Wiggins 2000, 49–61; Tal 2001). Other studies have suggested that the rise of home-based self-employment has more to do with the increasing availability and use of new ICTs, like PCs, mobile phones, fax machines, and the Internet, which have enabled individuals to work from home while remaining in close contact with clients and colleagues (Akyeampong and Nadwodny 2001). Whatever the reason for resorting to home-based work, ICTs play an undeniably important enabling role.

As with other impacts of ICTs, the implications and effects of increased home-based work, often called "telecommuting," are ambiguous and difficult to make generalizations about. Commentators like Mitchell, Negroponte, and Rheingold, for example, invoke bucolic scenes of "electronic cottagers" plying their electronic crafts in the comfort of their homes, while Gurstein and Menzies warn of the danger of homes being turned into silicon sweatshops. In the new economy, however, workers in conditions approximating both of these stereotypes exist at once. In fact, home-based telework appears inherently polarizing in terms of the nature of the work involved and kinds of working conditions, security, and remuneration it entails.

Of the kinds of work that might take place outside conventional workplaces, repetitive low-skill data entry and clerical work, on the one hand, and highly cognate "symbolic analysis" such as report writing, on the other, appear to be the most sustainable. Home-based telework in Canada features plenty of both. In 1991, for example, the largest occupational category for female home-based workers was clerical work, which accounted for over 110,000 positions, followed closely by service and sales positions at 98,000 and 34,000, respectively (Menzies 1997, 113). Home-based clerical workers at the time earned a mean income of around $7,000, according to one of the few studies available (Menzies 1997, 113). At the other end of the spectrum, high-paying professional and semi-autonomous positions in managerial, social science, and educational occupations are also well-represented among home-based workers. For example, fully 25 per cent of employed and 44 per cent of self-employed individuals in managerial occupations work from home (Akyeampong and Nadwodny 2001, 15; Peruuse 1998).

The polarization of the home-based labour force around the figures of the "cyberserf" and the professional "telecommuter" suggested by the above figures is reproduced at the level of working conditions. A semi-skilled single parent engaged in home-based teleservice work because she is unable to afford childcare is far more likely to be poorly paid, enjoy few benefits, and have little protection of the law. She is more likely to suffer job-related injury, will be cut off from vital social networks, training, advancement, and union-organizing opportunities available at conventional workplaces, and will experience the intrusion of surveillance and the blending of work and home-life as an imposition (Bernstein, Lippel, and Lamarche 2001; Felstead and Jewson 2000, 107–08; Gurstein 2002). The well-educated, self-employed, home-based consultant, meanwhile, often enjoys considerable flexibility and autonomy, opportunities for creative collaboration with associates, and generous tax write-offs for business expenses, including a portion of his or her home (Symons 1997, 203–05). Having said that, the story for each of these figures is often more mixed. The home-based tel-eservice worker can save on transportation, food, and clothing costs associated with working outside the home, and, ironically, may be in a stronger position to lever employer compliance with labour standards as a result of electronic monitoring, the record of which can be valuable as proof of time worked, wages owed, and the all-important "employment relationship" (Bernstein, Lippel, and Lamarche 2001, 12). The average professional "tel-ecommuter," meanwhile, also risks isolation and diminished access to social networks as a result of reduced face-to-face contact with clients and col-leagues (Gillespie and Richardson 2000, 230–32). And while touted as ena-bling workers to balance better their work and family commitments, ICTs have failed to halt a steady increase in the number of workers experiencing conflict and stress as a result of attempts to do so.[13] Indeed, new technologies are part of the problem, as they facilitate working at home after the regular work day and increase expectations of "24/7" availability (Duxbury and Higgins 2001, 8). In addition, the anticipated reductions in traffic conges-tion and other environmental advantages of telecommuting have not mate-rialized. All of which is to say that it is impossible to generalize about the experiences of those workers whom new ICTs have enabled to return to the "electronic cottage."

Mobile Work

In addition to contributing to the resurgence of home-based work, new ICTs like cell phones, pagers, PDAs, and mobile e-mail devices have enticed or compelled many workers into mobile work, where the closest thing to a regular place of work is their cars, delivery van, or truck. Innovations in ICTs have spawned new patterns of travel associated with work, in which workers find themselves increasingly working in their cars, at the premises of associates or clients, and "hot-desking" for brief periods at a central office. Reliable figures on the number of such nomadic, mobile workers in Canada are difficult to come by. Place of Work statistics from the 1996 Census reveal that just over one million workers have no fixed workplace address, but its figures are too broad to accurately capture the extent of the phenomenon, as they do not distinguish mobile teleworkers from other mobile workers, such as tradespersons, whose work is less dependent upon enabling ICTs. Assuming a figure in the range of 5 per cent to 10 per cent of Canada's workforce, the number of nomadic, mobile teleworkers could exceed one million.

Mobile work has obvious advantages for employers. Having workers spend less time in the office and more time in the field can help salespersons "get closer to the customer," reduce office overhead and increase productivity. However, not all managers are comfortable with it since, as with telecommuting, it diminishes opportunities for managerial oversight and surveillance of work. Mobile employees pay a certain price as well. Reduced time in a regular office also means diminished opportunities for face-to-face interaction, socializing, and networking with colleagues, and reduced visibility of the sort that can lead to advancement and promotion within the company. Finally, while ICTs have been traditionally portrayed as suppressing the need for travel, the phenomenon of mobile telework appears to be part of a trend toward what the authors of one study refer to as "hypermobility," in which new ICTs change the locational dynamics of work in such a way as to increase rather than decrease the car-dependence of work by, for example, increasing the number of car trips made during the day (Gillespie and Richardson 2000, 228, 243; Miller 2000). According to U.S. studies, the increased incidence of home-based work has also produced little net reduction in vehicle miles travelled and has resulted in an increasing number of trips throughout the day within residential neighbourhoods, leading to greater noise, pollution, and congestion at off-peak periods (Gillespie and Richardson 2000, 228–45). One can see this reflected in the fact that some of the "smartest" cities in North America in terms of labour force skills and ICT infrastructure, such as San Francisco, Seattle, and Ottawa, have experienced worsened traffic congestion (Hill 2000; Laucious, 2000; Singer 2000). With fewer workers engaging in traditional commutes while many are increasing their daytime car use, ridership on public transportation has dropped as well, threatening the future quality and viability of such services (Gillespie and Richardson 2000, 236–38).

High-tech "Clusters": The Geography of Work in the New Economy

The decoupling of work and place enabled by ICTs is also affecting the location of work and employment on a regional and international basis.

Within Canada, there are signs that the nature and location of work in the knowledge-based economy are having uneven effects on the development of regional, urban, and rural economies, and that the growth of the international teleservices market presents both opportunities and challenges for those aspiring to gain entry to or succeed within it.

One of the keenly anticipated benefits of new ICTs has been their potential to promote economic development in rural and remote locations throughout Canada, including aboriginal communities – areas traditionally dependent upon declining agricultural and primary industries. The vision, articulated most recently by the federal National Broadband Task Force, is of remote communities, connected by broadband digital networks, peopled by skilled knowledge workers able to overcome the barriers to employment and economic opportunity posed by distance. According to the Task Force:

> By reducing or even eliminating the economic costs tradition-
> ally associated with distance, broadband communications offer all
> Canadian communities the potential to capitalize on their natural
> and human endowments, and to compete effectively in markets of
> whatever scale in their areas of comparative advantage. (National
> Broadband Task Force 2001, 24)

However, notwithstanding concerted attempts by both federal and provincial governments to lever ICTs to lessen the economic disparities among regions and between urban and rural communities, such as New Brunswick's attempt at refashioning itself as the call centre capital of Canada, there is mounting evidence that the knowledge-based economy, and the importance of ICTs to it, reinforces rather than reduces historic patterns of regional disparity.

Even as rural and remote communities promote themselves as increasingly "wired" and ready to participate in the new economy, a consensus has emerged around the increasing importance of "clustering" the development of high-tech, knowledge-based industries around largely existing urban centres in order to compete internationally. Cities have become more rather than less important in the new international division of labour, as nodal points for controlling the flow of goods and services and as hubs for R&D and specialized economic activity such as international financial services (Castells 2000, 424–40; Huws, Jagger and Bates. 2001; Sassen 1998). Business leaders and policy makers alike now argue that so-called high-tech "clusters" or "learning regions" such as Kitchener-Waterloo,

Graham D. Longford and Barbara A. Crow

Ottawa, Toronto, and Montreal, are key to competing in the global economy, because it is in such places that innovative, job-creating companies have access to so-called "untraded interdependencies," which are specific to locales, including: a critical mass of highly skilled labour; communications and transportation infrastructure; access to public and private R&D institutions and potential partners; large pools of venture capital; and the kind of quality of life that attracts workers (Courchene and Telmer 1998, 268–96; Nankivell 2001, 85–91; Wolfe 2000). The emphasis on clustering the development of knowledge-based industries around existing urban centres and surrounding suburban zones, however, flies in the face of expectations that ICTs will produce a more even spatial distribution of work across Canada, and threatens to exacerbate existing regional economic disparity and tension as governments focus investment and services on the economies of already privileged clusters.[14] Meanwhile, attempts to incubate and foster high-tech clusters in historically "low tech" provinces have achieved limited success and have more often than not pitted jurisdictions against one another in intense "locational tournaments" involving competition for investment in low-wage industries such as call centre services, with each trying to outdo the other in offering tax holidays, regulatory concessions, and job subsidies to potential investors (Jang 2001; Joint Venture: Silicon Valley 1998; Savoie 2001, 102–5, 157–60; Tutton 2001).

High-tech cluster regions are noteworthy not only for their prosperity relative to rural areas, but for the heightened degree of economic and social polarization within, as local labour markets themselves become bifurcated between high-tech professionals and low-tech workers in janitorial services, electronics assembly, and personal services work. Castells refers to this as the phenomenon of the "dual city" increasingly characteristic of high-tech cluster regions (Castells 1999, 27–41). Silicon Valley and other high-tech clusters have increasingly taken on the form of what one commentator calls the "resort economy," in which a highly affluent minority enjoys fat salaries, lavish homes in gated communities, exclusive club memberships, and premium shopping and recreational opportunities insulated against the intrusions of the wider community, all supported and surrounded by the labour of a nearly invisible underclass of service and manual workers. While employees in the software industry, for example, routinely pull down salaries in excess of US$100,000, average salaries in the industry with the largest employment in Silicon Valley, local and visitor services, are under US$23,000 (Joint Venture: Silicon Valley 2000). Canadian communities such as Toronto and Ottawa–Hull are well down the path to social polarization laid down by high-tech meccas like Silicon Valley, as evidenced by overheated real estate markets, affordable-housing shortages, gentrification, and increased evictions and homelessness (Hill 2000; Solnit and Schwartzenberg 2000; Layton 2000; Goodell 1999).

Finally, combined with the liberalization of trade, the growing international trade in informational goods and services is reshaping the international division of labour and Canada's place within it. Canada has achieved some noteworthy successes exporting computer and software services and telemediated customer services. However, the ease with which such work can be outsourced or transferred elsewhere is a constant threat. In computer and software services, for example, Canada's trade balance has been narrowing throughout the 1990s, steadily eroding a modest surplus, suggesting that the time when Canada becomes a net importer of such services may be near (Prabhu 1998, 8–9; Industry Canada 2000, 27). The low-wage call centre industry in the Atlantic provinces and elsewhere, meanwhile, faces increasing competition from teleservice outsourcing firms in India and the Caribbean, where generally well-educated English-speaking employees can be hired for less than half of what it costs to pay Canadian workers (McElroy 2001). Places like New Brunswick may find such work disappearing through the very same network from which it came. While the magnitude of the threat remains small for now, the trend toward outsourcing teleservices to offshore locations such as India is accelerating.[15]

Electronic Monitoring and Workplace Privacy

Part of the allure of applying ICTs to work is not only the labour cost savings achieved through process automation, but the ability to use these same technologies to monitor the production process. Such technologies enable firms not only to track sales, inventory, and production speeds, but to track the performance, whereabouts, and, increasingly, private thoughts and personal communications of employees. Today, the location and activities of millions of workers are more closely monitored than ever, thanks to innovations such as GPS locators, computer keystroke logs, and software designed to monitor employee e-mail and Internet use. Indeed, technology is now available to employers to review the Web-surfing habits and histories of prospective employees even before they are hired (Privacy Commissioner of Canada 1999). Aside from the anxiety and atmosphere of suspicion that such moni-

Graham D. Longford and Barbara A. Crow

toring can foster among supervisors and employees, the intensification and spread of electronic monitoring poses a growing human rights challenge.

First, let us get a handle on the scope of the phenomenon. An initial indication of the spread of electronic monitoring and its effects on workers has been signalled by the rising frequency of media reports involving employee abuse of e-mail and Internet tools at work, uncovered by employer monitoring (CBC News Online Staff 2001; Canadian Press 2001). Firming up these anecdotal impressions of the increased use of electronic monitoring are recent statistics on employer uses of electronic monitoring. A recent survey of workplace monitoring and surveillance practices in the United States by the American Management Association (AMA) found that nearly 78 per cent of firms record and monitor employee communications and activities on the job, including their phone calls, e-mail, Internet site visits, and computer files (American Management Association 2001, 1). The U.S.-based Privacy Foundation, meanwhile, estimates that up to one-third of the online workforce, or roughly fourteen million U.S. employees, is under continuous surveillance for improper e-mail and Internet use (Privacy Foundation 2001). While no equivalent figures are available on the extent of the practice by Canadian employers, there is little doubt that it is widespread (Bryant 1995, 505–21).

Not only have the extent and intensity of surveillance changed with new technologies, but the targets as well. While the work of cashiers, data entry clerks, and call centre agents has long been susceptible to electronic monitoring, new software tracking workflow, e-mail communication, and Internet use facilitates increased surveillance of professional, managerial, and technical personnel as well.

The main reasons cited by employers for adopting such technologies are the need to limit legal liability, conduct performance reviews, measure productivity, and ensure the security of proprietary information against disclosure (American Management Association 2001). The AMA study showed that limiting liability was the primary reason for introducing such technologies. The proliferation of computers, e-mail, and Internet access in the workplace has given rise to inappropriate uses of the technology, including visits to gambling and pornography sites, and the transmission of harassing e-mails of a sexual, racial, or religious nature. Arguably, such monitoring systems have helped enforce policies against racism and sexism in the workplace. However, the trend toward continuous monitoring, which effectively casts a pall of suspicion over all employees, invites the question of whether employees' privacy rights and some form of the presumption of innocence should be sacrificed at the altar of limiting corporate liability.

Privacy legislation in Canada currently provides little protection to employees, particularly in the private sector. Canada's *Privacy Act* (1982) covers government uses of citizens' personal information, while the more recent *Personal Information Protection and Electronic Documents Act* (2001) focuses on protecting consumers, in order to shore up confidence in the beleaguered e-commerce sector. The latter signals the ascendancy of an e-commerce conception of privacy and the displacement of a rights-based conception from the current debate within Canada (Steeves 2001, 49–56).[16] Privacy advocates, including Canada's Privacy Commissioner, increasingly worry that Canadians surrender their privacy rights, often unwittingly, immediately upon entering the workplace. Workers should be entitled to some expectation of privacy in the workplace in order to communicate with family members and interact with colleagues in a natural manner, which may include venting frustrations about employers and working conditions; freedom to do so without fear of surveillance or reprisal is an essential ingredient of a reasonable quality of working life. Such a right to privacy, as one advocate argues, "cannot be conjured away by means of an employment contract" (Privacy Commissioner of Canada 2000).

Conclusion

This article provides a cursory overview of the complex and far-reaching effects and implications of ICTs for paid work in Canada. As a counter-narrative to the boosterism of high-tech gurus and leaders in business and government, it maps areas of pressing concern seldom acknowledged as anything more than "potholes" on the information highway. In our view, however, the connections between ICTs and workplace and employment trends like labour force polarization, the growth of non-standard employment, the gendered division of labour, increased stress and hours of work, and the social and environmental costs of clustered development raise serious doubts about how benign the information economy and society of our near future will really be. We conclude with a series of recommendations on ways to mitigate the more disturbing effects of ICTs on work and workers in Canada:

Graham D. Longford and Barbara A. Crow

- Modernization of legislation in areas like employment insurance, occupational health and safety, pensions and benefits, and employment standards in order to prevent the growing numbers of contingent workers from being excluded from enjoying full rights of economic and workplace citizenship.
- Funding for empirical research aimed at better understanding the various populations of teleworkers and the challenges they confront.
- Rededication by governments to long-term labour adjustment and retraining policies and programs abandoned in the 1980s and 1990s, especially for workers displaced by new technology.
- Facilitation of opportunities for the formation of institutions and mechanisms of collective representation, including trade unions, for contingent and home-based workers.
- Investigation of the health and environmental impacts of ICTs and the forms and locational dynamics of work they support.
- Development and enactment of privacy legislation related to individuals as workers, in addition to protection already in place for citizens and consumers.
- Recommitment by governments to regulating and planning the development of urban and suburban regions with a view to creating livable cities.
- Increased public investment in mass transportation.

Acknowledgment

Graham Longford wishes to acknowledge and thank Trent University's Social Sciences and Humanities Research Council (SSHRC) Committee on Research for generous financial assistance provided during the research for and preparation of this manuscript.

Works Cited

Akyeampong, Ernest, and Richard Nadwodny, 2001. "Evolution of the Canadian Workplace: Work from Home." Perspectives on Labour and Income 2(9) (September). Ottawa: Statistics Canada.
Alliance@IBM. Available: http://www.allianceibm.org.

American Management Association. 2001. *AMA Survey: Workplace Monitoring & Surveillance, Summary of Key Findings*. New York: American Management Association.

Andresky Fraser, Jill. 2001.*White Collar Sweatshop: The Deterioration of Work and Its Rewards in Corporate America*. New York: W.W. Norton.

Association of Canadian Search, Employment and Staffing Services (ACSESS). 2001., "National Staffing Industry Association Commends Repeal of Employment Agencies Act," Press Release, May 4, 2001.

Avon, Emmanuelle. 1996. "Human Resources in Science and Technology in the Services Sector." Services, Science and Technology Division, Statistics Canada, Analytical Research Paper No. 8. July Ottawa: Minister of Industry, July.

Barney, Darin, 2000. *Prometheus Wired: The Hope for Democracy in the Age of Networked Technology*. Vancouver: University of British Columbia Press.

Benner, Chris, and Amy Dean. 2000. "Labour in the New Economy: Lessons from Labour Organizing in Silicon Valley." In *Nonstandard Work: The Nature and Challenges of Changing Employment Arrangements*, ed. Françoise Carré, Marianne A. Ferber, Lonnie Golden and Stephen A. Herzenberg, 361–75. Champaign, IL: Industrial Relations Research Association.

Bernstein, Stephanie, Katherine Lippel, and Lucie Lamarche. 2001. *Women and Homework: The Canadian Legislative Framework*. Ottawa: Status of Women Canada.

Betcherman, Gordon, and Kathryn McMullen. 1998. "Impact of Information and Communication Technologies on Work and Employment in Canada." CPRN Discussion Paper No. 10. Ottawa: Canadian Policy Research Networks, February.

Bickerton, Geoff, and Catherine Louli. 1995. "Decades of Change, Decades of Struggle: Postal Workers and Technological Change." In *Re-shaping Work: Union Responses to Technological Change*, ed. Christopher Schenk and John Anderson, 216–32. Don Mills, ON: Federation of Labour.

Boston Consulting Group [Canada]. 2000. "Fast Forward: Accelerating Canada's Leadership in the Information Economy." Report of the Canadian E-Business Opportunities Roundtable. Toronto: Boston Consulting Group [Canada].

Brunet, J., and S. Prioux. 1989. "Formal versus Grass-Roots Training: Women, Work and Computers." *Journal of Communication* 39(3): 77–84.

Bryant, S. 1995. "Electronic Surveillance in the Workplace." *Canadian Journal of Communication* 20(4): 505–21.

Buchanan, Ruth, and Sarah Koch-Schulte. 2001. "Gender on the Line: Technology, Restructuring and the Reorganization of Work in the Call Centre Industry." Ottawa: Status of Women Canada.

Burke, Mike, and John Shields. 2000. "Tracking Inequality in the New Canadian Labour Market." In *Restructuring and Resistance: Canadian Public Policy in an Age of Global Capitalism*, ed. Mike Burke, Colin Mooers, and John Shields, 98–123. Halifax: Fernwood.

CBC News Online Staff. 2001. "Navy Officer Disciplined for Accessing Internet Porn." June 19. Available: http://www.cbc.ca/cgi-bin/templates/view.cgi?category=Canada&story=/news/2001.06/18

Canadian Policy Research Networks. Available: http://www.cprn.org.

———. JobQuality.ca. Available: http://www.JobQuality.ca.

———. 2002. JobQuality.ca. Indicators. Available: http://www.jobquality.ca/indicator_e/sec001.stm. [January 23, 2002]

Canadian Press. 2001. "New Brunswick Cracks Down on Unauthorized Surfing." *globeandmail.com*, September 5.

Castells, Manuel. 1999. "The Informational City is a Dual City: Can it be Reversed?" In *High Technology and Low-Income Communities: Prospects for the Positive Use of Advanced Information Technology*, ed. Donald A. Schön, Bish Saynal and William J. Mitchell, 27–41. Cambridge, MA: MIT Press.

———. 2000. The Rise of the Network Society: The Information Age. vol. 1, 2d ed. London: Blackwell.

Chun, Jennifer Jihye. 2001. "Flexible Despotism: The Intensification of Insecurity and Uncertainty in the Lives of Silicon Valley's High-Tech Assembly Workers." In *The Critical Study of Work: Labour, Technology and Global Production*, ed. Rick Baldoz, Charles Koeber, and Philip Kraft, 127–54. Philadelphia: Temple University Press.

Church, Elizabeth, 2001. "Workers' Priorities Changing after Sept. 11." *Globe and Mail*, October 15.

Citizenship and Immigration Canada, 2000. "Supporting Jobs in the High Tech Sector." News Release, January 21. Available: http://www.cic.gc.ca/english/press/00/0003-pre.html.

Conference Board of Canada. 1996. "Jobs in the Knowledge Based Economy: Information Technology and the Impact on Employment." Ottawa: Conference Board of Canada.

Courchene, Thomas. 2000. "A Mission Statement for Canada." *Policy Options* (July–August): 6–14.

——. 2001. "A State of Minds." Montreal: Institute for Research on Public Policy.

Courchene, Thomas, with Colin R. Telmer. 1998. *From Heartland to North American Region State: The Social, Fiscal and Federal Evolution of Ontario.* Toronto: University of Toronto Press.

Denton, Timothy, and Bert Pereboom. 2000. *Profile of the Information and Communications Technologies Sector.* Prepared for the Expert Panel on Skills, Advisory Council on Science and Technology. Ottawa: Industry Canada.

Duxbury, Linda, and Chris Higgins. 2001. "Work-Life Balance in the New Millennium: Where Are We? Where Do We Need to Go?" Discussion Paper No. W/12. Ottawa: Canadian Policy Research Networks, October.

Ekos Research Associates. 2001. "Canadians and Working From Home." May 18. Available: http://www.ivc.ca/part12.html.

Ertl, Heidi, 2001. "Beyond the Information Highway: Networked Canada." Ottawa: Statistics Canada.

Eyerman, Jane. 2000. *Women in the Office: Transitions in a Global Economy.* Toronto: Sumach Press.

Felstead, Alan, and Nick Jewson. 2000. *In Work, At Home: Towards an Understanding of Homeworking.* London: Routledge.

Forrester Research Inc. 2002. "3.3 Million US Service Jobs to Go Offshore." November 11, 2002, http://www.forrester.com/ER/Research/Brief/Excerpt/0,1317,15900,00.html [March 16, 2003].

Galabuzi, G. 2001. "Canada's Creeping Economic Apartheid: The Economic Segregation and Social Marginalisation of Racialised Groups." Toronto: CSJ Foundation for Research and Education, August.

Gillespie, Andrew, and Ronald Richardson. 2000. "Teleworking and the City: Myths of Workplace Transcendence and Travel Reduction." In *Cities in the Telecommunications Age: The Fracturing of Geographies,* ed. James O. Wheeler, Yuko Aoyama, and Barney Warf, 230–32. London: Routledge.

Goodell, Jeff. 1999. "Down and Out in Silicon Valley." *Rolling Stone,* December 9.

Guly, Christopher. 2000. "Cyber-Watchdog for Call Centres." *Ottawa Citizen,* July 4.

Gurstein, Penny. 2002. *Wired to the World, Chained to the Home: Telework in Daily Life.* Vancouver: University of British Columbia Press.

Hill, Bert, 2000. "Ottawa's Good-News Growth comes at Bad-News Price: Author." *Ottawa Citizen,* September 26.

Hughes, Karen, and Graham Lowe. 2000. "Surveying the 'Post-Industrial' Landscape: Information Technologies and Labour Market Polarization in Canada." *Canadian Review of Sociology and Anthropology* 37(1): 29–53.

Huws, Ursula, Nick Jagger, and Siobhan O'Regan. 1999. "Teleworking and Globalization." Report Summary, Institute for Employment Studies Report 358. Available: http://www.employment-studies.co.uk/summary/358sum.html

Huws, Ursula, Nick Jagger and Peter Bates. 2001. "Where the Butterfly Alights: the Global Location of eWork." Report Summary, Institute for Employment Studies Report 378. April. Available: http://www.employment-studies.co.uk/summary/378sum.html

Industry Canada. 2000. *Information and Communications Technologies Statistical Review: 1990–1998.* Spectrum, Information Technologies and Telecommunications Sector. Ottawa: Industry Canada, July.

Information and Privacy Commissioner/Ontario. 1992. "Workplace Privacy: A Consultation Paper." June. Available: http://www/ipc.on.ca

Information Highway Advisory Council. 1997. "Preparing Canada for a Digital World: Final Report of the Information Highway Advisory Council." Ottawa: Industry Canada.

InnoVisions Canada/Canadian Telework Association. 2001. "Canadian Stats and Facts." Available: http://www.ivc.ca/part12.html [October 15, 2001].

Jackson, Andrew, David Robinson, Bob Baldwin, and Cindy Wiggins. 2000. "Falling Behind: The State of Working Canada 2000." Ottawa: Canadian Centre for Policy Alternatives.

Jang, Brent. 2001. "Its Share of Pain belies Notion of Opulent Alberta." *Globe and Mail,* September 1.

Johnson, Karen, Donna Lero, and Jennifer Rooney. 2001. "Work-Life Compendium 2001: 150 Canadian Statistics on Work, Family & Well-Being." Guelph, ON: Centre for Families, Work and Well-Being, University of Guelph.

Joint Venture: Silicon Valley. 1998. "*1998 Index* Finds Silicon Valley Facing Challenges, But Community Starting to Respond." Press Release, January 11. Available: http://www.jointventure.org. [January 23, 2002].

———. 2000. *2000 Index of Silicon Valley.* Available: http://www.jointventure.org. [January 23, 2002].

Laucious, Joanne. 2000. "High-Tech Boom Faces Roadblocks: Road System needs Upgrades." *Ottawa Citizen*, August 3.

Layton, Jack. 2000. *Homelessness: The Making and Unmaking of a Crisis.* Toronto: Penguin/McGill Institute for the Study of Canada.

Lin, Zhengxi, Janice Yates, and Garnett Picot. 1999. "Rising Self-Employment in the Midst of High Unemployment: An Empirical Analysis of Recent Developments in Canada." Business and Labour Market Analysis, Analytical Studies Branch. Ottawa: Statistics Canada, March.

Longford, Graham. 2001. "Rethinking E-Government: Dilemmas of Public Service, Citizenship and Democracy in the Digital Age." Paper presented to the Canadian Political Science Association Annual General Meeting, Université Laval, Quebec City, Quebec, May 27–29.

Lowe, Graham, Grant Schellenberg, and Katie Davidman. 1999. "Rethinking Employment Relationships." CPRN Discussion Paper No. W/05, Changing Employment Relationships Series. Ottawa: Canadian Policy Research Networks.

Marshall, Katherine. 2001. "Working With Computers." *Perspectives on Labour and Income* 2(5). Ottawa: Statistics Canada.

McBride, Stephen, 2000. "Policy from What? Neoliberal and Human-Capital Theoretical Foundations of Recent Canadian Labour-Market Policy." In *Restructuring and Resistance: Canadian Public Policy in an Age of Global Capitalism,* ed. Mike Burke, Colin Mooers and John Shields, 159–77 Halifax: Fernwood.

McElroy, Damien. 2001. "Workers Know the Score." *National Post*, May 28.

McMullen, Kathryn. 2001. "Skill and Employment Effects of Computer Based Technologies." Canadian Policy Research Networks, Backgrounder.

McNally, David. 2000. "Globalization, Trade Pacts and Migrant Workers." In *Restructuring and Resistance: Canadian Public Policy in an Age of Global Capitalism,* ed. Mike Burke, Colin Mooers and John Shields, 268–70. Halifax: Fernwood.

Menzies, Heather. 1996. *Whose Brave New World? The Information Highway and the New Economy.* Toronto: Between the Lines.

———. 1997. "Telework, Shadow Work: The Privatization of Work in the New Digital Economy." *Studies in Political Economy* 53 (Summer): 103–23.

Miller, Eric J. 2000. "Transportation and Communication." In Trudi Bunting and Pierre Filion, *Canadian Cities in Transition: The Twenty-first Century.* 2d ed., 173–97. Toronto: Oxford.

Nankivell, Neville. 2001. "Why Canada's Capital is a High-Tech Hotbed." *National Pos*, April 18.

National Broadband Task Force. 2001. "The New National Dream: Networking the Nation for Broadband Access." Report of the National Broadband Task Force. Ottawa: Industry Canada.

Noble, David. 1995. *Progress Without People: New Technology, Unemployment, and the Message of Resistance.* Toronto: Between the Lines.

Ontario Ministry of Labour. Your Guide to the Employment Standards Act. Available: http://www.gov.on.ca/LAB/english/es/guide/

Peruuse, D. 1998. "Working at Home." *Perspectives on Labour and Income* 10(2) (Summer). Ottawa: Statistics Canada.

Peterson, Greg. 2001. "Electronic Commerce and Technology Use." Connectedness Series No. 5, Science, Innovation and Electronic Information Division, Statistics Canada. Ottawa: Minister of Industry.

Prabhu, Sirish. 1998. "The Software and Computer Services Industry: An Overview of Developments in the 1990s." Analytical Paper Series No. 17, Statistics Canada. Ottawa: Minister of Industry.

Privacy Commissioner of Canada. 1999. *Annual Report 1998–99.* Ottawa: Minister of Public Works and Government Services Canada.

———. 2000. *Annual Report 1999–2000.* Ottawa: Minister of Public Works and Government Services Canada.

Privacy Foundation. 2001. "One-Third of U.S. Online Workforce under Internet/E-Mail Surveillance." Privacy Watch, July 9. Available: http://www.privacyfoundation.org/privacywatch/report.asp?id=72&action=0

Putman, Carol, and Anne Fenety. 2000. "Who's on the Line?: Women in Call Centres Talk about their Work and its Impact on their Health and Well-Being." Halifax, NS: Dalhousie University, Maritime Centre of Excellence for Women's Health.

Rao, Badrinath. 2001. "Economic Migrants in a Global Labour Market: A Report on the Recruitment and Retention of Asian Computer Professionals by Canadian High Tech Firms." CPRN Discussion Paper No. W/13. Ottawa: Canadian Policy Research Networks.

Reid, Angus. 1996. *Shakedown: How the New Economy is Changing Our Lives.* Toronto: Doubleday.

Rheingold, Howard. 1994. *The Virtual Community.* London: Secker and Warburg.

Rifkin, Jeremy. 1995. *The End of Work: The Decline of the Global Labor Force and the Dawn of the Post-Market Era.* New York: G.P. Putnam's Sons.

Rubin, Jeffrey. 2001. "How Long will the Market Continue to Pay High Tech Multiples?" *Globe and Mail,* September 1.

Sassen, Saskia, 1998. *Globalization and Its Discontents: Essays on the New Mobility of People and Money.* New York: The New Press.

Savoie, Donald. 2001. *Pulling Against Gravity: Economic Development in New Brunswick During the McKenna Years.* Montreal: Institute for Research on Public Policy.

Sawchuck, Kim, and Barbara Crow. 1995. "Some Canadian Feminists Intervene in the Datasphere." Proceedings: Telecommunities '95 Equity on the Net, International Community Networking Conference. Victoria.

Schmidt, Lisa. 2001. "Canada Lagging Behind Many Countries in Adult Education finds Study." Canada.comNews, September 9. Available: http://www.canada.com

SchoolNet program. Available: http://www.schoolnet.ca/home/e/

Shalla, Vivian. 1997. "Technology and the Deskilling of Work: The Case of the Passenger Agents at Air Canada." In *Good Jobs, Bad Jobs, No Jobs: The Transformation of Work in the 21st Century,* ed. A. Duffy, D. Glenday, and N. Pupo, 76–96. Toronto: Harcourt Brace and Co.

Singer, Zev. 2000. "West-End Land Crunch hits Tech Sector." *Ottawa Citizen,* June 13.

Solnit, Rebecca, and Susan Schwartzenberg. 2000. *Hollow City: The Siege of San Francisco and the Crisis of American Urbanism.* London: Verso.

Stanford, Jim. 2001. "We can't all be Web Designers." *CCPA Monitor* 8(5) (October): 31.

Statistics Canada. 1998a. "1996 Census: Labour Force Activity, Occupation and Industry, Place of Work, Mode of Transportation to Work, Unpaid Work," *The Daily,* March 17, 3–6.

——. 1998b. "Cellular Telephone Service Industry: Historical Statistics," *The Daily,* April 1. Available: http://www.statcan.ca:80/Daily/English/980401/d980401.htm

——. 2001a. Labour Force Survey, August. Available: http://www.statcan.ca/english/Subjects/Labour/LFS/lfs-en.htm

——. 2001b. The Daily, August 27. Available: http://www.statcan.ca/Daily/English/010827/d010827b.htm

——. 2001c. "After the Layoff." The Daily, October 25. Available: http://www.statcan.ca:80/Daily/English/011025/d011025a.htm

——. 2001d. "Telecommunications Statistics: Third quarter 2001." *The Daily,* December 21.

——. 2001e. *Workplace and Employee Survey Compendium: 1999 Data.* Ottawa: Minister of Industry.

Steeves, Valerie. 2001. "Privacy Then and Now: Taking stock Since IHAC." In *E-commerce vs. E-commons: Communications in the Public Interest,* ed. Marita Moll and Leslie Regan Shade, 49–56. Ottawa: Canadian Centre for Policy Alternatives.

Stromber, M. H., and C. Arnold. 1987. "Computer Chips and Paper Clips: Technology and Women's Employment, Vol. 2: Case Studies and Policy Perspectives, Panel on Technology and Women's Employment." Committee on Women's Employment and Related Social Issues. Washington, DC: National Research Council.

Symons, Frank. 1997. "Network Access, Skills and Equity in the Workplace: Polarization in Social Policy." *Canadian Journal of Communication* 22(2): 195–215.

Tal, Benjamin. 2001. "Trends in Small Business as of October 2001." Economics Division, Canadian Imperial Bank of Commerce. Available http://www.cibc.com/

Tapscott, Don. 1996. *The Digital Economy: Promise and Peril in the Age of Networked Intelligence.* Toronto: McGraw-Hill.

Treasury Board of Canada Secretariat. 2000. Employment Statistics for the Federal Public Service: April 1, 1999–March 31, 2000. Available: http://www.tbs-sct.gc.ca/pubs_pol/hrpubs/pse-fpe/es-se99-00-1_e.html#_Toc501185760

Tutton, Michael. 2001. "N.S. Offering Record-Breaking Subsidies to Attract Call Centre Business." *Yahoo News Canada,* July 31.

Ullman, Ellen. 1995. "Out of Time: Reflections on the Programming Life." In *Resisting the Virtual Life: The Culture and Politics of Information*, ed. James Brook and Iain A. Boal, 131–44. San Francisco: City Lights.

United States General Accounting Office. 2000. "Contingent Workers : Incomes and Benefits Lag Behind those of the Rest of Workforce: Report to the Honorable Edward M. Kennedy and the Honorable Robert G. Torricelli," 18–30. U.S. Senate. Washington, DC.

Vosko, Leah. 2000. *Temporary Work: The Gendered Rise of a Precarious Employment Relationship.* Toronto: University of Toronto Press.

Walters, Gregory J. 2001. "Information Highway Policy, E-commerce and Work." In *E-commerce vs. E-commons: Communications in the Public Interest*, Marita Moll and Leslie Regan Shade, 78–83. Ottawa: Canadian Centre for Policy Alternatives.

Washington Alliance of Technology Workers/CWA. 2001. *Disparities Within the Digital World: Realities of the New Economy.* Prepared by The Worker Centre, King County Labor Council. Available: http://www.washtech.org

Whitaker, Reg. 1999. *The End of Privacy: How Total Surveillance is Becoming a Reality.* New York: The New Press.

Wolfe, David. 2000. "Social Capital and Cluster Development in Learning Regions." Paper presented to the XVIII World Congress of the International Political Science Association, Quebec City, August 5.

Wright, R. 1997. "Women in Computing: A Cross-National Analysis." In *Women in Computing: Progression: From Where to What?*, ed. R. Lander and A. Adam, 72–82. Exeter, UK: Intellect Books.

Notes

1   Statistics Canada reports that by 1999 Internet and cell phone penetration of Canadian households reached 42 per cent and 32 per cent, respectively. See Ertl (2001, 38, 40). Elsewhere, Statistics Canada reports that there were 9.9 million cellular phone subscribers in Canada by 2001 (Statistics Canada 2001d).

2   Betcherman and McMullen (1998) report as little as 16 per cent of workers using new ICTs like computers as recently as 1985.

3   This is not to deny the emergence of some disturbing trends, such as growing underemployment and rising unemployment among certain groups, such as single mothers and young, unskilled males (Burke and Shields 2000, 98–123; Jackson, Robinson, Baldwin, and Wiggins 2000, 47–73).

4   The Liberal Party Red Book of 1993 stated, for example, that "it is the information and knowledge-based industries with their new products, new services, new markets for old and new products, and new processes for existing businesses that are providing the foundation for jobs and economic growth." Quoted in McBride (2000, 163).

5   Betcherman and McMullen (1998, 11) find little proof of a direct connection between ICT use and overall job growth. Their study reveals the strongest influence on job growth to be sales growth rather than ICT investment.

6   Traditionally associated with agricultural and construction work, the use of temporary workers is high in "knowledge sectors" like management and administrative services (24 per cent) educational services (19 per cent) and public administration (15 per cent) as well: CPRN, JobQuality.ca, Available: http://www.JobQuality.ca.

7   See, for example, a report on wages and working conditions in the IT sector in Seattle: Washington Alliance of Technology Workers/CWA (2001).

8   For example, amendments to Ontario's *Employment Standards Act* in 2000 repealed provisions regulating and licensing temporary employment agencies, and raised from 44 to 60 the maximum number of hours in the work week. The latter provision was eagerly sought by the ICT industry, which had sought exemptions under the previous Act on a routine basis. See Association of Canadian Search, Employment and Staffing Services (ACSESS) (2001), and Ontario Ministry of Labour, *Your Guide to the Employment Standards Act*, available at http://www.gov.on.ca/LAB/english/es/guide/.

9   For more detailed demonstrations of this link, see, for example: Betcherman and McMullen (1998, 15–17); and Hughes and Lowe (2000, 29–53).

10   Research results from the U.K., however, suggest little impact so far. The proportion of U.K. teleworkers with disabilities stands at 9 per cent, which is roughly the same proportion as in the traditional workforce (Huws, Jagger and O'Regan, 1999).

11 The most serious consequences for accessibility are to be found at the university level, where undergraduate tuition fees have increased 120 per cent, on average, in Canada since 1990 (Statistics Canada 2001b).

12 Almost 60 per cent of Canadian workers with only high school diplomas reported receiving no training during 1999, whereas only 30 per cent of those with university degrees reported receiving no training (Statistics Canada 2001e, 30).

13 A 2000 survey found that 58 per cent of employees experience high levels of work–family role "overload," up from 47 per cent in 1990. Such stress is most acute among professional and managerial employees (Johnson et al. 2001, 53–54). Similar findings have been reported in Duxbury and Higgins (2001). See also Church (2001).

14 For the most part, decentralizing forces observed in the new economy have involved the movement of work and business away from central business districts to suburban nodes, rather than from metropolitan to rural or remote regions.

15 In November of 2002, the U.S.-based IT industry research firm Forrester Research Inc. issued a study predicting the loss of 3.3 million service jobs from the U.S. over the next 15 years due to off-shore outsourcing to countries such as India and China (Forrester Research Inc. 2002).

16 The clash between surveillance and basic legal rights in the workplace are discussed at length in Information and Privacy Commissioner/Ontario (1992).

NOTES ON CONTRIBUTORS

Maria BAKARDJIEVA

>is an assistant professor in the Faculty of Communication and Culture at the University of Calgary. Her research interests focus on how people use and have shaped the Internet.

Bart BEATY

>is an assistant professor in the Faculty of Communication and Culture at the University of Calgary. His research interests include popular culture, cinema, comic books, and Canadian cultural policy.

Vince CARLIN

>is an associate professor in the School of Journalism at Ryerson University. He was head of news and current affairs for CBC radio and was head of CBC Newsworld.

Barbara CROW

>is an associate professor in the Division of Social Science at York University. She specializes in the social, cultural, and economic effects of digital technology and the history and politics of the women's movement.

Christopher DORNAN

>is the director of the School of Journalism and Communication at Carleton University. He has worked as a journalist for the CBC, the Ottawa Citizen, and the Globe and Mail among other news organizations.

Marilynne HEBERT

>is an assistant professor in the Department of Community Health Sciences at the University of Calgary's Faculty of Medicine. Her research, consulting, and teaching interests focus on the understanding the impact of information and communications technology, more specifically, e-homecare applications in the community and applying these findings into practice.

Penny JENNETT

>is a professor and head of the Telehealth Program in the Department of Community Health Sciences at the Faculty of Medicine, University of Calgary. She is an international expert and health researcher in e-health, telehealth, continuing medical education, health education, and dissemination.

Malek KHOURI

>is an assistant professor in the Faculty of Communication and Culture at the University of Calgary. He is currently working on a filmography of the National Film Board and its depiction of working-class Canadians. He is also collecting an anthology on the topic of class and the Canadian cinema.

Graham LONGFORD

is an assistant professor in the Department of Political Studies at Trent University. His research focuses on the impacts of new communications technologies on Canadian politics and society.

Frits PANNEKOEK

is director of Information Resources at the University of Calgary. He is also an associate professor in the faculties of Environmental Design (Heritage Studies) and Communication and Culture. His research interests lie in public or applied history and the impact of digital technology and the commodification of information on marginalized cultures.

Richard SCHULTZ

is a professor in the Department of Political Science at McGill University. His research interests centre on broadcasting and telecommunications regulation and on Canadian public policy in general.

Richard SCOTT

is an associate professor and Fulbright New Century Scholar in the Department of Community Health Sciences at the University of Calgary's Faculty of Medicine. His research examines the role of e-health in the globalization of healthcare, pursuing the development of a global e-health policy matrix model.

Will STRAW

is director of the Graduate Program in Communications in the Department of Art History and Communications Studies at McGill University. He specializes in popular music and its impact on identity.

Rebecca SULLIVAN

is an assistant professor in the Faculty of Communication and Culture at the University of Calgary. Her research focuses on feminist media studies and on questions dealing with science, religion and technology.

David TARAS

is a professor in the Faculty of Communication and Culture at the University of Calgary. He is interested in mass media and their effects on Canadian politics and in broadcasting policy.

Aritha VAN HERK

is a professor in the English Department at the University of Calgary and noted author. Her novels include Judith, The Tent Peg, No Fixed Address, and Restlessness.

Cora VOYAGEUR

is an assistant professor in the Department of Sociology at the University of Calgary. She specializes in Canadian Aboriginal life and on the experiences of Aboriginal women in particular.

computer based composition. *See* music
computer technology. *See* information
   and communications technologies
   (ICTs)
concentration of ownership. *See*
   convergence
La Conférence des recteurs et des
   principaux des universités du
   Québec, 86
consolidation. *See* convergence
Consortia Canada, 86
Consortium of Ontario Libraries, 86
consumer choice, 32, 148, 152, 154–55,
   160, 163. *See also* Canadian content;
   cultural sovereignty
   government control, 18, 29–31
   limitation of, 28
consumers *vs.* citizens, 54, 61, 63
contingent workers, 275, 279, 283, 286
   labour laws, 282
   lack of employer-sponsored training,
      288
contract employment. *See* contingent
   workers
convergence, 15–16, 52, 58–60, 83, 112,
   163
   as business strategy, 65, 67
   Canada's leading media giants, 19
   of carriage and content, 42, 53
   conglomeration of Canadian television
      industry, 144, 152–53, 161
   cross-media holdings, 98
   definitions, 53
   failure, 55, 64
   libraries, archives, museums, 76–77,
      89
   media empires, 19–20, 144, 154,
      161–62
   music industry, 211, 213–14
   ownership, 53, 55–56, 98, 112, 117,
      153
   technological, 14–15, 53
   telecommunications and broadcasting
      media, 33
Coon Come, Matthew, 170, 174

Copps, Sheila, 194–95, 215
copyright
   digital, 84
   impact of new technologies, 138
   music, 211
Corus Entertainment, 52, 56, 154, 161
Council of Atlantic Librarians, 86
Council of Federal Libraries, 86
Council of Prairie and Pacific Libraries,
   86
Country Canada, 161
country music, 217
Cowan, Ruth Schwartz, 228
CRBC, 28. *See also* CRTC
Cree-Ative Media, 173
"critical skills," 284
Crouching Tiger, Hidden Dragon (film), 189
Crow, Barbara, 21–22, 306
Crown, 124
CRTC, 28, 38, 58, 144, 153, 162, 181, 206
   Alliance Atlantis/Salter Street rulings,
      154
   approval of digital channels, 14, 161
   Canadian content, 30, 155
   CanWest Global rulings, 59–60, 62
   competition, 37, 41, 55–56, 59
   laissez-faire, pro business attitude,
      155
   licenses, 155–56
   magazine policy, 45
   mandatory carriage regulations, 148
CSI (TV program), 158
CTV, 16, 42, 54–56, 59–60, 64, 100,
   117–18, 157–60
   and influx of specialty services, 151
   license renewal, 155
CTV Sunday Movie, 158
cultural democracy
   illusion of, 72
cultural sovereignty, 32, 35, 82, 155, 194,
   200
   American dominance, 19, 30
   privileging middle-brow dramatic
      programming, 143
Cyber Futures (Sardar and Ravet), 72

Independent Film Channel, 161
Indigo Books, Music, and More, 128–30, 134
  code of conduct, 131
Industry Canada, 39, 78
  "Connecting Canadians" initiatives, 75
  funding for telehealth, 264
  School Net projects, 76
Industry Canada website, 266
Infinity, 52
information
  access, 84
  commodification of, 75–76, 84–87, 91
  cost-per-view, 85
  as free, 56–57, 85
  monetarization, 57, 59
information and communications technologies (ICTs), 253–54, 275, 277. *See also* knowledge-based economy; telework
  "24/7" availability, 292
  balance of work and family commitments, 292
  business and government endorsement of, 276
  "delocation," 288
  deskilling and job loss, 279
  effect on clerical positions, 279
  effect on workplace skills, 283
  employment gains and losses, 280–81
  expenditures on, 279
  flexibilization of the workforce, 281
  gendered and racialized division of labour, 276, 278, 284–87
  imposed relevance in everyday lives, 229
  polarization, 276, 287
  positive aspects, 276
  public-sector organizations, 278
  recommendations for mitigating, 299
  regional economic disparity, 295
  relocation of work, 288–89
  remote communities, 294
  social diffusion, 230

  transfer of work out of Canada, 280
  and workplace privacy, 296
"The Information Deficit: Canadian Solutions," 87
Information Highway Advisory Council, 28, 41
information literacy, 89
"Injun Joe," 165
interactive entertainment business, 11
International Telecommunications Union, 38
international trade agreements, 46
  Free Trade Agreement, 33, 280
  General Agreement on Trade and Tariffs (GATT), 32, 35
  General Agreement on Trades in Services (GATS), 35, 41
  and independent action by government policy-makers, 42
  NAFTA, 13, 33, 35
  national sovereignty, 32–33
  World Trade Organization, 13, 34–35, 41–42
International Women's Day, 66
Internet, 14, 21, 32, 53, 145–46, 225–52, 276–77
  access to NFB films, 200
  advertising, 118
  broadband capabilities, 33, 37–40, 261
  Canadian material, 19
  children's use of, 10, 21, 241–43, 248
  commercial activity, 71
  for communication (e-mail), 232
  content creation and access, 72, 234
  cost to access, 71
  credit/income gap, 39
  culturally imposed relevance, 232
  democratic development, 250
  downloading music, 207, 209, 219
  e-health, 259
  and equality of opportunity, 234
  fantasy and reality, 11
  high-speed access, 59
  high-tech users, 233
  HSA Canadians, 233